FIRST EDITION

THE
WITH IDEAS AND
POWER

AN INVESTIGATION OF
ANTHROPOLOGY AND
HUMAN CULTURE

By John Sheehan

State University of New York at Cortland

Bassim Hamadeh, CEO and Publisher
Michael Simpson, Vice President of Acquisitions
Jamie Giganti, Senior Managing Editor
Jess Estrella, Senior Graphic Designer
John Remington, Senior Field Acquisitions Editor
Monika Dziamka, Project Editor
Brian Fahey, Licensing Specialist
Berenice Quirino, Associate Editor
Kat Ragudos, Interior Designer

Copyright © 2017 by Cognella, Inc. All rights reserved. No part of this publication may be reprinted, reproduced, transmitted, or utilized in any form or by any electronic, mechanical, or other means, now known or hereafter invented, including photocopying, microfilming, and recording, or in any information retrieval system without the written permission of Cognella, Inc.

Trademark Notice: Product or corporate names may be trademarks or registered trademarks, and are used only for identification and explanation without intent to infringe.

Cover image copyright © Richard Throssel / Museum of Photographic Arts / Copyright in the Public Domain..

Printed in the United States of America

ISBN: 978-1-5165-0412-1 (pbk) / 978-1-5165-0413-8 (br)

To Brenda,

For keeping the home fires burning during this project, and burning brightly!

CONTENTS

INTRODUCTION — v

CHAPTER ONE
THE NUTS AND BOLTS — 2

CHAPTER TWO
THE BIOLOGICAL CREATURE — 10

CHAPTER THREE
WESTERN "TRUTH" — 22

CHAPTER FOUR
SELF, US, THEM, AND LAND — 32

CHAPTER FIVE
CULTURAL ANTHROPOLOGY — 44

CHAPTER SIX
"TELLING" A STORY — 54

CHAPTER SEVEN
THE EVOLUTION OF CULTURAL ANTHROPOLOGY — 68

CHAPTER EIGHT
BONDING HUMANS TOGETHER: FAMILY, KINSHIP, AND MARRIAGE — 78

CHAPTER NINE
NATURE AND NURTURE: RACE, ETHNICITY, AND GENDER — 88

CHAPTER TEN
SOCIAL STRUCTURE, ART, AND RELIGION — 108

CHAPTER ELEVEN
AN ETHNOLOGICAL CASE STUDY AND APPLIED ANTHROPOLOGY — 122

CHAPTER TWELVE
ECONOMIES AND GOVERNMENT — 134

VI THE CREATURE WITH IDEAS AND POWER: AN INVESTIGATION OF ANTHROPOLOGY AND HUMAN CULTURE

CHAPTER THIRTEEN
THE MODERN WORLD 144

BIBLIOGRAPHY 163

INTRODUCTION

What is anthropology? Furthermore, why study it? These are familiar questions to many undergraduate students. Having been one myself, I am sympathetic to your plight. Few choose to take a cultural anthropology class for reasons other than "my advisor suggested it." My question to you is why did your advisor suggest it? My job in this book is to help you realize why that suggestion was a good one for your personal development as a student, as a worker, as a citizen, and as a functional and informed participator in the strongest democracy this planet has ever known. You have been endowed with power, power to access resources to build a successful life and power to affect the life of billions by the choices you make in a democratic society. I wonder how many at the undergraduate level have thought very deeply about that. I remember the football games, the parties, the angst, and the time devoted to studies, trying to balance all of the competing activities for my time, and trying to do it well. But now, with more years of experience under my belt, I think very deeply about how important each individual's role is in this "global village," hence, my self-envisioned role as a teacher and a mentor.

I see it as my task to help introduce you to your individual role, but really only in a small way, because each of you must figure that out for yourselves. That is the responsibility of each individual in a society that promotes the ideal of freedom. You have civil rights. That doesn't mean that the government owes you something just for being born. That is a sentiment smacking of unearned entitlement. What civil rights offer you, in the truest sense, is that no one can put arbitrary obstacles in your path, based on race, sex, gender, religion, etc., that can hamper you from becoming a fully functional, responsible, and contributing member of your family, community, nation, and planet. That is your privilege and that is the path to your happiness. We will refer to these ideas often in this course. Why study anthropology? It is a gilded doorway to help you know yourself. To know yourself, you need to know where you are, where you came from, and where you are going. The better you know yourself, the better your plans for the future can become very realistic and attainable. Your decisions will become wiser and your community will become stronger. Democracy is only an ideal that will survive as a result of well-educated and wise individuals. You, as an individual, have a great opportunity. Your education at this institution is a privilege that few on this planet can aspire to.

This course in cultural anthropology is part of a smorgasbord of disciplines that you will sample in four years to enable you to know the very basics of many things that will help you choose a career for which you are capable of performing well and happily. It is not a product that you have already paid for like a pair of shoes in a shopping mall. It is not a negotiating table to haggle for better grades. It is a doorway to your own self. It is up to you to make the most of this experience to expand who you are. The liberal arts by definition are those disciplines that enable those individuals within a community to explore, develop, and enjoy freedom of the mind and body. That is your privilege and your opportunity.

This book is designed to help you make the most of them, and to enjoy the football games and the parties too!

So much for the pep talk. This book contains 13 chapters. The following list of the chapters lays out the flow of information presented in this course.

Chapter 1: **The Nuts and Bolts** deals with the origins of the discipline of anthropology and defines its four main sub-fields.

Chapter 2: **The Biological Creature** talks about the essence of physical anthropology and biological anthropology: evolution, genetics, primatology, and the human mind.

Chapter 3: **Western "Truth"** deals with the contingent experiences of "reality" that all humans have to make sense of in their lives, both those living today, as well as our ancestors from the past. The focus in this chapter is the development of that notion of reality associated with Western culture.

Chapter 4: **Self, Us, Them, and Land** deals primarily with how early tribal peoples derived culture from their environmental experiences and how they defined themselves in relation to those environments.

Chapter 5: **Cultural Anthropology** discusses the basic elements that make human societies, both past and present, cohesive and how anthropologists study them.

Chapter 6: **"Telling" a Story** examines how artifacts removed from the ground and scientifically dated can augment the information humans share among themselves via oral and written communications.

Chapter 7: **The Evolution of Cultural Anthropology** traces how anthropology as a discipline came into being and how that discipline has evolved over time according to the cultural values of the changing times.

Chapter 8: **Bonding Humans Together: Family, Kinship, and Marriage** deals with those culturally derived bonds that "glue" humans together through time, space, and story.

Chapter 9: **Nature and Nurture: Race, Ethnicity, and Gender** discusses how our cultural bonds and our genetic inheritances are constructed to give humans a sense of community and legacy.

Chapter 10: **Social Structure, Art, and Religion** deals with how the structuring of a society is linked culturally to the religion that that society conceives, and the art that that society projects its belief through.

Chapter 11: **An Ethnological Case Study and Applied Anthropology** serves as an example of how all of the sub-disciplines of cultural anthropology come together to tell the story of a people, in this case, the Haudenosaunee.

Chapter 12: **Economies and Government** deals with how humans extract, use, and exchange natural and social resources, and what rules apply to those resource utilizations, both locally and non-locally through time.

Chapter 13: **The Modern World** grounds the student in the contemporary world. Ideas of modernity, international integration, and environmental and ecological issues will be discussed.

CHAPTER ONE

THE NUTS AND BOLTS

Let's return to the question, what is anthropology? **Anthropology** is the study of humans, the biological and mental creature that humans are, as well as all of the collective activities of that creature past and present. The word anthropology is derived from two Greek roots: *anthropos*—"man" or "human"—and *logos*—"the study of" or "derived from reason." So everything that humans are, think, and do fall under the umbrella discipline of anthropology. It is a pretty big field. In fact, it is the largest field of study in the liberal arts, since all other fields of human endeavor fall within its domain. Hence, every other field of study is in some way anthropological. Because of this, one of the key terms in the discipline of anthropology is holism. **Holism** is a perspective in anthropology that attempts to study a culture by looking at all parts of the system and seeing how those parts are interrelated. Incidentally, any study that a student wishes to pursue, and any paper that a student wishes to write, can ultimately be justified as an anthropological study.

The discipline of anthropology attempts to put human beings in a perspective that makes sense to the individual as well as to the society.

FIG. 1.1. The Scream by Edvard Munch is the iconic image of angst.

It attempts to answer the contingent questions that each of us asks in the course of our lifetime to make sense of things, to create for ourselves that which is "real." Who am I? Why am I alive? What am I supposed to do? Am I important? How am I like some people? Why am I different from others? And perhaps the most important question, where do I go when I die? To me, an even more important question is what should I do with the finite time I have remaining in this physical container I call my body? These are called contingent questions. **Contingent**, derived from the Latin word *contingere*, is derived from the prefix *con*—"with"—and *tingere*—"to touch" and means "to have contact with" or "befall." Contingency has to do with those tangential factors in our lives that impinge upon us daily and may or may not be out of our control. These include all events that are possible but uncertain. Contingent feelings can lead us to inspiration and drive so that we can "rise to the occasion." Or, they can fill us with angst and dread and lead us to self-doubt, indecision, and paralysis. **Angst** is a feeling of anxiety and is quite uncomfortable.

In dealing with feelings, humans construct symbolic images and artifacts to help channel those feelings away from destructive patterns and into organized, and often, but not always, constructive

FIG. 1.2A AND 1.2B. Gangs such as the Crips and the Bloods identify themselves via their "colors," which on the face of it seems to be a benign way of identifying their respective groups via graphic symbols. But, woe betide the gang member wearing the wrong "color" in the wrong territory. In this sense, gang colors are "religious" symbols; they are strongly embedded with cultural meanings.

FIG. 1.3. Roman Legion.

communally enacted rituals, customs, histories, polities, and religions. A **polity** is simply a political organization and is derived from the Greek word *polis*—"city-state." The term religion is both a very simple and a very complex word due to its common use in meaning a spiritually organized group. In its basic sense, **religion** is a Latin word *religare*, derived from the prefix *res*, which means the "idea, the concept, or the essence" of something, coupled with the root l*igare*—to bind. Hence, a religion is a set of ideas and ideals to which one binds one's mind via an act of "ligio," much like a ligament binds muscle tissue or a ligature binds up wounds with stitches. The idea of ligatory binding can be expanded to the mental concept of "legis"-lation—the ideas that bind people together in a polity, an act of "legio." The term republic is derived from the prefix *res*, which means the "idea, the concept, or the essence" of something coupled with the root *publicus*—the people. A **republic** is quite literally "the thing of the people." Religious ideas can also bind people to a spiritual set of commandments and rituals such as in Judaism, Christianity, Hinduism, Islam, and Witchcraft as much as they can bind Democrats and Republicans in a constitutional democracy. Gangs such as the Crips and the Bloods or fraternities and sororities follow "religious" rules and rituals by the types of "colors" they wear or the types of initiations they perform.

And ultimately, in ancient Rome itself, the religious ideals of the Roman people were upheld by the "binding" enforced by the legion itself—that famous instrument of military binding.

Even modernity essentially practices science as a "religion," by conforming to the rules and rituals of the scientific method. By saying this, I am not declaring that fundamentalist monotheism and evolution are equally true and valid religions. What I am saying is that both sets of ideas, mutually antagonistic to many in contemporary culture, are, by definition, religions. I leave the reader to discern how true any religion is. Scientists ascertain truth by a self-corrective process called the scientific method.

The **scientific method** is a means by which to investigate the natural and social world involving critical thinking, logical reasoning, and skeptical thought. This approach to garnering knowledge is in contrast to personal opinion as well as religious or spiritual revelation and religious or spiritual faith. An **opinion** is a belief or judgment that rests on grounds insufficient to produce complete certainty. An opinion is not, by definition, scientific, though it may be. Testability of phenomena and verifiability of conclusions

FIG. 1.4A. Albert Einstein.

FIG. 1.4B. Isaac Newton.

according to prescribed norms by the scientific community are mandatory for ideas to become accepted and scientific. Others must be able to come to your conclusions for science to contribute to the body of knowledge accepted as "truth." The beauty of scientific truth is that it is malleable; it is susceptible to change and refinement according to more thoughtful and sophisticated experiments. Hence, the body of human knowledge based on reason is self-corrective as it increases. The scientific method is fundamental to the human notion of "progress," an idea that will be developed more fully in Chapter 4.

Unlike scriptural and spiritual religion, skepticism lies at the heart of scientific inquiry. **Skepticism** is the doctrine that true knowledge is uncertain. Incidentally, scriptural religions do change over time. Although the Dead Sea Scrolls may be codified on paper, which means that the words cannot change over time, social circumstances do change over time, and scriptural "truth" changes while the words do not. For example, both the Hebrew Old Testament and the Greek New Testament forbid women to speak in a synagogue or a church, yet many reformed Jewish and Christian denominations do ordain women to speak and preach in "holy" places. What has changed with time in these instances is the culture, hence the interpretation of language, not the language itself. Place, along with time, will be discussed in Chapter 4. Ironically, I do not claim that all scientists accept the discoveries of others without prejudice and dispassion, especially radically new theories. Scientists are human after all and the products of the cultures in which their minds were trained. Charles Darwin was hounded and lampooned in his day by his "scientific" contemporaries, that is, until his ideas grew to become the norm. Albert Einstein too was vilified for assailing the sacrosanct laws of Isaac Newton with his new-fangled ideas about relativity, until repeated and increasingly sophisticated tests continually confirmed Einstein's formulas. Ironically, Einstein failed to carry through to the logical conclusions the possibilities that his theories opened up because they would do away with the notion of God that he had learned as a child. Others were left to take up the reins of unsentimental science and pioneer onward where he feared to tread.

In the scientific method, there are two dispassionate and logical philosophical means of testing proposed ideas—the inductive method and the deductive method. For the **inductive method** of investigation, a scientist first makes observations, then collects data, and then proceeds to formulate a hypothesis. For the **deductive method** of investigation, a scientist first develops a theory and then develops a specific hypothesis before finally testing it. The data collected in scientific experiments are called **variables**. Variables are measured as carefully as possible with the highest degree of sophistication possible for accuracy. Statistical analyses discern patterns among variables. Researchers use the observations about different variables to develop their hypotheses. A **hypothesis** is an idea that correlates proposed patterns and relationships among observed data. Testing these relationships and patterns is the fundamental operation of the scientific method. If the conclusions of a hypothesis are found to be repeatable and valid, then that hypothesis can be integrated with other repeatable and valid hypotheses into a theory. A **theory** is an accepted pronouncement that explains natural and social phenomena. In this way, the corpus of human knowledge is progressed.

Anthropology is one of the social sciences, along with history and sociology. The history of the discipline of anthropology begins with the Medieval Period in Europe. Truth at that time was garnered both spiritually and physically, that is, by the Bible and by scientists. Medieval scientists often used the deductive method in experimenting with natural phenomena, that is, they reasoned from God as the "Prime Mover" in all things, and all variables that conflicted with their scriptural notion of deity were deemed corrupt and discarded. This type of "spiritual" science was termed Scholasticism. Scholasticism attempted to wed the rational discernment of the natural human mind, which included the great "pagan" Classical Greek and Roman philosophers, with the revelation of codified scripture. The Catholic philosopher Thomas Aquinas was the most noted Scholastic thinker of the age.

This method of inquiry came under fire during the Renaissance and the Protestant Reformation when literacy became the hallmark of all those thinking intellectuals who were "protesting" against the ideas of the Catholic Church. Religious reform led to political reform and social reform. By the seventeenth century, observant scientists, such as Isaac Newton, had begun to codify the laws of physics after repeated hypotheses and theories continuously led to the same observable phenomena. With the irretrievable split between the Catholic and Protestant churches during the Wars of Religion, science and the scientific method displaced religious revelation from scriptures as the source of truth in the natural world. This had profound consequences.

FIG. 1.5. Thomas Aquinas.

Since public truth was no longer to be found in the Bible, humans and their scholarly activists, the Humanists, were determined to reconstruct European societies on the principles of scientific observation. Spiritual belief became a private affair. Church and state were to become separated. This new philosophical view of the cosmos and its organization was called **positivism**. Untrammeled by the dictates of organized religion, scientists grew excited and optimistic about the new scientific pursuit of truth, hence the term positivism. The eighteenth century French philosopher August Comte has been called "the apostle of positivism."

FIG. 1.6. Auguste Comte.

What Comte optimistically believed was that humans, by themselves and using science as their guide, could develop egalitarian, prosperous, and happy utopian societies throughout Europe and the world.

To develop these utopias, European leaders would wed the technological advancements coming from the laboratories of mathematicians, biologists, chemists, and physicists to the scientists of the new societies. These scholars of society were called sociologists. **Sociology** became the discipline that studied the origin, development, organization, and functioning of the new human societies. Historians would help ground these new social ideas upon the bedrock of the lessons learned from old, documented, and analyzed events. **History** is the branch of knowledge that records and explains past events. These physical and social scientists were men who lived in urban societies; that is, they were specialists who were enabled to use their daily hours in study and experimentation and not use their labors to work the fields in order to put bread on their tables. That would be the social function of the peasants. It is ironic that the urban scholars became the men to ponder natural law and not the brute workers in the fields. Their conclusions, therefore, should not be surprising. Rather than live in a holistic harmony with a spiritualized nature, as tribal societies do, these positivists demystified nature into a warehouse of physical objects free for the taking by progressive societies. Progress entailed material expansion of goods, extension of trade, acquisition of lands, and evangelization of progressive ideas. In this process of progressive Western growth, social scientists bumped up against people as "primitive" as their own tribal ancestors. What could be learned from them in order to holistically round out their body of scientific knowledge and create the fully integrated and benign human "utopian" civilization? Positivists needed to study these peoples. Thus anthropology was born. We will have much more to say about positivistic progress.

Anthropology then, by studying humans through time, is really a study of how we all see ourselves in the here and now. Traditional anthropology is comprised of four main sub-fields: physical anthropology, archeology, linguistic anthropology, and cultural anthropology. This book and this course will focus primarily on the latter, cultural anthropology, but will include heavy dollops of the other sub-fields in fleshing out the discipline. Here are the nuts and bolts:

Physical anthropology studies the human creature as a biological species. It focuses on the evolution of humans through time and the resulting variations in the human creature that exist today. This will raise the thorny questions about race and ethnicity that are prevalent today as well. The word physical is derived from the Greek root: *physica*—"of nature" or "natural."

Archeology studies prehistoric and historic life forms and cultures through the excavation of fossils, artifacts, and material remains. It endeavors to tell the story of human lifestyles and history where no written documents remain or ever existed. The word archeology is derived from two Greek roots – *archein*—"to begin"—and *logos*—"the study of" or "derived from reason."

Linguistic anthropology studies the nature of language, both oral and written. In addition, linguistic anthropology studies how humans understand reality through language. The word language is derived from the Latin root l*ingua*—"tongue."

Cultural anthropology studies the mental, social, and spiritual constructs of human societies in both the past and the present. It focuses on how values, morals, and ethics are derived from the environment and from our ancestral norms. These mental structures are collectively termed "culture." The word culture, derived from the root word "cult," is ultimately derived from the Latin root *cultus*—"to plant." Culture is a set of ideas that are "planted" into our minds.

Having atomized the discipline into its major sub-fields, let's look a little closer at each sub-field in turn in the following chapters, after a chapter that looks at how contingency drives humans to orient themselves in their environments and experiences.

KEY WORDS

Angst
Anthropology
Archeology
Contingent
Cultural anthropology
Deductive method
History
Holism
Hypothesis
Inductive method
Linguistic anthropology
Opinion
Physical anthropology
Polity
Positivism
Republic
Religion
Scientific method
Skepticism
Sociology
Theory
Variables

IMAGE CREDITS

- Fig. 1.1: Edvard Munch / Copyright in the Public Domain.
- Fig. 1.2: ScottSteiner / Wikimedia Commons / Copyright in the Public Domain.
- Fig. 1.2: Mattho69 / Wikimedia Commons / Copyright in the Public Domain.
- Fig. 1.3: Copyright © 2006 by CristianChirita / Wikimedia Commons, (CC BY-SA 3.0) at http://commons.wikimedia.org/wiki/File:Roman_turtle_formation_on_trajan_column.jpg.
- Fig. 1.4A: Oren Jack Turner / Copyright in the Public Domain.
- Fig. 1.4B: Godfrey Kneller / Copyright in the Public Domain.
- Fig. 1.5: Carlo Crivella / Copyright in the Public Domain.
- Fig. 1.6: Copyright in the Public Domain.

CHAPTER TWO

THE BIOLOGICAL CREATURE

This chapter addresses the concepts that are related to the anthropological sub-field of physical anthropology. As stated in Chapter 1, physical anthropology studies the human creature as a biological species.

In his studies of finches on the Galapagos Islands in the mid-nineteenth century, the naturalist Charles Darwin observed the various species of finch inhabiting the islands. In particular, he pondered how each finch species sported a different type of beak that allowed its members to gather different food sources from different environmental niches that enabled all of the species to maximize their food intakes. **Environmental niches** are the advantageous localities made by specific life forms to stresses in a particular environment, as a result of genetic adaptations, that enable them to successfully live in a particular time and space. From these observations, he formulated a progressive hypothesis about life on earth, that is, that the various life forms observed today developed from less sophisticated life forms over the ages, back to a common life form in the remote past. **Evolution** is derived from the Latin root *evolvere*—"to unroll." It is defined as a theory in which various types of animals and plants that are observed today have their origin in other preexisting types, and that the distinguishable differences among them are due to modifications in successive generations.

Darwinian evolution is based upon the concepts of mutation and natural selection. A **mutation** is a permanent and physical change in a life form that may or may not be passed on to its progeny, and may or may not better suit that species to survive within a specific environmental niche. **Natural selection** is a natural process that tends to cause the survival of individuals or groups best adjusted to the conditions under which they live. But, despite his sound reasoning, Darwin did not discover the mechanisms by which mutation and natural selection functioned. Scientific instruments were still too crude for that to occur in his lifetime, as were the modern methods of dating geological rock formations. The discovery by Gregor Mendel that biological traits could change and be passed on to offspring in mathematically predictable patterns, called the **Mendelian Inheritance**, put teeth in the mouth of Darwin's theory; however, Mendel could only describe inheritance, not demonstrate its mechanism. The door to that answer would be unlocked by James Watson and Francis Crick when they cracked the code of deoxyribonucleic acid (DNA) and discovered how the blueprints for life forms were recorded and changed within the chromosomes of cellular nuclei in quantized packets of information called genes. Genetics was born. **Genetics** is that branch of biology that studies genes, heredity, and variation in living organisms. At last, evolution now had a mechanism.

FIG. 2.1A. Charles Darwin.

FIG. 2.1B. Gregor Mendel.

FIG. 2.1C. James Watson and Francis Crick (on the right of the photo).

Physical anthropology is actually a sub-field of the umbrella discipline biological anthropology. **Biological anthropology** studies all life forms in its attempt to understand the human creature. Physical anthropology focuses its lens primarily on humans and their primate and hominid kin. Let us look at biological anthropology first.

The word **biology** is derived from two Greek roots: *bios*—"physical life"—and *logos*—"the study of" or "derived from reason." Prior to the development of genetics, biologists in the sub-field called **embryology** studied the variations in embryos and fetuses of numerous creatures to discern the morphological patterns inherent in each species. An **embryo** is a vertebrate—a creature with a backbone—at an early stage of development prior to birth or hatching, but which cannot be determined as any distinguishable species from its outer form. For instance, chicken, horse, and human embryos look similar under the microscope. A **fetus** is a later stage in the development of an organism prior to birth or hatching in which its genetic material has given it distinguishable outward features. The fetuses of a chicken, a horse, and a human can now be distinguished. From these observations, the nineteenth century scientific adage, "Ontogeny recapitulates phylogeny," was born. This means that in the course of developing vertebrate offspring, **ontogeny**—the development of embryos—follows through each stage of **phylogeny**—the evolutionary history of a kind of organism. Although some pundits argue that the development of embryos is not lockstep with its ancestral genetic forebears in its phylogenic progressiveness, there is certainly enough evidence that this is what does occur during embryonic development. And, it is a strong prop of the theory of evolution. From these

THE BIOLOGICAL CREATURE   13

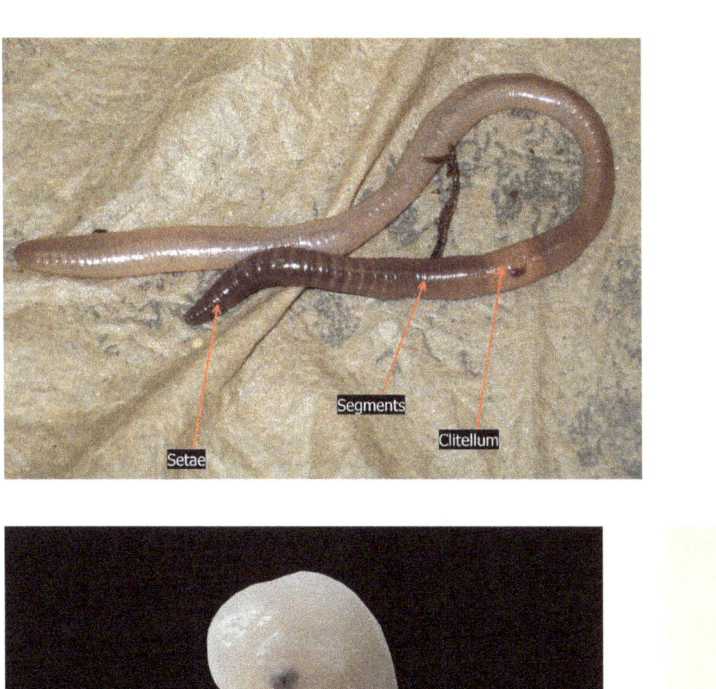
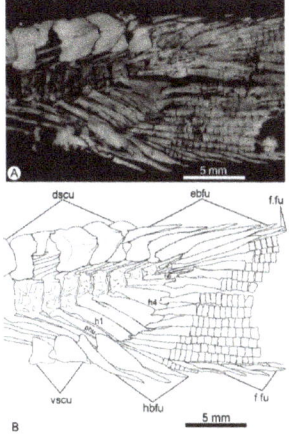
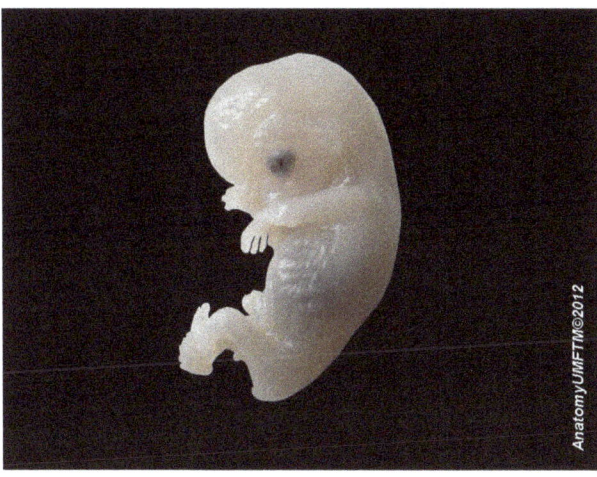
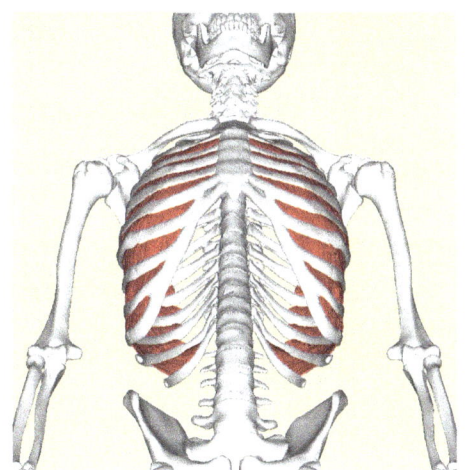

FIRST ROW: FIG. 2.2A. Segmented Earthworm, FIG. 2.2B. Segmented Fish Vertebrae.
SECOND ROW: FIG. 2.2C. Human Embryo, 4 Weeks, FIG. 2.2D. Human Intercostal Muscles.

studies, the field of **comparative anatomy** was born. Comparative anatomy is the study of similarities and differences in the morphology—bodily forms and structures—of different species. As an example, let us examine the anatomies of several species according to these ideas, specifically the phylogenic concept that large aggregates of cells functioning together as a viable organism developed segmentation to duplicate and elongate their bodies. Large **invertebrate** creatures—those creatures with no backbones, but which possess types of neural, circulatory, digestive, and muscular systems—evolved into still larger **vertebrate** creatures that possessed all of the same systems in more efficient networks that are anchored together around a strong and segmented backbone. Notice in the following series of photos how human intercostal muscles and ribs recapitulate the segments of worms, fish, and human embryos.

FIG. 2.3A. A tarsier is a good example of a primate.

FIG. 2.3B. A chimpanzee is a good example of a hominid.

FIG. 2.3C. The Australopithicine "Lucy" is a good example of a hominin.

The collective work done by evolutionists, geneticists, and comparative anatomists augment are, in turn, augmented by the work done by physical anthropologists. Let us now examine physical anthropology more closely. Remember, physical anthropology focuses on humans and their primate and hominid kin. **Primatology** is the study of primates. A **primate** is that taxonomic group of mammalian vertebrates, whether alive or extinct, that utilizes opposable thumbs on their forelimbs to manipulate objects. These include Homo sapiens, Neanderthals, Australopithecines, chimpanzees, gorillas, orangutans, monkeys, lemurs, lorises, and tarsiers. A **hominid** is that family of primates, whether alive or extinct, that includes Homo sapiens, Neanderthals, Australopithecines, chimpanzees, gorillas, and orangutans. A **hominin** is that family of primates, whether alive or extinct, that includes Homo sapiens, Neanderthals, and Australopithecines. **Paleoanthropology** is the study of human evolution through the analysis of fossilized human, hominin, and hominid remains. We will see more of paleoanthropology in Chapter 4.

The study of genetics has opened up fields in physical anthropology that include forensic anthropology, epidemiology, and population anthropology. **Forensic anthropology** utilizes the skills and tools of physical anthropology in the examination of human skeletal remains to help law enforcement agencies determine the identify of unidentified bones. **Epidemiology** is the study of the occurrence, distribution, and control of diseases in various populations. **Population biology** is the study of the interrelationships between population characteristics and environments. Such genetic studies have determined that even after the invasions and settlements of the Normans, the Vikings, the Anglo-Saxons, and the Romans, the genetic composition of the common "Englishman" is still 80 percent Celtic. I apologize if that is an unwelcome revelation to some. And due to the martial and ravenous worldview of the Mongol leader Genghis Khan, perhaps 1 male in 100 living today is a direct genetic descendent of him. would be the same as for males, that is, 1 person in 100, for a grand total of 32 million people!

FIG. 2.4. Genghis Khan.

As we will see in the next few chapters, humans construct their environments according to symbols, and language is basically a set of symbols recorded in sound, while writing being a more abstract way of recording sound in symbols recorded in texts. Let's examine one particularly crucial symbolic representation that sets humans apart from their primate kin. These are the consonants **M** and **N** used in a basic Indo-European root **MN**. (Vowels were invented much later than the guttural consonants to make language more fluid and responsive to human cultural needs.)

MN is the foundational root in the Latin word *Homo humanus*—"hu**MaN**" or "**MaN**kind." This root reveals much about how our ancestors defined themselves culturally. **MN** is the root also for the Latin word **MaN**us—"hand," that instrument located on the forelegs of upright and bipedal primates that is used to **MaN**ipulate objects. In Spanish, the word is "**MaN**o." The hand is that appendage that allows humans to correlate rational **MeN**tal activities in the human mind—Latin "**MeN**tis"—to dominate extrasomatic space, that is, the area outside of the human body that can be controlled by applying thought to objects in order to control ever-greater concentric rings of territory. The hand-mind connection allowed humans to develop clubs for efficiency in hunting and protection, then spears, then javelins and bows and arrows, eventually leading up to guns and missiles. Other mammals with huge cerebral cortices in the brain, such as whales and porpoises, cannot accomplish these feats. This is the greatest advantage of human beings over other creatures. And a third quality of humans, applicable to only half of our species, our females, make them special and "holy" creatures as we will learn in Chapter 5. That is **MeN**strus. Without the ability to propagate our species into the future via repeatable generative acts, our species would be soon extinct. The triune qualities of **MeN**talization, **MaN**ipulation, and **MeN**struation are what make us truly hu**MaN**.

Although it is not only the mind that separates humans from other animals, it is in the mind that we construct our collective cultural worldviews as well as our individual places in it. It is in the mind where we create culture. Human culture is the great legacy of our species. It is time to examine the human brain and that quality of human experience associated with that human mind that can create culture. In the figure below, please note the differences and similarities between the skulls of our hominin ancestor, Homo habilis, and ourselves, Homo sapiens.

Homo habilis was a bipedal creature and its name means the "human"—*Homo*—that was "handy"—from the Latin *habere* "to make." Homo habilis was the first hominin toolmaker. By taking skull castings of the inside of a Homo habilis skull, anthropologists have determined that this ancestor had language centers in its brain in the same areas as modern humans do. It is assumed that Homo habilis had language. Further evidence gleaned from the comparative anatomy of habilis and human skulls support this. The mandible, the lower jaw, of both species are roughly the same size. That has been interpreted to mean that the spherical volume of the interior of the mouth encompassed by the mandible of both species was naturally selected for in evolution because language was a huge benefit for our bipedal kin. By keeping the vocal chamber the same size over eons, speech centers and the tonal qualities of sound inherent in language would be maintained in the mental capabilities of our hominin line. Hence, the capacity to generate culture and other cognitive functions became an adaptive trait that contributed to the survival of our genus and was thus maintained in the genome. (A **genome** is an organism's complete set of DNA.) In fact, these traits are perhaps the greatest adaptations that humans made to their environmental stresses. And, as a corollary to that point, all of the locations of the taxonomic sensory organs of the faces of habilis and human are in roughly the same places and are nearly the same sizes. Nature has prepared this taxonomic line to be aware of the contingent facets of reality that our species has had to ponder and deal with over time. (**Taxonomy** is a field of science that encompasses the description, identification, nomenclature, and classification of organisms.) The nature of human contingency will be examined in the next chapter. Incidentally, Homo habilis was the first hominin that developed distinguishable differences between the morphologies of the left and right hemispheres of its brain. (**Morphology** is a branch of biology dealing with the study of the form and structure of organisms and their specific structural features.) As the human brain increases in size through evolution, the differences between its left and right brains becomes more pronounced as do the sexual differences among the sexes within the species. Humans exhibit the greatest degree of sexual dimorphism among all primates. **Sexual dimorphism** is the presence of different characteristics in males and females of the same species. Again, the evolution of brain hemispheres will be discussed in the next chapter and sexual dimorphism in Chapter 9.

The "triune brain" model posited by the neuroscientist Paul McLean offers further evidence supporting the evolution of the brain in the hominin line. The triune brain is composed of three successive layers of neural development that have been accreted on top of one another, from the brain stem to the skull, like layers on a cake. The three layers are: reptilian complex, paleo-mammalian complex (the limbic system,) and neo-mammalian complex (the neocortex.)

THE BIOLOGICAL CREATURE   17

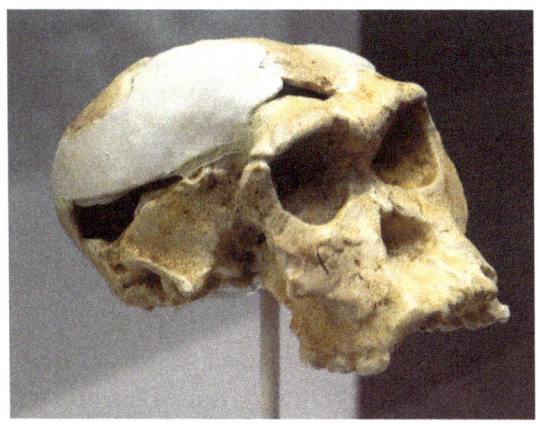  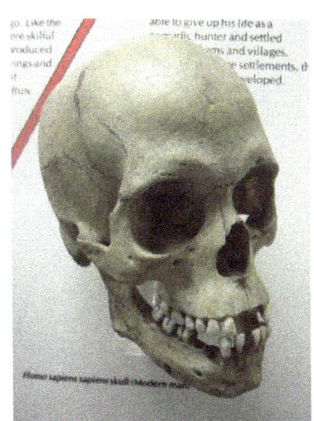

FIRST ROW: FIG. 2.5A. Homo Habilis Skull. FIG. 2.5B. Homo Habilis. FIG. 2.5C. Homo Sapien Skull.
SECOND ROW: FIG. 2.5D. Asian Man, FIG. 2.5E. White Man, FIG. 2.5F Black Woman.

The reptilian complex, or R-complex, is homologous to the brain in reptiles and is responsible for instinctual behaviors such as aggression, dominance, territoriality, and ritual displays. A **homology** is a characteristic shared by two or more species that is similar because of common ancestry. Good examples of a homology are the wing of a bat, the flipper of a whale, and the hand of a human, all of which share the same number of and positions of bones on their forelimbs. This is evidence for the environmental effects on species that cause mutation and natural selection in order to enable species to adapt.

The paleo-mammalian complex arose early in mammalian evolution and is responsible for the motivation and emotion involved in feeding, reproductive behavior, and parental behavior. The neo-mammalian

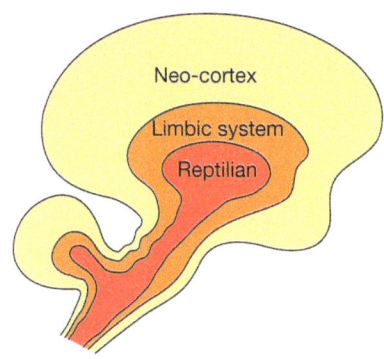

FIG. 2.5. Symbolic representation of the triune brain.

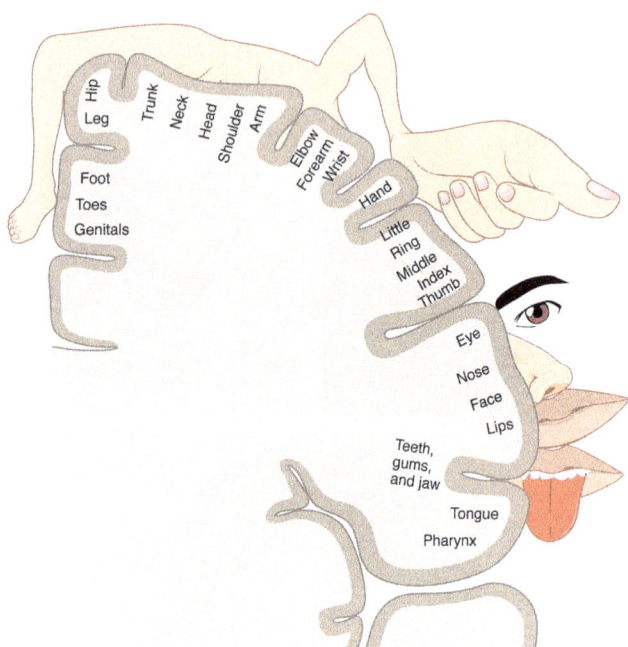

FIG. 2.7. The computer image of the sensory "homunculus," and a partial map of the sensory regions on the human neocortex from which the sensory "homunculus" was generated.

complex is the cerebral neocortex found in higher mammals, especially humans, and is that part of the brain responsible for perception and the higher cognitive functions of language ability, abstraction, and planning. Humans, therefore, are creatures of instinct, emotion, and intellect.

As we saw earlier in the discussion on the skulls of Homo habilis and Homo sapiens, the sensory organs have remained relatively similar in position and function on our heads, and the electro-chemical sensory impulses from them that reach our brains and are processed there have been mapped on in the regions of our cerebral cortices. Notice in the accompanying diagram where the brain centers in our cortices receive this sensory information and process, and understand that our left and right brains process this information slightly differently. Using computers, anthropologists have determined how much energy our bodies give to processing our senses—sight, smell, taste, touch, and sound—and have generated the image of the sensory "homunculus," or "little human" as seen. Notice how much importance natural selection has placed on our hands—the **MaN**us—for touching, and somewhat less in our hind limbs, our legs, which are certainly necessary for locomotion, but not **MaN**ipulation; our ears for hearing; our eyes for seeing; our noses for smelling, although human olfaction centers have decreased in evolutionary importance and given space in our brains to our huge logical centers; and our mouths, both for tasting and reproductive selection, but mostly for the purposes of constructing particular sounds in a particularly spherical chamber in order to produce language.

In the next chapter, we will take this biological creature, the human, and wrap him and her in the various sensuous experiences that he or she is and has been confronted with through time, and how those experiences have been codified into culture.

KEY WORDS

Biological anthropology
Biology
Comparative anatomy
Embryo
Embryology
Environmental niches
Epidemiology
Evolution
Fetus
Forensic anthropology
Genetics
Genome
Homology
Hominid
Hominin
Invertebrate
Mendelian Inheritance
Mutation
Morphology
Natural selection
Ontogeny
Paleoanthropology
Population biology
Primate
Primatology
Phylogeny
Sexual dimorphism
Taxonomy
Vertebrate

IMAGE CREDITS

- Fig. 2.1A: Herbert Rose Barraud / Copyright in the Public Domain.
- Fig. 2.1B: Copyright in the Public Domain.
- Fig. 2.1C: Copyright © by Marjorie McCarty, (CC BY 2.5) at http://commons.wikimedia.org/wiki/File:Maclyn_McCarty_with_Francis_Crick_and_James_D_Watson_-_10.1371_journal.pbio.0030341.g001-O.jpg.
- Fig. 2.2A: Copyright © 2012 by Iceclanl / Wikimedia Commons, (CC BY-SA 3.0) at http://commons.wikimedia.org/wiki/File:Earthworm_segments_Labeled_Segments.jpg.
- Fig. 2.2B: Copyright © 2013 by Paulo M. Brito and Jesus Alvarado-Ortega, (CC BY 3.0) at http://commons.wikimedia.org/wiki/File:Cipactlichthys_scutatus_caudal_fin.tif.
- Fig. 2.2C: Copyright © 2012 by Anatomist90 / Wikimedia Commons, (CC BY-SA 3.0) at http://commons.wikimedia.org/wiki/File:Human_embryo.jpg.
- Fig. 2.2D: Copyright © 2012 by the Database Center for Life Science, (CC BY-SA 2.1 JP) at http://commons.wikimedia.org/wiki/File:Internal_intercostal_muscles_below.png.
- Fig. 2.3A: Copyright © 2007 by Kok Leng Yeo, (CC BY 2.0) at http://commons.wikimedia.org/wiki/File:Tarsier_Hugs_Mossy_Branch.jpg.
- Fig. 2.3B: Copyright © 2011 by Tony Hisgett (CC BY 2.0), at http://commons.wikimedia.org/wiki/File:Chimpanzee_1d_(5512034715).jpg.

- Fig. 2.3C: Copyright © 2013 by Momotarou2012 / Wikimedia Commons, (CC BY-SA 3.0) at http://commons.wikimedia.org/wiki/File:Skeleton_and_restoration_model_of_Lucy.jpg.
- Fig. 2.4: Copyright in the Public Domain.
- Fig. 2.5A: Copyright © 2014 by Nachosan, (CC BY-SA 3.0) at http://commons.wikimedia.org/wiki/File:OH_24_replica_03.JPG.
- Fig. 2.5B: Copyright © 2007 by Sargoth / Wikimedia Commons, (CC BY-SA 2.5) at http://commons.wikimedia.org/wiki/File:Homo_habilis-cropped.jpg.
- Fig. 2.5C: Copyright © 2013 by Rept0n1x / Wikimedia Commons, (CC BY-SA 3.0) at http://commons.wikimedia.org/wiki/File:Homo_sapiens_sapiens_(Modern_man),_World_Museum_Liverpool.JPG.
- Fig. 2.5D: Copyright © by Depositphotos / monkeybusiness.
- Fig. 2.5E: Copyright © by Depositphotos / curaphotography.
- Fig. 2.5F: Copyright © by Depositphotos / jbryson.
- Fig. 2.7: Copyright © 2013 by OpenStax College (CC BY 3.0), at http://commons.wikimedia.org/wiki/File:1421_Sensory_Homunculus.jpg.

CHAPTER THREE

WESTERN "TRUTH"

This chapter has to do with the contingent questions that faced Western humans. Contingency, remember, deals with those tangential factors in our lives that impinge upon us daily and may or may not be out of our control. Contingent questions deal with orienting one's self in time, in space, on land as well as who is one's friend and who is one's foe. It is in answering these questions that humans have contrived their cultures. It is also how humans through time have contrived their "truth." **Absolute truth** is the notion that there is only one type of universal reality and its laws are binding upon all things and everyone. It is the type of truth supported particularly by fundamentalist religions. The secular mind and in particular, multicultural social scientists, propound the notion of relative truth. **Relative truth** is the idea that total and universal truth is not fully known and is perhaps ultimately unknowable, but people can know some facets of it and contrive their belief systems accordingly. They often do this by "filling in the blanks" with non-demonstrable "truths" and myths based on non-testable faith. Scientific minds are not hostile to the concepts of absolute truth and relative truth, since not even science claims to know all "truth." In fact, science seeks to know the absolute truth supporting the universe, and it must assume that natural law has not changed over time in order to do so. At the same time, science realizes that any set of scientific hypotheses, theories, and laws are only contingent, "step-by-step" approximations of the "truth." That is a healthy stance to take from which to investigate the tangential factors that impinge upon the human creature. Science makes cultural mistakes only when it tries to ossify ideas like religious fundamentalists do, which turn out to be insufficient and perhaps erroneous upon later investigation. Lamarckian ideas about evolutionary change through acquired characteristics are no longer in vogue in the scientific community, although Lamarck did have his proponents then, and he still does today.

From earliest times, humans have been trying to answer their contingent questions and the religions they have developed are their best attempts to put form to these contingent needs. Religion, in the traditional sense, is based upon supernatural ideas. **Supernatural ideas**—derived from the Latin prefix *super*, meaning "above" or "beyond" and the root *natura*, "nature"—are those unverifiable explanations of observable phenomena that are "above" or "beyond" our current cultural and scientific methods of inquiry. I will add the distinction that supernatural concepts may not be unnatural at all, but may be ideas attributed to spirits and phenomena that one day turn out to be "purely" scientific and "purely" natural. But from the worldview of the spiritually-minded humans of the past and present, whether "deity" listens to their prayers concerning contingent needs in the various languages in which the petitions are sent, for example, English, Spanish, French, Arabic, Hebrew, Hindi, etc., is a fundamental

FIG. 3.1. Pythagoras was a: (A) philosopher, (B) mathematician, (C) priest, (D) scientist, or (E) all of the above.

way to orient themselves in time and space. These same humans however rarely claim to hear a voice in response to their prayers. What praying humans look for, whether we choose to admit it or not, are "signs," whether "positive" or "negative," to determine the mind and the will of deity in their lives. This social phenomenon is as old as human culture itself, and is the original basis for it. But, the greatest "sign" from deity, if you will, is the physical universe itself. Deity is "the Creator" and the universe is deity's *magnum opus*. If deity's job description is "Creator," then the "proof" of that creator is the creation itself. This is the fundamental premise of the Scholastics like Thomas Aquinas as I mentioned earlier. We will discuss this deductive nature of investigation shortly. The early scientists of nature, in order to discern the nature and the mind of deity, looked for predictable patterns operating within nature. Physical scientists, social scientists, and early theologians all did this. Men like Pythagoras explored nature as priests in order to understand the divine nature of reality. That was the worldview in which Pythagoras lived. We have re-created him—I mean Pythagoras—in our image, that is, in the worldview of the modern secularist. **Secularism** is the principle of the separation of the governmental and physically-derived institutions of the "State" (representing "the people") from the spiritual and ecclesiastically-derived institutions of the "Church" (representing "deity"). To us as secular moderns, Pythagoras was a mathematician, a philosopher, and/or a scientist, not a priest.

Pythagoras and other Greek natural scientists did discover many of the mathematical principles that govern nature, and the Classical Greeks and Romans, and for that matter, Mayans, Hindus, Muslims, and Chinese, did likewise. These natural scientists encompassed their conclusions in a body of knowledge called natural law. **Natural law** is a deterministic system of laws governed wholly by forces operating within nature and so is universal. Scholastics had to balance their mathematical and scientific observations of natural law—to them, the mind/"*logos*" of God—with scripture—the "Word" of God, theologically—a task often wrought with contradictions and tensions. Natural scientists operating within this paradigm included both Newton and Einstein. Secular scientists today exclude deity as a "prime mover" of natural phenomena; they rely solely on observable and repeatable patterns and measurements. Einstein, remember, had trouble being a "pure" secularist. Does that make him an "impure" scientist? Is it possible to be both? The answer to these questions depends upon the perspective we take, and our perspectives, if we look at ourselves candidly, are highly culturally derived. We will explore these culturally derived facets of human cultures and their "rules," such as morals, ethics, values, norms, etc., in Chapter 8.

To continue, mathematicians such as Pythagoras and Euclid founded the modern sciences upon very powerful and verifiable natural laws. One of the most profound understandings of nature and the universe was also one of the first discovered. That is the notion of "phi." Phi is basically the recognition of a naturally occurring ratio, a ratio that appears to be one of the foundational blueprints for the construction of the universe. Pythagoras discovered that if one breaks a stick in such a way that the relationship of the whole stick to the bigger piece of the broken stick relative to the larger piece of the broken stick to the smaller piece is always 1.62/1, *ad infinitum*. This ratio is called the "Golden Ratio," and has been deemed a "sacred" mathematical principle by numerous ancient peoples, including the Egyptians, the Mayans, and the Greeks. A secular and scientific way of visualizing this ratio, as portrayed in the accompanying diagram is: a + b/a is proportional to a/b = 1.62.

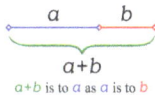

FIG. 3.2. The Phi Ratio or "Golden Ratio."

When utilizing this ratio in increasing fractal units, many structures of the physical universe reveal this "secret." A **fractal** is a natural phenomenon or a mathematical set that exhibits a repeating pattern at every scale.

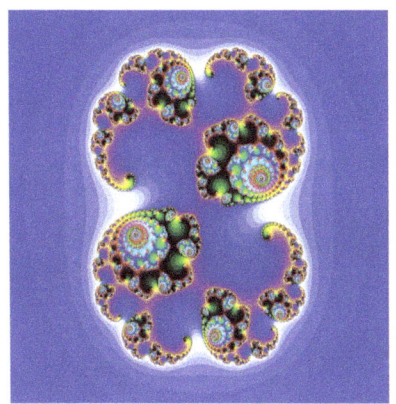

FIG. 3.3. A fractal.

The Fibonacci Series is based on fractals and represents the basic formula that adding the successive two numerals in the sequence gives the next number in the sequence. That is, 0 + 1 = 1, 1 + 1 = 2, 1 + 2 = 3, 2 + 3 = 5, 3 + 5 = 8, and so on to 13, 21, ... This Fibonacci Series is the pattern by which plants whorl like spokes in a wheel, or verticillate, as they grow, thus maximizing the spatial distribution of each leaf, and thus maximizing the amount of sunlight that the fractal array of leaves can absorb. Rivers meander according to Fibonacci fractals, similar to the way the long bones in our bodies fan out at the ends to distribute weight efficiently, and similar to the way galaxies unfurl.

The mathematical formulas of Pythagoras and Euclid became cultural norms that were used by traditional contemporary Greek architects to utilize this sacred geometry in the construction of their contemporary divine edifices. Phidias constructed the Parthenon by using a "Golden Rectangle" as his template. The Mayans were also aware of the Golden Rectangle and constructed their temples according to similar cultural parameters. These structures are good examples of how humans view their universes culturally and proceed to landscape their environments according to their cultural visions. Humans **MaN**ipulate the universe according to their visions, whether they are Haudenosaunee longhouses, as we shall see, sacred temples, or Art Deco skyscrapers.

How culture can be contrived from mathematical principles is again greatly evidenced by the Greeks. Using fractals as templates for form, Greek artists sculpted "perfect" human bodies that conform to phi fractals. Both the "classical" male sculpture *Doryphoros*, the "spear thrower," and the goddess Venus were sculpted according to these ideals.

FIG. 3.4. Notice how Fibonacci ratios underlie patterns in nature: (a) a galaxy; (b) an unfurling fern; (c) a human long bone; (d) a meandering river; and (e) the verticillation—three-dimensional unfolding—of tree leaves.

The Greek notion of "beauty" seems not to have been in the eye of the beholder, as we egalitarian postmoderns would wish it to be. (Postmodernism will be discussed in Chapter 13.) Rather than a matter of personal choice or whim, beauty seems to be mathematically encoded into our mental memories. Perhaps we (post)modernists should say, "Beauty is in the 'phi' of the beholder." Ironically, we moderns have rediscovered this ancient Greek norm when we respond to visual stimulations of someone we find attractive. A plastic surgeon in Hollywood made great sums of money by re-sculpting the faces of already beautiful women desiring to be truly beautiful. What a conundrum for him. What is beauty? According to what parameters would he re-sculpt their faces? He decided to research the contours of modern runway models—Asian, Caucasian, and Black—and the contours of "beautiful" women through time depicted in art. Using computer analysis, he constructed the model of the "perfect" human face, according to fractal patterns based on the pentagon. Ironically, the five-pointed pentagram used by fertility worshipping Wiccans today is the age-old five-pointed Star of Venus. It seems Greek culture knew best all along. The Greeks constructed their goddess of fertility and beauty according to the mathematical principles that appear to be encoded in our unconscious minds. To put that in evolutionary terms, pentagonal fractals operated archetypally in the evolutionary line that sculpted from the spatially-oriented

 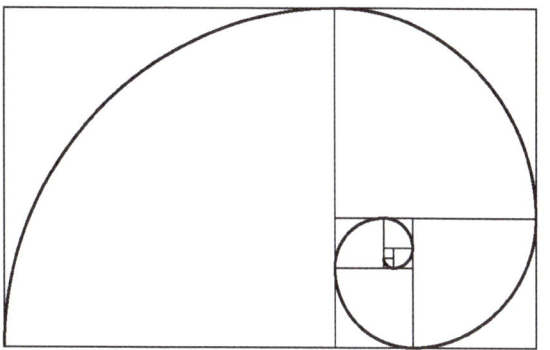 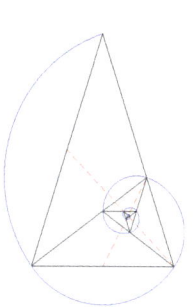

FIGS. 3.5A, 3.5B, AND 3.5C. Phi fractals in a nautilus shell and in Golden Triangles and Rectangles.

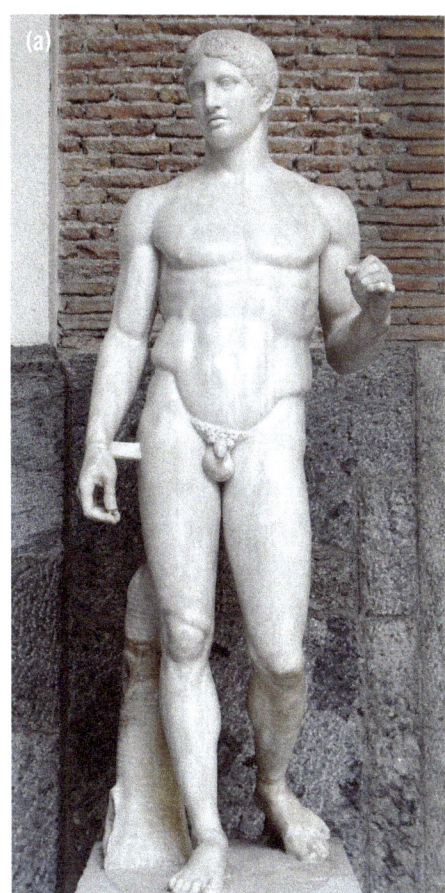 

FIGS. 3.6A AND 3.6B. The Greek sculptures (a) *Doryphoros* and (b) Venus.

sensory organs on the face of Homo habilis, the face of modern Homo sapiens, and made it "beautiful." We will discuss this further when we discuss psychological theory.

The Greeks extrapolated their observations about nature to create a culture based on personal and collective inquiry. Socrates inherited the mathematical philosophies of his forebears and conceived a methodology for his fellow Athenians to know "truth." He was a philosophical mentor of the youth of Athens. The word philosophy is derived from two Greek roots—*philos*—"lover of"—and *Sophia*—"wisdom." **Philosophy** is the love of, and study of, knowledge in order to gain wisdom. Wisdom is knowledge that has been tested in the fires of experience. According to legend, the methodology Socrates used to gain wisdom was derived from the god Apollo, which among his various titles was the "god of truth and prophecy." The **Socratic method** is a form of inquiry and discussion between individuals based on asking and answering questions to stimulate critical thinking and to illuminate ideas. Generally, one point of view is questioned and one participant may lead another to contradict himself in some way, thus leading to the limits of one's knowledge and a desire to seek additional information to increase the understanding of one's "truth." To Socrates, knowing truth is a personal journey and society can benefit from the fruits of each person's personal journey. Two hallmarks of Socrates' philosophy are "To know thyself," and "Get rid of garbage." That is, the purpose of life, and therefore of philosophy, is to know who one truly is, embrace those values and lifestyles that contribute towards one's happiness and utility, and dispose of those behaviors that lead to dysfunction. This not to say that one should flout societal norms, but that individual wisdom is more valuable than conventional custom. Ironically, the conservative Athenian authorities forced Socrates to commit suicide because he contributed to the so-called corruption of the minds of the youth of Athens, by training them to think for themselves. This is a cautionary lesson about what happens when ossified "religious" ideals are used to trump the human spirit, even when those ideals were argued to save the democracy of Athens in a time of crisis.

Socrates' legacy was not lost to posterity with his death. One of his pupils, Plato, wrote down the lessons of his mentor and used them to devise his own. Plato believed in archetypes. **Archetypes** are those mathematical blueprints of "reality" contained within the fabric of natural law from which all physical forms are copied, as poor "rubber stamps," hence our bodily differences. Based on the notion of archetypes, Plato's contribution to Western logical and scientific reasoning would come to be known as deductive reasoning. **Deductive reasoning** proceeds from theory and develops conclusions that are logically drawn from the premises of the theory. This type of reasoning is called *a priori* reasoning, in that one starts from a given and accepted known to "deduce" further truth from it. For Plato, the given known was an archetype. For Thomas Aquinas and the Scholastics, the given known was the Prime Mover, "the Christian God." Plato's disciple Aristotle turned the method of his mentor on its head. Rather than proceeding from known givens, Aristotle would make known previous unknowns by inductive reasoning. **Inductive reasoning**, or **empiricism**, proceeds from experience and experimentation and draws conclusions from them. That is, a scientist should gather all of the variables about a hypothetical idea, subject them to statistical analysis, and thus "induce" new conclusions. This type of reasoning is called *a posteriori*, or after the

FIGS. 3.7A, 3.7B, AND 3.7C. The founders of the scientific method of the Western heritage: (a) Socrates, (b) Plato, and (c) Aristotle.

fact, reasoning. Modern scientists use both deductive and inductive reasoning in their methodologies.

As a pioneer in the Renaissance, Leonardo da Vinci was just such a scientist, and as seen in the diagram, his "Vitruvian Man" displays the phi ratio in its formulation. He re-discovered that if one measures a human from the top of the head to the navel and divide that number by the measurement from the navel to the bottom of the feet, one gets the number 1.62, or phi. Human beings are products of math, and da Vinci emphasized this by encapsulating the "perfect" human form in a "perfect" circle as well as a "perfect" square.

Having analyzed the mentality that formed the bedrock of Western cultural thinking, let's go back even further to the primordial days of human investigations in their pristine environments and see how they structured the contingent questions that confronted them. It is from these "primitive" tribal peoples that the values of civilized thinking will flower. **Primitive**, derived the Latin root *primus*, means "first" or "original," hence the original cultural constructions by the human mind. Incidentally, in this context it is not a stigma denoting inferiority.

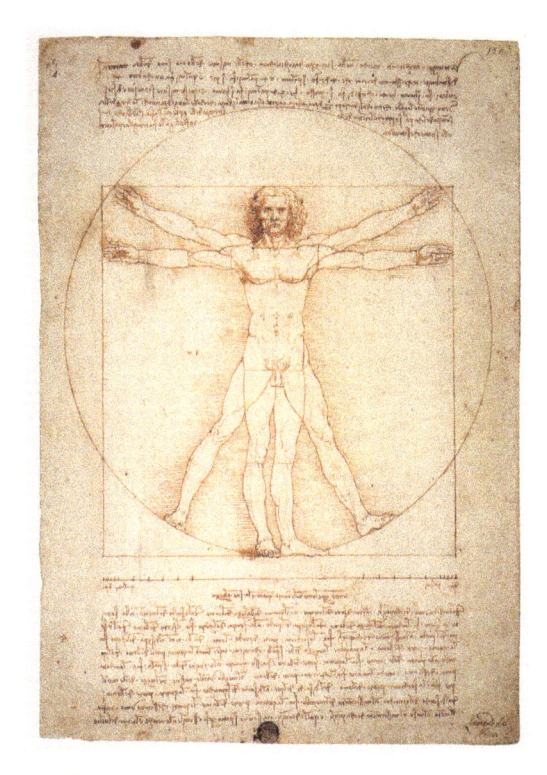

FIG. 3.8. Leonardo da Vinci's "Vitruvian Man."

KEY WORDS

Absolute truth
Deductive reasoning
Fractal
Inductive reasoning
Natural law
Philosophy
Primitive
Relative truth
Secularism
Socratic method
Supernatural ideas

IMAGE CREDITS

- Fig. 3.1: Szilas / Wikimedia Commons / Copyright in the Public Domain.
- Fig. 3.2: Eisnel / Wikimedia Commons / Copyright in the Public Domain.
- Fig. 3.3: Solkoll / Wikimedia Commons / Copyright in the Public Domain.
- Fig. 3.4A: NASA / ESA / Copyright in the Public Domain.
- Fig. 3.4B: Copyright © 2008 by Rror / Wikimedia Commons, (CC BY-SA 3.0) at https://commons.wikimedia.org/wiki/File:Athyrium_filix-femina.jpg.
- Fig. 3.4C: Johannes Sobotta / Copyright in the Public Domain.
- Fig. 3.4D: Copyright © 2007 by Andrew Smith, (CC BY-SA 2.0) at https://commons.wikimedia.org/wiki/File:The_River_Forth,_Craigforth_-_geograph.org.uk_-_318675.jpg.
- Fig. 3.4E: Copyright © 2007 by Piotr Konieczny, (CC BY-SA 3.0) at https://commons.wikimedia.org/wiki/File:Shaped_tree_branches_Tenerife.JPG.
- Fig. 3.5A: Copyright © 2014 by Dicklyon / Wikimedia Commons, (CC BY-SA 4.0) at
- http://en.wikipedia.org/wiki/File:Nautilus_Cutaway_with_Logarithmic_Spiral.png.
- Fig. 3.5B: Dicklyon / Wikimedia Commons / Copyright in the Public Domain.
- Fig. 3.5C: Personline / Wikimedia Commons / Copyright in the Public Domain.
- Fig. 3.6A: Copyright © 2011 by Marie-Lan Nguyen, (CC BY 2.5) at http://commons.wikimedia.org/wiki/File:Doryphoros_MAN_Napoli_Inv6011.jpg.
- Fig. 3.6B: Bibi Saint-Pol / Wikimedia Commons / Copyright in the Public Domain.
- Fig. 3.7A: Szilas / Wikimedia Commons / Copyright in the Public Domain.
- Fig. 3.7B: Copyright © 2014 by Wellcome Images, (CC BY 4.0) at http://commons.wikimedia.org/wiki/File:Portrait_of_Plato;_bust._Wellcome_M0005618.jpg.
- Fig. 3.7C: Szilas / Wikimedia Commons / Copyright in the Public Domain.
- Fig. 3.8: Leonardo da Vinci / Copyright in the Public Domain.

CHAPTER FOUR

SELF, US, THEM, AND LAND

The psychologist Carl Jung claimed that the collected memories of our species' wisdom lay encoded within the unconscious memory of each individual human. He termed this "the million-year-old mind" and all humans inherit it. According to Jung, the human psyche is composed of several elements: the conscious, the unconscious, and the collective unconscious. All three elements constitute the Jungian **Self**. The **conscious** is the arena wherein the cognitive mind reflects upon itself in its daily activities. The **unconscious** is the non-cognitive and symbolic arena of the mind submerged beneath, but interwoven with the conscious. Though based upon personal experience, its wisdom generally lies beyond recall, yet it strongly motivates human behavior through dreams and intuition. The **collective unconscious** is the repository of the psyche that possesses the psychic wisdom of the ancestors that is inherited by each individual consciousness. What Freud called the "ego" and Jung called the conscious is only the tip of the iceberg of the true Self that swims deeply in the various levels of the unconscious and feeds the conscious. But, it is the ego/conscious part of the mind that reflects upon and reacts to contingent "reality." This collective wisdom of the human species is encoded in the shadows of the collective unconscious. This "million-year-old mind" is the arena in which the archetypes dance. This is where Jung incorporates the concepts of Plato into a modern context. Archetypes are symbolic propensities for thought within the human psyche. They are "thought-images" that are charged with emotion by the "primitive" mind and thereby gain **numinosity** or psychic energy, which results in their manifestation as conscious symbols. Archetypes are not definable, static symbols transmitted as irrefutable stock themes from generation to generation. Rather, they are psychic propensities, malleable models, which influence and characterize the collective human psyche. Thus, the human psyche is not a *tabula rasa*, a blank slate, informed only through sensory perceptions; rather, it is an individual reflective conscious that is holistically buoyed and informed by an inter-penetrating web of unconscious archetypal patterns. Each generation within a cultural heritage adorns these archetypes with symbols according to its needs. Always dynamic and subject to various environmental and social factors, archetypes provide the templates for the creation of myths, religions, and philosophies worldwide. Primordial man was moved to deeds by age-old unconscious factors that were both mysterious and spiritual, and that was how he understood the universe.

All things, whether they be gods, spirits, humans, animals, trees, mountains, rivers or stars, were infused with the spirit-breath of deity and thus were inter-connected in the universal "world-soul," which is the consciousness of the divine. The human psyche was "inspired," from the Latin word *inspirare*, "to breathe in," by the "spirit-breath" of the divine, and was thus able to commune with the "all that is." And the divine inspired humanity through unconscious archetypes. The most typical archetypes are the **animus**, the protective and active/"aggressive" aspects of the eternal masculine in the human psyche; the **anima**, the altruistic and nurturing aspects of the complementary eternal feminine; and the **hero**, the divinely born "savior," who, with supernatural help, overcomes malevolent forces in a virtuous quest that typifies not only the struggles of whole peoples for deliverance, but also the struggle of "Everyman" for holistic unity of the rational and spiritual aspects of the psyche during the course of his or her life. All humans struggle to fit their personal identities into the rubric of cultural values and have done so for as long as there have been humans and cultures. The wisdom tales of our societies help us to do this. The composers of the Bible did this in their social and cultural environments; so did the philosophers like Socrates, the composer of Beowulf, the Scholastics like Aquinas, the positivists like Comte, the psychologists like Jung, the secularists like Erikson, and the social Darwinists like Hitler. All of these cultural paradigms will be examined in upcoming chapters.

The following discussion on cultural differences between "tribal" and "civilized" peoples must first be prefaced by an introductory discussion of human brain anatomy. It is well known that the human brain is asymmetric in its physiology and is divided into two hemispheres. The right hemisphere controls predominantly visual and spatial activities and the recognition of shapes and patterns, hence the holistic, qualitative, and abstract views of humans, including the realm of spirituality. These qualities are influenced by a hormonal wash that influences our emotions. The left hemisphere controls verbal and linguistic activities and practical, concrete, analyzing, detail-oriented rational activities, and hence the quantitative, structuring and legalistic views of humans. These brain functions are identical in both males and females of the human species. However, here the similarities diverge and subtle, but salient differences in the cerebral morphology of the two sexes of Homo sapiens are discernable. Women innately possess the intellectual abilities to both master the mechanics of language and grammar and explain ideas more completely than do men who are hard-wired more for terse, specific phrases. By nature, women are better at overall communication than men are. Men tend to be more highly developed in assessing visual-spatial depth perceptions than women are; a man has more frontally-oriented rods and cones in his retina that attune his awareness for this, while a woman has more rods and cones in the sides of her retina for greater peripheral vision. Women's left-brained rationality is more easily associated with emotion because they have emotional centers in both hemispheres and a larger *corpus callosum* connecting both hemispheres than men do. Men's brains divorce the rational left brain from the emotional center, located only in the right. A man, it seems, is equipped to throw a football at an intended moving receiver or loose a javelin at an elusive enemy or prey, while more easily distancing himself from the ethical, moral, and emotional pollutions that accrue to such acts than a woman can. A woman can multi-task at several chores at once, while being more vigilant of the goings-on of the neighbors and children in her surroundings than a man can. These sexual characteristics are hard-wired by physiology. The similarities and differences in brain morphology have given rise to the notions of the left brain as the male, or masculine brain, and the right as the female or feminine brain; these categorizations reveal the overlap and the amorphous liminal boundary between sex and gender and genetic inheritance and social construct. These ideas will be discussed more fully in Chapter 9.

Neuroscientist Jill Bolte Taylor experienced a severe stroke while researching the human brain and her insights help support the current theories of human brain geography. In her work, she has described the left brain as a serial processor, that is, it acts like a computer network that focuses massive amounts of energy on intellectual activities and deals with them sequentially, like the step-by-step premises that lead to logical conclusions in both deductive and inductive reasoning. The right brain acts like a network of parallel computers that assay information from a variety of sources and tries to see the "big picture." Please view her presentation on TED Talks, titled "My Stroke of Insight."

Long before the invention of the alphabet, human beings transmitted their cultures orally. Oral-based cultures are "right-brained" cultures because the auditory centers of the brain are located there and the incoming wisdom of a storyteller's tale is first filtered there. Thus, these cultures tend to be qualitative, creative, and holistic in nature. Peoples of such cultures observe their natural environments and conform to their rhythms. Thus, they also tend to think of life and time as periodic, seasonal, and cyclical events; their values are conservative in general, striving to preserve the heritage of the ancestors and live in harmony with all things. As a result, their cultural mentalities tend to be non-progressive. This does not mean that right-brained cultures are pacifistic. On the contrary, by their very natures, oral-based cultures ground their identities in "us-versus-them" cosmologies. In such cultures, knowledge is structurally derived. Natural phenomena are observed and classified in a process called **operations**. Much like a computer, the human mind makes sense of the world by imposing an analogical structure upon

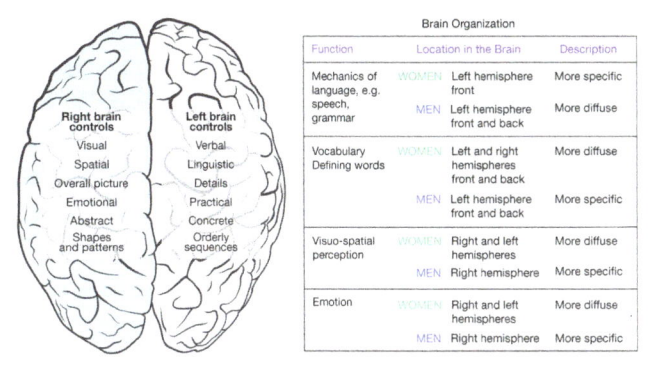

FIGS. 4.1A AND B. (a) The diagram on the left shows how the human brain is divided into two hemispheres—the right and the left. The right brain deals with human emotional, artistic, spiritual, and holistic sensitivities, while the left brain deals with human logical and rational qualities. All humans possess the same attributes in their left and right hemispheres. (b) The chart on the right depicts the subtle differences between human males and females in their brain geographies.

FIG. 4.2A. Jill Bolte Taylor holding a human brain and demonstrating its two hemispheres, left and right. http://www.ted.com/talks/jill_bolte_taylor_s_powerful_stroke_of_insight?language=en

the invisible and underlying order of reality. Through binary opposition—juxtaposing various pairs of opposites—mental linkages are made among natural phenomena and relationships that typify something else. Once these relationships become dogmatic, they become symbols—and in the cross-referencing of symbols, culture is born. Typically, clans and tribes find their identities in certain stock symbols that are unique to them. In times of cultural cataclysm, these archetypally-derived stock themes generally survive the kaleidoscopic shifts of alien acculturation and act as the **bricolage**, or symbolic nuclei of shattered operations, around which traumatized cultures will rally and accrue new ideas. These communal stock symbols are what set one tribal people apart from other tribes and peoples. They are ethnically-derived mental constructs that often obliterate erstwhile racial affiliations. They make "others" different and sometimes not even human. Hence, tribal cultures tend to conservatively protect "closed cells" of wisdom, which often pit tribe against tribe. Virtually all tribal cultures have a warrior class that answers the psychic needs of the animus globally and serves their societies functionally. Incidentally, slaves, who were seen as "others" in the right-brained tribal worldview, were often the booty of a successful martial foray. It is in this context, then, that one can make sense of the Navaho adage, "The Navajo are the only human beings in the world." It is also the tribal mentality that allowed the Crow Native Americans to act as scouts for Lieutenant Colonel George A. Custer against their bitter non-human enemies, the Sioux. Modern notions of "racial" and nationalistic affiliations are just that, modern. We will discuss these ideas in more detail in later chapters.

Across eons of time, early human tribesmen and women lived their days of birth, growth, and death in a verdant and teeming environment, and pondered them deeply. They noted the cycles and rhythms of life, of which they felt themselves a part, and their analogical minds began to structure their universe. Archetypal animals were selected for the properties that humans shared with them as well as for the totemic powers they coveted from them. In the awesome dome of the sky, birds soared, especially aquatic birds, exalted creatures that could ride the breath of the world-soul and unite the three regions of the cosmos—the upper, the middle, and the lower, the sky, the earth, and the waters. As a three-in-one singularity or as a series of three, these creatures of the wind would mediate between man and the deities of the sky. Three became a sacred number and trinitarianism an archetype in the proto-Indo-European mind. In time, as human behavior came to be bound by culture, the spirits of nature would be anthropomorphized into archetypal cult deities and supplicated or appeased as circumstances dictated. There would be many "trinities" in the centuries ahead.

The awareness of both life and death charged human thoughts with both thanks and dread. Women were special creatures. They experienced their fertility cycles with a periodicity that synchronized exactly with that of the moon—twenty-eight days per cycle and thirteen cycles per year, respectively. This coincidence reassured humans greatly. Man was born from the sacred womb of woman; he lived his days and died, his essence returning to the sacred. Also, from the birth of the first crescent, the moon waxed older for thirteen days to its fullness, then waned for thirteen days to its last ebb, before disappearing completely into the sacred. But methodically and miraculously, a new moon would again be birthed from the old. The power of this symbolism inspired in humans their creed of birth, death, and rebirth. Fertility became ensconced in the image of "the mother" on a universal scale. The creation of the cosmos from chaos was hence a feminine principle. The Creatrix was "the Great Mother." All things flowed from her and all things flowed to her, and from this idea, humans created the first recorded religion based on reincarnation. One of humanity's great contingent questions found an answer: "What happens to me when I die?"

Creation is a sacred act, a passage from the non-manifest to the manifest, from chaos to cosmos. Yet always the wheel continues its periodic and inexorable turn, reducing the ordered cosmic state to the primordial disorder of chaos, out of which the cosmogenic act is repeated over and over again, *ad infinitum*. **Cosmogeny** is any theory concerning the origin of the cosmos—the physical universe—and/or the reality of sentient beings. Chaos became the domain of the serpent, the masculine symbol of the unformed, the realm of the archetype. Cosmos became the domain of the mother, the feminine symbol of order, wherein the archetype is made manifest. To the archaic Greeks, this ideology constituted the myth of "the eternal return," an image of "indestructible life." Life is eternal; it transcends the individual mortal creature. To express this concept, the Greek language has two words for life—*zoe* and *bios*. *Zoe* is immortal, archetypal life and is "the time of the soul." *Bios* is specified, physical life and moves in the course of its births from one manifestation to another. From the cultural operations inherent in the Paleolithic mind, body and brain differences between males had been culturally structured into a "gendered" universe of complementary/opposing masculine and feminine principles that led to gendered landscapes, gendered religions, and gendered social roles. The **Paleolithic**, derived from the Greek prefix *paleo*—"old"—and the root *lith*—"stone"—was "the old Stone Age" that lasted about 2.5 million years when primitive stone implements were used.

Homo sapiens living in the Paleolithic era constructed the first recorded human religion in their cave art.

Paleolithic humans' first experience of life indestructible was the Great Mother; to commune with her was to commune with all creatures. Sensitive humans could enter this "communion" among the divine, the ancestors, and animals, and procure totemic wisdom, especially since all was not bliss in the world of contingent mortal existence. At any moment, death might seize someone, young or old, weak or strong. Perhaps most feared was the swift attack of a predator. Predators are hunters, stalkers, disordering creatures full of guile and power. In the cosmos, they are man's equals, in the hunt, his prey—and totemic strength is needed for them to be bested. Contingent reality divided the tribe's territory into zones of the safe "**center**" and the dangerous "**periphery**." Buttressed by endocrine-generated physiology, archetypal gender roles developed to fill social needs. Man was equipped by nature to be a guileful hunter and warrior at the periphery, the area of "masculine" disorder and the encroachment of danger. Woman was equipped by nature to be the moral-conscious guardian of the hearth, the area of "feminine" order and community, in the "center." The Creatrix ramified into a "Mother Earth" goddess and numerous kindred goddesses associated with the feminine concepts of fertility, productivity, and sovereignty. In a cosmos increasingly imposed

FIG. 4.3. In the accompanying images, notice how the Paleolithic human mind structured its understanding of the universe into gendered images of the "masculine" deity, a horned and powerful Animal Master that male hunters and warriors could commune with in fulfilling their social roles as "sacrificial" elements in their societies. In the sculpted "feminine" deity, notice how the ideas of fertility are shown by the abundance of her body. Also notice that in her hand she holds a cornified crescent moon that starts at a point—nothingness—the new moon, has thirteen scratches in it that waxes to its full end—the full moon—and then wanes again until it "dies" into the new moon, only to be "born again" each month. One day, plus 13 days, plus another one day, plus another 13 days add up to 28 days. The birth and death of one period of the life of the moon coincides exactly with the 28-day menstrual cycle of a human female. This "secret" of the universe reassured contingent Paleolithic humans that they had an afterlife and they developed a religion based on reincarnation. And Paleolithic culture also gained two powerful gendered symbols, the life-giving "feminine" moon and its dialectic opposite, the hot and energizing "masculine" sun.

upon by patriarchal connotations, that is, as the left-brained—rational—human mind domesticated the bountiful fertility of nature via agriculture and husbandry, as well as its right-brained feminine mother goddess, the sky became associated with the masculine principle and "Father Sky" became its sovereign, a god called *dyeus*, or Zeus. The masculine periphery became the domain of gods whose worship took place in nature. They were the "Masters of Animals" and the "Men of the Woods" who imparted totemic wisdom to the hunters and warriors. From them would come the archetypal and beneficent horned-god Cernunnos of Celtic mythology, later demonized by monotheists as Satan, and the sylvan Green Man, whose face was sculpted of foliage and berries. These peripheral deities would reappear as the mysterious Green Knight of Arthurian lore and the legendary archer Robin Hood. Women provided the nurturing focus for the group, the cosmic center for the community, the haven for the jaded warrior returning from the chaotic traumas of the periphery; her holistic mindset suited her for the archetypal task of feminine "communion." The ethic of the warrior entailed that a man should become proficient in martial arts, be his people's "champion," the defender of its culture, its heritage, and its honor. If necessary, he was to "sacrifice" himself, that is, to let his blood flow, to re-immerse himself in the "sacred," in their cause, and his gifts of intense and narrow focus suited him for the archetypal task of masculine "sacrifice." Representing a harmonization of the animus and anima archetypes in cultural values everywhere, religions universally link the ideas of communion and sacrifice. As societies domesticated grains and herds, ceased from their nomadic migrations, and sunk roots into definable territories, they sought to arrest the primordial cosmogenic cycle and preserve their community, throughout its generations, from pollution and decay. Hence, propitiatory sacrifices, either humans or substituted animals, would be made to interdict the periodic re-immersion of the cosmos into the pollution-cleansing abyss of chaos and extend, instead, one's heritage into the future indefinitely. Humans liked their domestication of nature and they wanted to see it continue. In fact, they wanted to continue experimenting with resources to make life even easier for themselves in the future. Thus was born the notion of "**progress**." However, with the advent of linear time, pollution would accrue to an unrecycled cosmos, and at some point, humanity would become hopelessly lost in its "sins" and need a super-human archetypal hero, a sacrificial savior, to wash away the "sins of the world."

All of these ideas reflect the subliminal processes by which humans struggle to figure out their own places in the cosmos. A universal unconscious archetype for the unknown contingent forces that operate on the dangerous periphery of the land of the "true humans," and later the "chosen people," is the circle (o). The circle encapsulates the safe and sacred space of the controllable center. The circle represents the holistic uncontrolled space out there; it is the domain of chaos that constantly encroaches on the cultural accomplishments of humans and it is the domain of the right brain. It also represents the Jungian Self. The area within the boundary of the circle is the safe center. It is the place where humans can control nature and "cosmicize," that is, domesticate it according to their needs. It is the feminine space of culture and progress. It is the domain of the left brain. It also represents the ego, or conscious. The safe center, wherein humans can orient themselves, has traditionally been represented as an (x) like the crosshairs in a gun sight.

FIG. 4.4. Traditional Native American societies have oriented themselves by a symbolic (x) in the domestic space termed the "center," the place of ego and consciousness, within an uncontrollable peripheral cosmos, the realm of Jung's Self, symbolized by a circle (o).

As societies settled into territorial lands, they stratified into social classes, castes, or estates dependent upon the charismatic gifts of the gods to each individual at his or her birth. There was little consciousness of a modernesque sense of social injustice concomitant with the development of hierarchical societies. One accepted the fact that one's station in life was ordained by destiny. There were "those who ruled," the priests and kings who were endowed with the spiritual and physical qualities of "communion" requisite for the vicars of deity on earth; "those who fought," the warriors endowed

FIG. 4.5. The Ancient Celts developed cultural ideas that envisioned the fertile landscape upon which they dwelled as feminine, and gave her a name—Erin. Erin was defended by physical men at the periphery.

FIG. 4.6. The Zulu constructed circular settlements called *kraals*, outside of which warriors defended women who foraged for food.

with the prowess and ethics necessary to satisfy the "sacrificial" needs of society; and "those who worked," the laborers whose productivity satisfied the "fertility" qualities of society. Societies were thus symbolically structured to conform to the archetypal and "trinitarian" ideals of communion, sacrifice, and fertility. Georges Dumézil has deconstructed the primal Indo-European society as a trinitarian society, and it is from our Indo-European ancestors that Western culture developed, and from that, modern world culture, as we shall see.

Among the ancient Celts, whose frenetic passions mimicked the latent, but explosive energies of the universe, each new king as "sovereign," the physical embodiment of the land's masculine fertility, would ritualistically "mate" with the goddess of "sovereignty," the principle of feminine fertility inherent in the land itself, and re-energize the cosmos. Later, when the king's "fecund" powers waned, he would be sacrificed, initially literally, to make way for heartier royal stock. As an abstract adaptation of the "eternal return myth" of Mircea Eliade, the indestructible sovereign fecundity of the nation would be regenerated through the perpetual reincarnation of its sovereign. Thus, the prosperity of the people would be assured in a chaotic cosmos, and hence the chant, "The king is dead; long live the king!"

The father-mother-son "trinitarian" incest-cycle inherent in the anthropomorphized eternal return myth is woven deeply into the European collective unconscious. To perpetuate life indestructible, the fecund Eternal Mother mates with the ephemeral fertilizing father who regenerates himself as the "born-again" son in the endless cycle of archetypal life. The Osiris-Isis-Horus and Zeus-Persephone-Dionysos trinities accommodate this archetype. Even Christianity conforms to this sacred symbolism. Of necessity, the virgin Mother Mary is deified through an "immaculate conception" in order to birth the Son of God from the heavenly Father. The birth of a salvific son-god who insures cosmic fertility and prosperity for his people by atoning for their chaotic pollutions through an ecstatic and empathetic sacrifice can be traced back to the initial wisps of European culture. The first sacrificial savior was a bull-god, which is a symbol of the masculine periphery. Paleolithic cave paintings in Lascaux, France depict an entranced shaman communing with a bull that oversees the heavenly herds and is gored by a spear. Peripheral bull-gods were sacrificed to feminine vulture-goddesses in propitiatory rites at Catal Huyuk in Turkey. The Celts chose their kings through a sacrificial druidic ritual called the "bull feast," and Athenian hostages were sacrificed to the Minotaur—the "bull-god of Minos"—in a cosmicizing, that is, pollution-cleansing, labyrinthine dance in ancient Crete. The ancient peoples colonized by the Greeks in the lands south of Latium called themselves in the Oscan tongue *Uitelieu*, or Italians, the "sons of the bull-god." The savior-god Mithras slew the sacred bull of heaven in order to procure cosmic prosperity for his people, and even the horned bull-god Dionysos, whose name means "the twice-born one" or "the one born again," would become a suffering god, taking on his people's pollutions through his sacrifice. Such was the sacred origin of the **drama**, a Dionysian ritual to recapitulate the unpolluted *dromenon*, "the thing done in mythic time." To this day, the Spanish unwittingly recapitulate this primordial drama in their bullfights. And not surprisingly, the word "messiah" itself derives from a Sumerian root meaning "raging bull."

Having analyzed how early peoples codified their contingent questions in time, space, and on land, and saw themselves as Self, us, and them, let us now examine how these ideas come together in cultural anthropology.

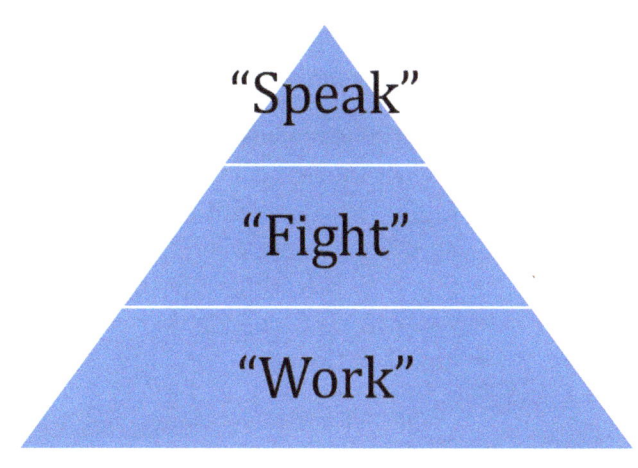

FIG. 4.7. Diagram of Dumézil's social structure for the primal Indo-European culture.

KEY WORDS

Anima
Animus
Archetypes
Bricolage
Center
Collective unconscious
Conscious
Cosmogeny

Drama
Hero
Operations
Paleolithic
Progress
Self
Unconscious

IMAGE CREDITS

- Fig. 4.2: Copyright © 2008 by Steve Jurvetson, (CC BY 2.0) at http://commons.wikimedia.org/wiki/File:Jill_Bolte_Taylor_-_observing_a_stroke_from_within.jpg.
- Fig. 4.3A: Jean Clottes and David Lewis-Williams / Copyright in the Public Domain.
- Fig. 4.3B: Copyright © 2008 by 120 / Wikimedia Commons, (CC BY 3.0) at http://en.wikipedia.org/wiki/File:Venus-de-Laussel-vue-generale-noir.jpg.
- Fig. 4.5: H.R.Millar / Copyright in the Public Domain.
- Fig. 4.5: El Comandante / Wikimedia Commons / Copyright in the Public Domain.
- Fig. 4.6: George French Angas / Copyright in the Public Domain.

CHAPTER FIVE

CULTURAL ANTHROPOLOGY

Two developments would transform the hero-god archetype of right-brained and conservative tribal cultures into secular, futuristic, and progressive left-brained "Western" cultures. The first was the invention of the Northern Semitic, and from it the Greco-Roman alphabet. The alphabet shifted the intake of knowledge from the oral tales of the storyteller to the written word of the scribe. Sensory information now passed through the eyes, which funneled its signals to the left hemisphere of the brain for initial processing. Hence, knowledge filtered there tended to be analyzed, sequenced, categorized, and quantified before being shared with the holistic right brain. By being encapsulated in written symbols, language no longer danced with the speaker's breath on the world-soul. On papyrus or parchment, language lost its magic. Hence, knowledge would be garnered by rational, logic-chopping individuals ruminating over books in isolation, not in communal orations. Left-brained cultures would undermine the clannishness of the tribes and eventually elevate the individual human as its hero. Cultures that derive their wisdom from books develop a sense of history that is linear and progressive. Recorded history marches on. Sequential chronicles overpower the periodicity of history. Left-brained cultures transcend the non-progressive and conservative world-views of their ancestors. Gone will be the reverencing of the wisdom of the patriarchs in the pristine golden days, whose morality their sons and daughters could only hope to mimic, not better. Instead will be fostered a progressive morality in which the world of their sons and daughters will build on the recorded accomplishments of the ancestors and surpass them. Not only will language lose its magic in a rational mindset, but also nature itself will lose its holistic sacredness and become the warehouse of resources for human progress. Only in the West will the alphabet prove simple enough to be eventually mastered by the masses, which, with the new mindset will eventually tear down the barriers dividing the classes in charismatic, hierarchical societies. **Charisma**, derived from the Greek root *charis*, connotes the idea of "grace" as a unique and personal "gift" that each human is endowed with at birth. Today, we would equate it with "personality." From its very beginning then, left-brained culture, which I deem Western culture, will be sown with the seeds that from tribal soils will bloom those rational, scientific, and progressive societies. In turn, these societies will ultimately foster the ideals of individual maximization and political liberalism that are the cornerstones of all nations that adhere to the tenets of modern one-world internationalism today.

    The second development that fostered the genesis of Western civilization was the formulation of a radically dualistic sense of morality in the ancient Near East. In the ever-rebellious polyglot empire of ancient Persia, the "King of Kings," Darius I, realized that the religious toleration of his ancestors, like

Social Construction

"Right-Brain"	"Left-Brain"
• Experiential, Holistic	• Analytical, Logical
• Spoken	• Written
• Oral Traditional	• Books
• Nature	• Literary, Scientific
• Cyclical	• Linear, Progressive
• Tribal	• Civilized
• Past-oriented	• Future-oriented
• Conservative	• Liberal
• Charismatic, Communal	• Individual, Democratic
• Non-western	• Western

FIG. 5.1. In the chart, notice how all cultures start out as environmentally sensitive right-brain cultures because tribal humans filter their sensory input from their environments through the holistic and emotional right brain before passing the information on to the left brain. As a result, languages are oral and cultural lore must be memorized and passed on correctly from generation to generation. Hence, right-brained cultures are nature honoring, conservative, past-oriented, and communal in their worldviews. With the invention of writing, visual stimuli pass through the analytical left brain first, where they are de-mystified and sequentially processed, fostering a cultural worldview that is linear, futuristic, progressive, and as a result of private studies, individualistic. These cultures are the "modern" cultures and are characterized by their secular, democratic, and socialistic ideologies.

Cyrus who allowed the Hebrews to return to Jerusalem, would never unite his unwieldy domains, and eagerly embraced the new leveling religion of Zoroaster. Zoroastrians preached that all morality was ordained of the one god of truth, Ahura Mazda, and was recorded in scriptures. All those who lived according to the dictates of those scriptures were righteous; all those who didn't were sinners and unwitting minions of Ahriman, the god of lies, Ahura Mazda's adversary and history's first Satan. In the heavenly battle of good against evil throughout history, the servants of Ahura Mazda must not only live exemplary lives themselves, but must also crusade against and destroy the minions of Ahriman while they cleanse themselves of unrighteousness. This will, then, cleanse their lands of pollution and chaos.

In their transition to an oral-derived culture, the tribes of ancient Israel imbibed these mores in the formulation of their own scriptures. And in the welter of ancient Near Eastern power politics, the Kingdom of Israel would suffer civil war, dismemberment and captivity, and would pine for an archetypal hero-deliverer, a messiah. To some, he would appear in the person of Jesus Christ, who would act on their behalf as a substitute sacrifice. But, in a left-brained Hellenized world adhering to Plato's notions of archetypes, Christ's sacrifice would transcend the tribal and parochial "us-versus-them" worldview of the Jewish people to become the abstract, progressive, and final propitiation through flesh of the savior-god of all humankind. Christians were commanded by their savior and "King of Kings" to evangelize all the world, cleanse it of satanic pollutions, and make disciples of all nations. In order to make monotheistic, left-brained disciples of all nations, Western warriors would have to overwhelm right-brained warriors who were reluctant to give up their polytheistic religions and suffer their cultures to be reduced to westernized bricolage. That the West was able to field evangelical warriors that were able to do just that is a reflection of the amalgamation of the right-brained archetypal symbols of "pre-Western" Europe with the left-brained scientific progressivism of "Western" Europe.

CULTURAL ANTHROPOLOGY 47

In the 3,700 years since the advent of the alphabet began nuancing the evolution of the left-brained Western culture, many subliminal mental constructs have become interwoven into a single skein to produce the particular Western worldview. Millennia-old masculine and feminine symbols grounded ancient European cultures, endowing them with sacrificial warriors and communal nurturers, as we have seen. Such is true of all non-Western cultures. But, what shifts with the onset of left-brained literacy is the development of an offensive and evangelical warrior code from a defensive and protective one. This reflects a subliminal but profound shift in one's mindset from a closed "us-versus-them" tribal ethnocentrism to the adherence of a "chosen people" to a monotheistic deity's plan of universal pollution cleansing. Incidentally, this is true of both "spiritual" Christian and Muslim "evangelists," as well as the secular "evangelists" of democracy and Communism during the Cold War. "Progress" will be manifested in spiritual religion, secular politics, capitalism, industrialism, etc.

FIGS. 5.2A AND 5.2B. The dualistic deities of righteousness and evil in the Zoroastrian religion, (a) Ahura Mazda and (b) Ahriman (or Satan).

In Europe, ancient Greek history spanned the transformation of its various regional cultures from tribal and oral ones to ones that were oral-derived, urban, and literate. From an early modern European linear and progressive point of view, they were evolving from "inferior" cultural mores toward "superior" ones. As a result, ancient Greece bequeathed to Western civilization an ideological oxymoron, a legacy of equality and democracy for state citizens and enslavement for barbarian others. As a result of its traumatic and martial birth, Rome gave to the Western mentality not only its triumphant ideal of republican governance, but also its concomitant ideology of imperialism. **Imperialism**, derived from the Latin word *imperium*, means "the god-given right to rule others." Warriors no longer defended the sacred center at the periphery; they would expand the center by expanding the periphery to eventually encompass a "one-world system." The civic expansionism of the left-brained ancient Mediterranean world was justified by an ironically enviable acculturation of barbarian "others" to Hellenistic culture and the beneficent perquisites of the Pax Romana that were dangled before provincials in the linear progression of civilization. In an effort to rejuvenate popular adulation of the flagging Pax Romana, the Roman imperial government embraced Christianity, a left-brained "religion of the book," the tenets of which were enticingly more compatible with a centralizing ideology of progressive *imperium* than with the parochial cosmology inherent in the old tribal pantheon of Palatine Rome. In a process of psychic transformation, the burgeoning left-brained Western world-view pulled from the collective unconscious the disparate strands of the hitherto right-brained cultural symbols of the animus, anima, and hero archetypes and amalgamated them into a new Western worldview. In the new cosmology, devotion to the Roman Empire meant devotion to the aspirations of the universal, that is, "catholic" will of the savior-god. In the ideology of salvation of the Roman Catholic Church, "making disciples of all nations" equated with successful imperialism; in its application, the propagation of the gospel would be spearheaded, literally, by the cast of the javelin.

The successful fifth-century onslaught of the Germanic barbarians that toppled the Roman Empire re-leavened Roman Catholic Western Europe with dollops of right-brained paganism to create a medieval cultural heritage that was a curious mix of Western and pre-Western influences. The Holy Roman Empire was its offspring and its chivalric code launched sacrificial martial artists onto evangelical hero-quests and crusades. The hero-quest will be discussed more fully in Chapter 9. Christ remained the hero of Europe's urban centers, but in more pagan areas, old myths were resurrected and shape-shifted to meet current needs. Artio, the totemic bear-god of primeval Europe became King Arthur, the messianic *Restitutor Orbis*, the World Restorer, who would re-awaken in a time of national emergency and herald in a new age of Brythonic greatness. Revered leaders also conformed posthumously to the dictates of the hero archetype; in legend, both Charlemagne and the emperor Barbarossa would become "world restorers." Indeed, even in the twentieth-century, Adolph Hitler, in a time of reactionary anti-liberalism, would cast his gaze back to a Teutonic "golden age" and see himself as a messianic "world restorer" of the German people.

Cultural anthropology developed out of this welter of intellectual effort by Europeans attempting to create a Kingdom of "Man" on earth, and put deity on a political "back burner." The thinkers who pondered this new civilization were called humanists. **Humanism** is a philosophy that rejects spiritual revelation as the basis of knowledge and emphasizes the agency of critically thinking human beings in the attainment of human endeavors. As we saw earlier, the positivist Auguste Comte was instrumental in promoting an in-depth analysis of contemporary civilized European culture as well as its interactions with the primitive tribal peoples with which it was coming into contact with in its colonial domains. Among these peoples, Europeans saw their own cultural origins and desired to explore their "own" roots through them for any lessons that might prove helpful in devising their own humanistic "Kingdom" on earth. Thus, cultural anthropology was born and cultural anthropologists began their studies of aboriginal peoples. An **aboriginal** is a person inhabiting a land from the "earliest times," or from before the arrival of the colonists. It is derived from the Latin prefix *ab*—"from"—and the root *origine*—"the beginning." Aboriginal is synonymous with the word "indigenous."

Everyone today and everyone who has ever lived have faced the same contingent questions, and all answer those questions through culture. A **culture** is a way of life that includes the material and the mental products that are shared within a particular society and transmitted from generation to generation. Each human culture is a product of its environment and circumstances. How humans see those environments, manipulate them, analyze those circumstances, and draw lessons from them comprise the fundamentals of the term culture. Culture, remember, means to plant. What is planted in our individual and collective cultures is an amalgam composed of three elements: material resources, intellectual ideas, and behavior patterns. Pacific Islanders may hunt fish with harpoons made from shaped bone, stone, wood, and sinew. Their "good" deity may be a large fish or whale because it provides them with many of the basic resources necessary for survival. The shark may be deemed a "bad" deity because it not only denies the Pacific Islanders the resources they need, but it may eat them as well and prod them to think of contingent life now, and in a life that follows. Three elements—physical objects, mental ideations, and collective behavior—are the "strong forces" around which cultural "nuclei" aggregate.

In their specific environments, each culture uses the binary oppositions and the process of operations discussed in Chapter 4 to create symbols. **Symbols** are arbitrary units of meaning, whether verbal or nonverbal, which represent different concrete or abstract phenomena. Because of their violent volcanic environment, ancient Mesoamericans viewed volcanoes as a source of sustenance manifested from a nurturing mother. From her, mineral-rich ash overspread the landscape and enabled her "chosen" humans to produce their corn staple, *maize*. She also gave black obsidian glass—the scab of her bleeding—which was fashioned into sacrificial knives from which to remove the beating hearts of sacrificial victims whose blood replenished hers and which was freely given for the sake of her children. This reciprocity of ritualistic blood-letting kept the cosmos from collapsing back into chaos.

To return to the South Seas, when European ethnographers first encountered the Maori people on what would become New Zealand, they were captivated by the intense tattoos of the people. In a famous comparison of portraits, a British ethnographer sketched a Maori chieftain and then the Maori chieftain sketched himself. The British ethnographer utilized da Vinci's mathematical techniques of perspective in order to capture the three-dimensional features of the chieftain on a two-dimensional sheet of paper (an example is seen below). Whether he himself believed in supernatural ideas or not, he certainly could not capture spirit on paper. His was a secular sketch by a scientist. The chief, however, cared nothing for his physical and mathematical representation. He conveyed in his sketch his spiritual role as the conduit of divine forces that would bring sustenance, rain, food, and offspring to his people. His tattoos are not "art"; they are the insignia embedded within his body that connected into and channeled the divine. This is perhaps the classic example of tribal right-brained culture interfacing with left-brained Western culture.

A famous concept shared by many peoples is the idea that "we are one people made up of many." The United States has the motto "*E Pluribus Unum*" on its money – just look at the back of a penny. It is a Latin phrase that means "One"—*Unum*—"Out of"—*E*—"Many"—*Pluribus*. This particular version of the symbol

FIG. 5.3. Mesoamerican obsidian knife.

FIG. 5.4. A portrait of a Maori chieftain.

FIG. 5.5. Treaty between the people of the United Kingdom and the Fante Asafo tribe.

is distinctly Western because it is characterized by Latin letters and grammar. It is an entirely secular symbol. In the accompanying image, the British flag is really composed of three flags superimposed onto each other: the thick red cross on a white field is the emblem of St. George, the patron saint of England; the white saltire cross (diagonal) on a blue field is the emblem of St. Andrew, the patron saint of Scotland; and the red saltire cross on a white field is the emblem of St. Patrick, the patron saint of Ireland. Put together, they signify an abstract British way of conveying the idea *E Pluribus Unum*. The flag is unconsciously portraying a sacred right of the British people(s) to an "evangelical" empire in its flag. It is *imperium* brought to form. In its nineteenth century incarnation, British imperialism would promote less the spiritual religion of the gospel than the secular religion of "the White Man's Burden."

Often, different peoples can look at the same object and construct vastly different symbols for their cultures. For example, the primeval Europeans looked up at the most recognizable constellation in the night sky and envisioned their Great Bear Grandfather God—*Artio*—*Ursa Major* (the Great Bear)—the intercessor for them against the greatest predator in their environments, the bear. It was for them a construction that assuaged a contingent fear of death. Likewise, the ancient Mesoamericans looked up at the same constellation and saw Seven Macaw (so named for the seven stars of which it is comprised) a demon-bird pretending to be the sun in the night, a symbol of chaos encroaching upon the cosmos, which was restored to stasis by an ancient Maya hero who shot it with a blowgun. This story assuaged the angst of the Maya by teaching them that, although change is inevitable, community continues. We moderns look up at the same constellation and see a big spoon, the Big Dipper. This name for the constellation reveals that we are secularists and give more attention to material resources than to other contingent needs.

To gather data in order to understand the operations, symbols, and structures of cultures, anthropologists must go out into the field and investigate cultures on site. Anthropologists who do this are called ethnographers. **Ethnography** is a description of a society written by an anthropologist who conducts field research in that society, collects data on that society, and draws scientific conclusions about that society. Ethnographers have travelled far and wide over the past few centuries and have given Western culture

FIG. 5.6. The Great Bear or the Big Dipper?

many literary gems about specific cultures, "beads" if you will. It is the job of the ethnologist to run the "string" through these "beads." **Ethnology** is the sub-field of anthropology that focuses on the cross-cultural aspects of ethnographic studies. For example, the conclusion that might state, "tribal people are examples of right-brained cultures and civilizations are left-brained cultures" is an ethnological perspective culled from the work of many ethnographers. Having said that, the ethnographer must strive to put away his or her cultural biases and take on the view of the people being studied in order to represent, as accurately as possible, the viewpoints of those people. This is called the **emic** view. For example, an ethnographer might write that the South Seas Pacific Islanders believe that the whale is their benevolent deity. The ethnologist might take the academic **etic** viewpoint, the viewpoint prevalent in the current anthropological body of accepted knowledge, and conclude that the Pacific Islanders need whales to survive and project their uncontrollable contingent needs onto a marine mammal in order to assuage their angst about predatory sharks.

FIG. 5.7. Seven Macaw.

Intrinsic to ethnographic and ethnological studies is the viewpoint of the observer, that is, the anthropologist. A cultural anthropologist must be careful about being ethnocentric in one's studies. **Ethnocentrism** is the practice of judging another society by the values and standards of one's own. This was the bugbear of cultural anthropological studies one hundred years ago, as we shall see in Chapter 7. Today, in the post-colonial and "globalized" age where migrations and diasporas have caused formerly closed cells of cultural lore in "us-versus-them" tribal communities to interact with hegemonic cultures in pluralistic societies, cultural relativism has replaced the notion of ethnocentrism. A **diaspora** is the dislodging of any large number of people from their historical homeland to other places where they continue to maintain their original identity. **Hegemony** is the dominance of one group over another. **Pluralistic societies** are those societies that are composed of a number of different cultural or subcultural groups. A **subculture** is a portion of a larger ethnic culture that shares some features with the dominant culture, but which also differs with it in some respects. **Cultural relativism** is the viewpoint that the traditions that any cultural group constructs are valid and that no group's "truth" can be imposed on another as long as international law is obeyed. Today, this ideal is called multiculturalism. **Multiculturalism** is the public policy that all cultures are legitimate and equal.

Cultural ideas are exchanged through a process called cultural diffusion. **Cultural diffusion** is the spreading of objects, ideas, and behaviors from one society to another. Cultural diffusion brings change to a society. One change in a culture can induce other changes in a culture; these are called **linked changes**. Remember, bricolage is the attempt by an oppressed culture to save as much of its heritage as possible from being destroyed by the hegemonic culture. Such radical changes can produce culture shock. **Culture shock** is a psychological disorientation experienced when attempting to operate in a radically different cultural environment. And culture shock can lead to dysfunction. **Dysfunction** is a stress or imbalance induced within a cultural system by external pressures and may result in aberrant behaviors among individuals as well as the culture itself. Changes in culture from external influences do not always have to be dysfunctional. Cultures survive by adapting to these influences. One means of adapting to a culture is called acculturation. **Acculturation** is that form of learning in which a subordinate culture takes on many of the cultural ideals of the hegemonic culture. The idea of assimilation is related to this process. **Assimilation** is the process of absorbing a subordinate group into the dominant group. Once subordinate groups are assimilated into the dominant culture, all people in that culture will thereafter learn their values through a process called enculturation. **Enculturation** is the means by which human infants learn their culture.

In homage to the positivistic idea of studying the human creature in all of its cultural manifestations, when ethnographers go into the field to conduct research they sift among the various expressions of culture in various physical environments to distill out the cultural universals that all human groups must structure in order to meet their contingent needs. These universals include kinship structure, gender structure, family structure, religious structure, political structure, and social structure as well as access to resources, sex, and reproduction. **Cultural universals** are those cultural traits that are found in all societies around the world, not only today, but all through time. The notion of time will be discussed in the next chapter.

KEY WORDS

Aboriginal
Acculturation
Assimilation
Charisma
Cultural diffusion
Cultural relativism
Cultural universals
Culture
Culture shock
Diaspora
Dysfunction
Emic
Enculturation
Ethnocentrism
Ethnography
Ethnology
Etic
Hegemony
Humanism
Imperialism
Multiculturalism
Linked changes
Pluralistic societies
Subculture
Symbols

IMAGE CREDITS

- Fig. 5.2A: Copyright © 1991 by Ziegler175 / Wikimedia Commons, (CC BY-SA 3.0) at http://commons.wikimedia.org/wiki/File:AhuraMazda-Relief.jpg.
- Fig. 5.2B: Copyright © 2014 by ZxxZxxZ / Wikimedia Commons, (CC BY-SA 4.0) at http://en.wikipedia.org/wiki/File:Text-pal-Ahlmn%27-ahreman.png.
- Fig. 5.3: Copyright © 2009 by Simon Burchell, (CC BY-SA 3.0) at https://commons.wikimedia.org/wiki/File:Aztec_or_Mixtec_sacrificial_knife_1.jpg.
- Fig. 5.4: Syndey Parkinson / Copyright in the Public Domain.
- Fig. 5.5: Akwa Osei / Copyright in the Public Domain.
- Fig. 5.6: Copyright © 2013 by Siamaksabet / Wikimedia Commons, (CC BY-SA 3.0) at http://commons.wikimedia.org/wiki/File:Ursa_Major-siamak_sabet.jpg.
- Fig. 5.7: Siyajkak / Wikimedia Commons / Copyright in the Public Domain.

CHAPTER SIX

"TELLING" A STORY

"Once upon a time," … so every good story begins. But let's stop at time for a moment. What is time? Some non-academics would answer with assurance, "the fourth dimension." And, some academics would answer with non-assurance, "it is one of those relative truths." Time, in the Western heritage, moves in one direction. Anthropologists call this ideal of time **monochronic**. It is linear. It moves toward the future, through each present moment, from the past. "Time marches on." There can be no return to the past to change or observe events and there can be no reading of the future. Several scientists today are questioning how correct this notion of monochronic time really is. They suspect from their research that time is a symbolic construct of the left-brained mind and that there are no unilinear limits to time. Time and space act together as a single amalgam—"time-space"—and it is malleable. This new scientific idea corresponds to the notion of time held by many tribal peoples and by many ancient peoples. To them, there are no boundaries to time and shamanic practitioners can travel to the past as well as the future. Shamanic ideologies will be discussed in Chapter 10. Anthropologists call this ideal of time **polychronic**. Polychronic peoples tend to look back at the wisdom delivered to them from the ancestors. An aphorism of such old wisdom is "March toward your destiny by following in the footsteps of your ancestors."

An awareness of time is essential for establishing the setting of any story. So how can a positivist anthropologist tell the story of an ancient oral peoples who have no story to tell, peoples whose cultures have since vanished and/or who had no writing with which to record their ideas for posterity? These erstwhile mute peoples may yet have their stories told or at least parts of it through those anthropologists called archeologists. **Archeology** is the sub-field of anthropology that focuses on the study of prehistoric and historic cultures through the excavation of material remains. Before any archeological excavation can be begun, a research design must be conducted. A **research design** is a proposal for an anthropological endeavor that sets out the objectives of the proposed project, the means of accomplishing that project, the questions to be explored, and the methods by which the answers will be discerned. Reading the relevant anthropological literature, seeking the advice of experts, political leaders, and financial backers relevant to any project fall within the scope of a research design. Some archeologists search for fossils. **Fossils** are the preserved remains, impressions, or traces of living creatures from past ages left behind when the organic material of which they were composed decays and is filled with minerals that harden into rock and can be later identified by their characteristic patterns. If an archeologist is looking for fossils, knowledge of taphonomy is necessary. **Taphonomy** is the study of the natural and behavioral processes that lead to the locations where fossils may be found. This includes knowing where

FIG. 6.1. An archeological excavation of a tenth century Haudenosaunee site in 2008. Please note the grid layout, the unit sites in square-meter boxes, and the midden pile in the foreground.

FIG. 6.2. Midden "treasure."

FIG. 6.3. Documenting a unit containing a feature from which artifacts have been collected.

humans preferred to live and why, where predators hunted and killed prey, and where they deposited the remains. It also includes knowledge of the types of soils and environments likely to produce fossils. An archeologist who is studying humans will look for artifacts. An **artifact** is a type of material remain that has been made or modified by humans. Artifacts can include arrowheads, tools, eating utensils, etc. Before an archeological dig intended to excavate artifacts from the ground or underwater can begin, a thorough survey must be conducted. A **survey** is the systematic examination of a particular area, region, or country to locate the most likely sites for human activity and its remains to be found. Surveying sites can include high-tech aids that don't break the ground prior to a sponsored dig. These aids can include ground-penetrating radar, proton magnetometers, and electrical resistivity meters which use various "echo" images of items in the ground that differ from the regular images of the subsoil.

Once a particular site has been funded to be excavated, a grid is constructed by using a global positioning system (GPS) device to pinpoint a datum point. A **datum point** is a permanent marker set into the ground from which all measurements at the site are made. From the datum marker, a plumb line is run through the site. From this plumb line a grid is marked off in square meter boxes that will be used in correlating artifacts in the ground with a grid map of the excavation. Not all human "footprints" left in the ground are artifacts that can be mapped and taken away. Some that cannot be moved are called features. **Features** are parts of archeological sites that have been made or modified by humans and cannot be easily moved. Village sites, fire pits, and temple complexes are all examples of features. All artifacts and features encountered in the ground must be photographed, mapped, and recorded in their contexts before being moved and stored. **Context** refers to the exact location of a fossil or artifact in relation to the soil and any associated materials.

Some archeologists fantasize about being another Schliemann, who discovered ancient Troy in the nineteenth century, or an Indiana Jones, who can whisk away a crystal skull in less time than it takes to throw a punch and wield a six-shooter. But, most archeologists find more treasure by meticulously wielding a whisk broom in a trash pile left behind by the peoples who inhabited the archeological site. An archeology trash site is called a **midden**. Imagine trying to find out how a typical undergraduate student thought and lived; would you rather see the re-painted empty room that was left after he or she departed for the summer or the bag of trash containing posters, beer bottles, pizza boxes, and perhaps some old notes?

An important way in which a site, a feature, and an artifact can tell a story is through the determination of their dates. One family of dating methods is called relative dating. **Relative dating** is a method of dating that finds similarities among artifacts, features, and sites that can be cross-linked with other artifacts, features, and sites that both overlap in certain respects and dates as well as differ, whether older in part or younger in part, to build a chronological chain of dates. A good example of relative dating is dendrochronology. **Dendrochronology** is the study of tree rings, whether fossilized or from live trees, whose cross-sectional ring patterns can be calibrated to extend dates far into the past. The same idea applies to rock formations. According to the **law of superposition**, any succession of rock layers will have its lowest layers deposited first; thereafter, each successive layer added on top is younger. This law provides the basis for **stratigraphic dating**, that is, dating each successive layer of rocks according to its place in a formation. Dating rock strata can also date the fossils found within each layer. Again, the law of superposition states that the fossils of earlier life forms will be found in the lowest layers and more advanced life forms in the layers on top. This type of dating animal fossils is called **faunal succession**. The other family of dating methods is called absolute dating. **Absolute dating** uses the chemical nature of elements and compounds to date them. The most common form of absolute dating is based on radioactivity. All radioactive isotopes decay at a predictable rate, according to their half-lives. Radiocarbon dating, potassium-argon dating, and thermoluminescence all operate on these principles.

Two other archeological methods need to be mentioned. The first is palynology. **Palynology** is the study of pollen grains. It is a valuable means of helping in the reconstruction of past environments. The second is seriation. **Seriation** is a relative dating method that studies how cultural fashions in artifacts such as pottery styles, architectural techniques, etc., come into vogue, reach a peak, and go out of vogue, only to be replaced by another style. It is in the comparison of these serial changes that the ages of these styles and cultural tastes can be determined.

In our modern times, discovering historical sites buried underground excites not only archeologists, in a good way, but also businessmen and real estate speculators—probably not in a good way. They are likely having a site excavated for commercial development, not for academic reasons. Hence, they do not want to stop operations for archeological examination and thereby lose money. That is why most nations today have safeguards in place to postpone further digging at a commercial site until archeologists can come in, glean any valuable information, and save as many artifacts as possible. This is called **cultural resource management.** Cultural resource management is a form of applied anthropology that identifies, evaluates, and often excavates archeological sites before modern roads, dams, and buildings that would deform or destroy them can be built. Ireland did this when it incorporated the old medieval wall into the modern shopping mall built on top of it in Galway City. Generally, the "window of opportunity" for a cultural resource management project is short due to the commercial pressures involved.

FIG. 6.4. Medieval wall in a shopping mall in Galway City, Ireland.

One caveat about the way archeology can tell a story is that archeological data provides evidence to support a theory; it rarely can prove one. **Evidence** is a thing or things helpful in forming a conclusion or judgment. **Proof** is something that shows that something is true or correct. For example, many of the stories of the Bible take place in a city called Nineveh, but nobody knew whether it really existed or not. But in the early twentieth century, Nineveh was discovered and excavated and many claimed that the "truth" of the Bible was "proved." This type of conclusion is fallacious and illogical; evidence was only provided that the biblical stories had a real setting. It did not and cannot prove spiritual truth. Likewise, if in a post-apocalyptic world, an archeologist unearths a map of Kansas, it will not prove that there was a Wizard of Oz. It can only provide evidence that there was a wizard.

Also, when the fossil record failed to support the generally-accepted "gradual" ideas about Darwinian evolution, Stephen Jay Gould filled in the large "gaps" in the fossil record with his punctuated equilibrium theory. **Punctuated equilibrium** is a theory that proposes that most species will exhibit little net evolutionary change for most of their histories, while remaining in a condition of phenotypic stasis for an extended period of time. A **phenotype** is the composite of an organism's observable characteristics or traits. When significant evolutionary changes accrue, these species experience rare and rapid branching speciation. **Speciation** is the evolutionary process by which new biological species arise. The current understanding of the fossil record provides only evidence, but strong evidence that punctuated equilibrium is true, not proof.

Another way of telling a story is through language, both oral and written. Remember, the word language is derived from the Latin word for tongue and the tongue is instrumental in forming arbitrary sounds into meaningful symbols that

FIG. 6.5. Looking for the Wizard of Oz.

can become codified into a language. The cerebral cortex of humans expends enormous amounts of energy processing sensory information that reach it from the tongue and the mouth. Recall the *homunculus* image in Chapter 4. A recent study has determined that the typical American woman speaks 22,000 words per day, while the typical American male speaks 7,000. Some would raise the accusation of sexism, but it seems sexually dimorphic biology is the culprit. Women's brains are constructed to be more communicative than men's brains are. Recall the brain charts in Chapter

2. Language is perhaps the single most important component of human cultural constructions. In fact, Sapir and Whorf have postulated that the very way you think, the very way you see "reality" is determined by the way your culture constructs language, and not the other way around. This is called the **Sapir-Whorf Hypothesis**. This is quite an amazing idea—the way language is recorded in your brain in some ways pre-programs your behavior, and thus, your freedom. To understand this hypothesis further, let us examine the vocalizations of our animal kin.

Animals possess communicative skills. These are called closed systems of communication. A **closed system of communication** is a form of communication based on instinct in which the user cannot create new sounds or words. Humans use an **open system of communication**. An open system of communication is a form of communication in which the user can create new sounds or words. Human languages are distinct from closed systems of communication because they have the ability to speak about things that are remote in time and space. This phenomenon is called **displacement**. Human groups assign symbolic meaning to arbitrary sounds, although not all sounds and words may be arbitrary. For nine months a human fetus hears the sound of its mother's heartbeat in its warm and nourishing aqueous environment in the womb. After the trauma of being violently expelled into a frigid world, that is, being born, an infant seeks the reassurance of his mom's heartbeat and is placed on her chest where he hears the familiar heartbeat and where her breasts nurture him. This is perhaps the first symbolic linkage in the newborn's post-natal memory. And when that newborn acts on that linkage of heartbeat and nipple and begins to suck, he makes a cooing sound that everywhere sounds like "mmmmmmmmm." Mothers in cultures across the planet are called moms, mama, *mater*, etc. because of this sound. The "mmmm" sound is associated with and connoted with symbols such as woman, feminine, nurturing, the anima, etc., and still plays out in adulthood after a nurturing Thanksgiving dinner when we say, "Yummmmmmmy!" That other creature in the child's initial pantheon is called "pa," and as a child will soon learn in China or any other "pa"triarchal society, father, or *pater* is the physical expression of force, activity, and "po"wer. To make this sound, one must purse the lips and forcefully explode air out of the mouth in contrast to the soothing "mmm." With "ma" and "pa," gender will be extrapolated into culture in the periphery and the center, in social roles, and in parenting. Extrapolating these two basic and perhaps instinctual sounds with other arbitrary sounds gives us symbolic sounds. These symbolic sounds are called phonemes. A **phoneme** is the smallest bit of sound that distinguishes meaning. Examples of phonemes include the long *a*, the short *a, b, c, d*, etc. and diphthongs such as *th, sh*, etc. Phonemes are built up into morphemes. A **morpheme** is the smallest linguistic form that conveys meaning. Morphemes are composed of **free morphemes**, a linguistic form that can covey meaning by standing alone (and are usually words, such as *heat*) and **bound morphemes**, a linguistic unit that can convey meaning only when combined with another morpheme (usually prefixes, suffixes and gerunds, such as *re-* and *–ed*). **Morphology** is the study of the rules governing how morphemes are formed into words, such as *re-heat-ed* like my leftover dinner. The rules governing how words are arranged into phrases and sentences are called **syntax**. These rules are unique for each language and can contain idioms and other features of language that combine all of the parts of speech into a comprehensive whole. That comprehensive whole is called **grammar**. The accompanying diagram illustrates the comprehensive scheme of how languages are constructed.

Anthropologists who study languages are called linguistic anthropologists. **Linguistic anthropology** is the study of how languages have formed, how they have evolved, and how they are utilized today. The branch of anthropology that studies how languages emerge and change over time is called **historical linguistics**. The branch of anthropology that studies how languages are structured is called **descriptive linguistics**. The branch of anthropology that studies how language is used in different social contexts is called **sociolinguistics**. Anthropologists who study cultural data at a single point in time engage in a type of analysis called **synchronic analysis**. Sociolinguists tend to specialize in synchronic analysis. For example, a court case involving the communication, or miscommunication, between a dominant cultural use of language and a subcultural use of language may call for the expert testimony of a sociolinguist. Anthropologists who study sociocultural data through time engage in a type of analysis called **diachronic analysis**. Historical linguists tend to specialize in diachronic analysis. Historical linguists study changes in the both the structure and meaning of languages. The French linguist who accompanied Napoleon's army to Egypt in the early nineteenth century discovered and cracked the linguistic structure of ancient Egyptian hieroglyphics by comparing and contrasting the symbolic images encoded in three written languages on the Rosetta Stone: Ancient Greek, Classical Greek, and Egyptian hieroglyphics.

Language

Phonemes (h,e,a,t)

Morphemes (heat)

Free morphemes (heat) + Bound Morphemes (re-, -ed)

= Morphology (reheated)   +   Syntax

= Grammar

FIG. 6.6.   The holistic structure of language.

Languages are gathered into groups called family trees. In the following three diagrams, please note how the same generic information is presented in each, but notice how each of those diagrams is composed in such a way that reflects the contemporary notion of "truth," or subliminal cultural bias, that each of the anthropologists carried in his unconscious. These differences in interpretation are consistent with the conclusions of Sapir and Whorf. The first diagram is the oldest and traces the dissemination of languages from a common Indo-European parental language.

FIG. 6.7.   The Rosetta Stone.

This diagram can unconsciously be superimposed on a map of the Old World. If one traces all the linkages back to their origins, like spokes on a wheel, they intersect in Mesopotamia where the ancient city of Babel was said to exist. This diagram subliminally presupposes the truth of the biblical story of the Tower of Babel and constructs its "scientific" reality according to that numinous mental construct. The second diagram likewise does so for Darwinian evolution in which all languages evolve from a single parental root and "speciate." It deals with the exact same data as the first diagram does, but deals with it chronologically, not spatially as the first diagram did. The third diagram is the most contemporary and is a product of the modern global world. Notice how the data are arranged in a scheme that is reminiscent of the family trees used in genealogies, and conveys the subliminal message that we are all one multicultural global family inhabiting this planet.

Turning abstract sounds into oral language was the greatest invention in human history. Turning abstract sounds into writing was the second. Writing allowed humans to record thoughts and words in a mnemonic way, which allowed them to free up their minds for other thoughts. A **mnemonic** is a device, such as a pattern of letters, ideas, or associations that assists in remembering something. Rosary beads are considered mnemonics. Multiple mnemonic recordings of ideas on stone, papyrus, or parchment allowed knowledge to surpass the memorized, conservative corpus of collective wisdom of tribal peoples and thus increase exponentially. This fostered in humans their ideas of time marching forward, progress marching forward, and positivism marching forward. Writing was at first pictographic, that is, that the idea connoted in the image was an attempt to recapitulate that image. For example, the word "ox" was drawn to look like an ox. But over time, scribes designed more abstract shortcuts in depicting ideas in sound. The ox, the Paleolithic and Neolithic Middle Eastern symbol for the masculine deity, became more linear and flipped its head upside-down to become the alpha, a letter in the Greek alphabet that still connoted the new monotheistic male deity of Christianity before becoming the truly secularized letter "A" in Latin. As a true and simple alphabet evolved, it grew less "inspirational" and more practical, hence more secular. Please see the accompanying diagram for the evolution of the alphabet from pictographs.

China never developed a true alphabet, but clung to its several-thousand-character pictographic writing style for centuries, which allowed only the superior leisure classes the many years needed to master it. This not only led to the strictly hierarchical Confucian social structure of Chinese civilization, but also ensured that China would remain highly patriarchal. Men owned the land, symbolized by the pictograph of a tilled field:

According to Sapir and Whorf, the very structure of the written language predisposed China to its conservative and filial Confucian social structure of men ruling in a strictly hierarchical progression and submissive and docile women. We will talk more about the nature of language, gender, and social and political structures in upcoming chapters. Language is not a monolithic entity within a culture. Different areas in a region or country may speak different dialects. **Dialects** are variations of a language that are similar enough to be mutually

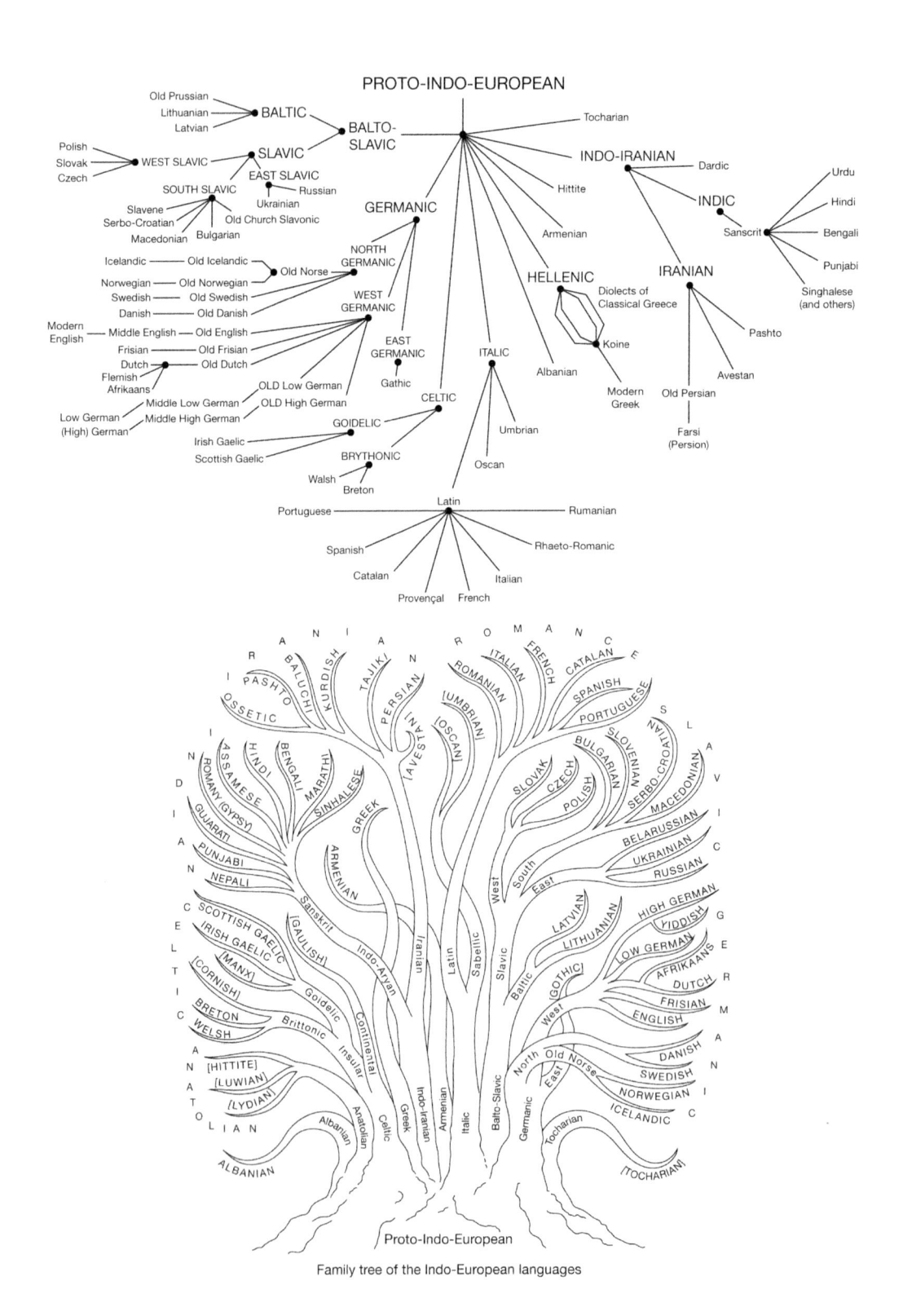

62 THE CREATURE WITH IDEAS AND POWER: AN INVESTIGATION OF ANTHROPOLOGY AND HUMAN CULTURE

Family tree of the Indo-European languages

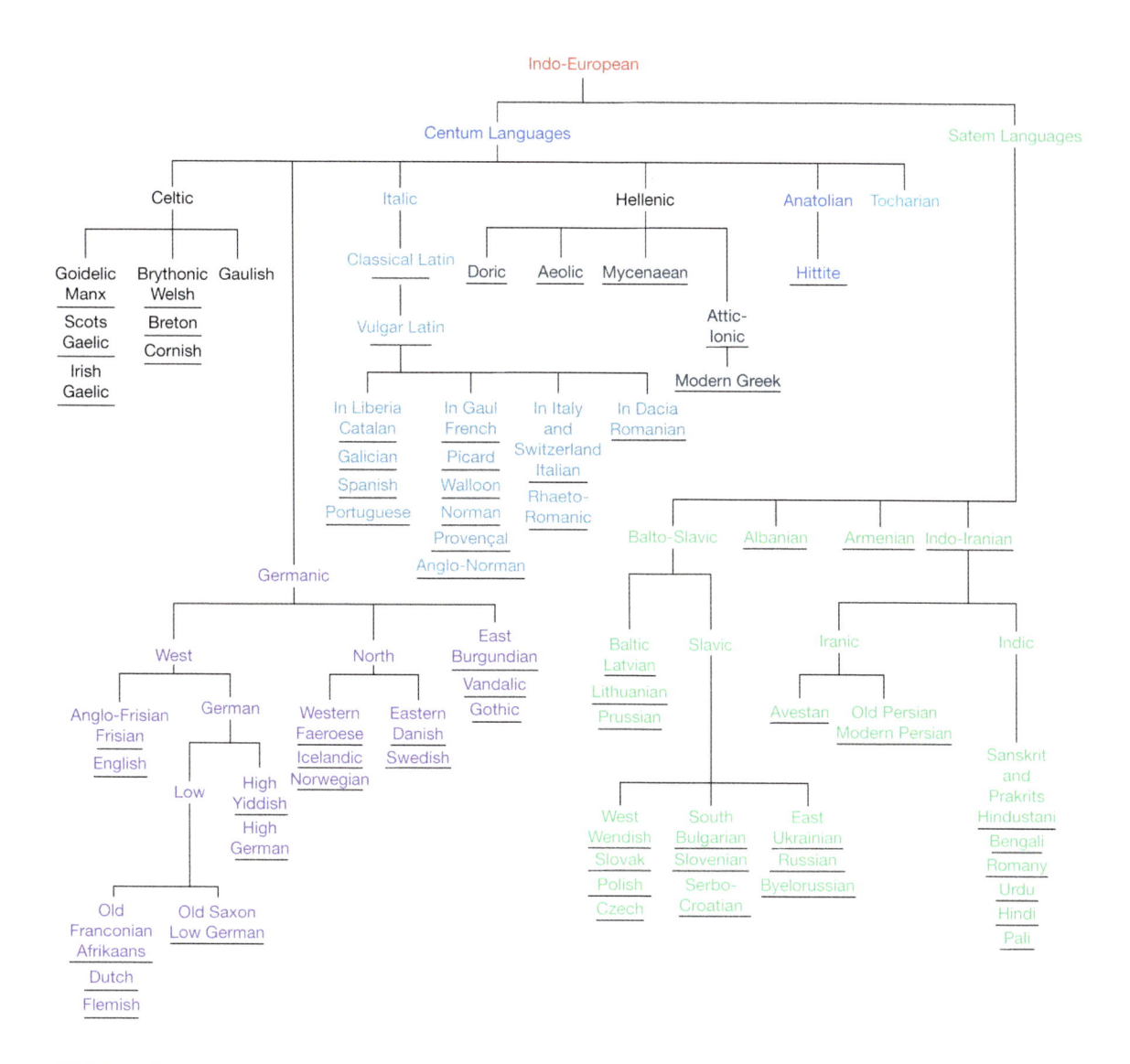

```
                                    Indo-European
                                          |
                    ┌─────────────────────┴─────────────────────┐
                Centum Languages                            Satem Languages
                    |
    ┌───────────────┼───────────────┬───────────────┐
  Celtic          Italic         Hellenic        Anatolian    Tocharian
    |               |               |                |
┌───┼───┐     Classical Latin   ┌───┼───┬──────┐   Hittite
Goidelic Brythonic Gaulish         |   Doric Aeolic Mycenaean
Manx     Welsh                  Vulgar Latin              |
Scots    Breton                     |                   Attic-
Gaelic   Cornish                    |                   Ionic
Irish                               |                     |
Gaelic                              |                Modern Greek
```

In Liberia   In Gaul   In Italy and   In Dacia
Catalan   French   Switzerland   Romanian
Galician   Picard   Italian
Spanish   Walloon   Rhaeto-
Portuguese   Norman   Romanic
              Provençal
              Anglo-Norman

Germanic
┌──────────┬──────────┐
West   North   East
                      Burgundian
                      Vandalic
┌──────┐ ┌────┬────┐ Gothic
Anglo- German Western Eastern
Frisian   Faeroese Danish
Frisian   Icelandic Swedish
English   Norwegian
┌───┬───┐
Low High Yiddish
     High
     German
┌────┬────┐
Old   Old Saxon
Franconian Low German
Afrikaans
Dutch
Flemish

Balto-Slavic   Albanian   Armenian   Indo-Iranian
┌─────┬─────┐   ┌──────┬──────┐
Baltic Slavic   Iranic   Indic
Latvian   ┌────┬────┐
Lithuanian   Avestan Old Persian
Prussian   Modern Persian
                                                            Sanskrit
                                                            and
                                                            Prakrits
┌──────┬──────┬──────┐   Hindustani
West   South East   Bengali
Wendish Bulgarian Ukrainian   Romany
Slovak Slovenian Russian   Urdu
Polish Serbo-   Byelorussian   Hindi
Czech   Croatian   Pali

FIGS. 6.8A, 6.8B., AND 6.8C. Three different cultural depictions through time of the same linguistic data. In each, anthropologists have constructed the "truth" in their own image.

FIGS. 6.9A, 6.9B, AND 6.9C, AND 6.9D. The evolution of the letter A from the pictograph of an ox.

understood. Also, humans conduct themselves differently and speak differently in different social situations. For example, at Thanksgiving dinner, a student may speak with his or her cousins about the experiences of college life and switch to an entirely different mode of speaking when talking to grandma. This is called code switching. **Code switching** is the practice of adapting one's language to the social situation. When humans deliberately seek to hide their thoughts and motives, they may engage in doublespeak. **Doublespeak** is the use of euphemisms to confuse or deceive. And when all is said and done about language, most of human communication is nonverbal, up to 70 percent of it. **Nonverbal communication** is the various means by which humans send and receive messages without using words, such as touches, gestures, displays, and facial expressions. The fact that most of our communication is nonverbal takes us back to studying our primate kin.

FIG. 6.10. The symbol for "land."

FIG. 6.11. The symbol for man became the symbol for land upheld by a typical stick figure of a human.

FIG. 6.12. The pictograph of a woman is that of a house, the domestic center of any man's land, which encloses a bowing stick figure.

KEY WORDS

Absolute dating
Archeology
Artifact
Bound morpheme
Closed system of communication
Code switching
Context
Cultural resource management
Datum Point
Dendrochronology
Descriptive linguistics
Diachronic analysis
Dialects
Displacement
Doublespeak
Evidence
Faunal succession
Feature
Fossils
Free morpheme
Grammar
Historical linguistics
Law of superposition

Linguistic anthropology
Midden
Mnemonic
Monochronic
Morpheme
Morphology
Nonverbal communication
Open system of communication
Palynology
Phenotype
Phoneme
Polychronic
Proof
Punctuated equilibrium
Relative dating
Research design
Sapir-Whorf Hypothesis
Seriation
Sociolinguistics
Speciation
Stratigraphic dating
Survey
Synchronic analysis
Syntax
Taphonomy

IMAGE CREDIT

- Fig. 6.1: Copyright © 2008 by Tina Stavenhagen-Helgren. Reprinted with permission.
- Fig. 6.2: Copyright © 2008 by Tina Stavenhagen-Helgren. Reprinted with permission.
- Fig. 6.3: Copyright © 2008 by Tina Stavenhagen-Helgren. Reprinted with permission.
- Fig. 6.5: Neelix / Wikimedia Commons / Copyright in the Public Domain.
- Fig. 6.7: Copyright in the Public Domain.
- Fig. 6.9A: Nohat / Wikimedia Commons / Copyright in the Public Domain.
- Fig. 6.9B: Pmx / Wikimedia Commons / Copyright in the Public Domain.
- Fig. 6.9C: Nathan Fisher / Copyright in the Public Domain.
- Fig. 6.9D: OsamaK / Wikimedia Commons / Copyright in the Public Domain.
- Fig. 6.10: Arlas! it / Wikimedia Commons / Copyright in the Public Domain.
- Fig. 6.11: Arlas! it / Wikimedia Commons / Copyright in the Public Domain.
- Fig. 6.12: Arlas! it / Wikimedia Commons / Copyright in the Public Domain.

CHAPTER SEVEN

THE EVOLUTION OF CULTURAL ANTHROPOLOGY

Anthropology, as we have stated, is an academic discipline that grew out of the positivistic concept of human progress. In order to arrive at a "perfect" society in the here-and-now, conceived of and implemented by cognitive rationalists, anthropologists were dispatched to conduct a systematic comparison of the varieties of human social groups outside the western purview in order to gather and analyze data.

The first major attempt at studying tribal peoples was filtered through an anthropological version of Darwinian thought, labeled **evolutionism**, by Lewis Henry Morgan. Morgan believed that all cultures passed through similar stages of development from primitive savagery to intermediate barbarism to advanced civilization. He divided and defined the stages by technological inventions, such as fire, the bow, pottery, etc., in the savage stage; metallurgy and domestication of plants and animals in the barbaric stage; and the development of the alphabet, city life, massive construction projects, and progress in the civilized stage. Social development was therefore unilinear; peoples could only develop civilization after first developing barbarism from tribal roots. This Darwinian approach to anthropology in the mid-nineteenth century reflects several social developments responsible for producing it. Western culture had jettisoned the Kingdom of "God" to construct its own Kingdom of "Man." This was called Social Darwinism. **Social Darwinism is the theory that persons, groups, and races are subject to the same laws of natural selection as Charles Darwin had postulated operates in plants and animals.** In the context of its day, evolutionism, at its worst, was used to claim that the colonization and exploitation of "inferior" tribal peoples by civilized "superior" Western peoples was only "natural." At its best, it fostered a paternalistic ideal of a "civilizing mission" or a "burden" of the "White Man" to bring civility to benighted "savages." It certainly justified imperialism. Imperialism, remember, is the economic and political domination and control of other societies. Morgan's approach was etic, that is, that the educated perspective of the civilized ethnographer was better able to describe the culture of the primitive more accurately than a primitive could. Morgan was a product of his age and so was his theory.

FIG. 7.1. Lewis Henry Morgan.

Morgan had drawn on history to cull terminology for his evolutionism theory. The English King Henry II had given his blessing of the Anglo-Norman invasion of tribal Ireland in the twelfth century

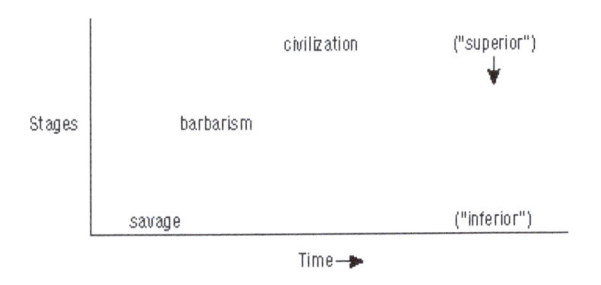

FIG. 7.2. Morgan's stage theory of cultural development. Note that it is "progressive" through time.

FIG. 7.3. "Savage" Irish tribesmen ambush an isolated Norman knight in twelfth century Ireland. Note that the band of Irish "savage-stage" warriors do not possess the requisite technological achievements of the more "civilized" Anglo-Normans who possess mail-armor, sword, shield, saddle, and stirrups, the trappings that a more efficiently organized society can produce. Guerrilla warfare and terrorism will ultimately have their roots in an unequal access to resources, but more importantly, in an unequal use of these resources "scientifically." Only through the diffusion and acculturation of Western ideas will non-Western peoples become capable of such "progress." These ideas will have practical consequences with regard to the ability of a people to apply force against others, as we will explore in Chapters 12 and 13.

by instructing his conquistadors to subjugate "*les irois sauvage, nous ennemis*" (the savage Irish, our enemies).

A corollary to Morgan's theory is the concept of cultural diffusion. **Cultural diffusion** is the idea that all societies change as a result of cultural borrowing from one another. Morgan's ideas were challenged in the latter part of the nineteenth century by Franz Boas who believed that all peoples need not pass unilinearly from one stage of "progress" to another to become a "Western" culture in their own turn. He claimed instead that ethnographers should get out and gather data on the unique cultures of peoples developing in response to unique and particular environments and via deductive reasoning determine how each culture defined itself. Boas' concept came to be called **American historicism**. His approach was emic, that is, the ethnographer must see the culture of the people being studied from their perspective, not the perspective of the ethnographer. American historicism, it must be pointed out, is a manifestation of the unconscious pride of nineteenth century America as a unique and particular people who cherish "freedom" and so distinguished themselves from the cultural trappings of Europe. Boas was a product of his times and so was his theory.

With the advent of the twentieth century, times would change and so would the unconscious worldview of anthropology. The gobbling up of tribal societies in Africa, Asia, and the Americas by industrial societies in Europe, Japan, and the United States had run its course. There were no "easy pickings" left for resource acquisition by the big powers to stock their warehouses in an arms race for a war all knew was coming, and feared. This was the time of the "powder keg" of Europe and the "end-of-the-century" frenzy of angst that characterized Europe. It was the time of Edvard Munch's "Scream."

As World War I raged, a Polish ethnographer named Bronislaw Malinowski was studying the Trobriand Islanders in the Pacific. As a historicist, Malinowski was a strong advocate of fieldwork, but he was less interested in how a culture evolved than in how contemporary cultures operated or functioned. During his studies, Malinowski had been impressed with the fact that the customs of the Trobriand Islanders all seemed to serve their everyday needs for food, shelter, companionship, etc., and this led him to develop the theory of functionalism. **Functionalism is the idea that all aspects of culture serve to fulfill the biological and psychological needs of individuals and each aspect contributes to the maintenance of the whole.** Marriage exists to satisfy sexual needs and magic and ritual allay otherwise uncontrollable anxieties.

Malinowski's functionalism to some degree transfers European "utilitarian" concepts to "primitive" societies, that is, as a rule in determining the needs of life, "the useful is considered to be the good." A weakness of functionalism is that to comprehend all the mutually supportive facets of a culture, that culture must be conceived of as an ossified, inflexible entity that must be studied via a synchronic "slice of time" approach. Any change introduced into one part of the system will change the integrated nature of the functionalist's ethnological construction. This goes hand-in-hand with the notion of the organic analogy of culture. The **organic analogy** is the idea that cultural systems are integrated into a cultural whole in much the same way as the various organs and systems of a biological organism function to maintain the health of the organism.

At the same time as Malinowski was hashing out his theory, English anthropologist A.R. Radcliffe-Brown reshaped Malinowski's functionalism and made it more abstract. Instead of some aspect of culture functioning to fulfill a specific biological and psychological need, Radcliffe-Brown saw the function of the same aspect of culture in the part that it played in maintaining the social structure of a group. Relationships and obligations became more important than biology. This method is called **structural functionalism**. Again, due to its synchronic nature, structural functionalism is unable to neatly fit cultural change, a constant feature of human life, into its paradigmatic scheme. In addition, it did not live up to Radcliffe-Brown's claim that it would eventually enable positivists to discover laws governing human social behavior. Despite these limitations, functionalism and structural functionalism remain viable theoretical orientations in anthropology because they reveal much about individual societies and their relative uniquenesses It is proper to note that both men were products of their times. Malinowski was born in a Poland dominated by Czarist Russia and wanted his country to be liberated and experience its own "organic" viability. Radcliffe-Brown was born into the height of the British Empire with its need to keep the social relationships of lord, commoner, citizen, subject, and colonial, all in their proper bounds. The study of unique societies was, and is, often run through a somewhat biased and often unconscious filter.

FIG. 7.4. Bronislaw Malinowski.

FIG. 7.5. Franz Boas.

FIG. 7.6. Margaret Mead.

Yet, what was it that made cultures and societies similar or unique? Intuitively, scholars knew they had to plumb the workings of the human mind for these answers, and cognitive anthropologists, in particular, sought to explain cultures by examining the different categories people create to organize the universe. When Locke had rejected the Hobbesian notion of an inherently "evil" human nature, which needed a strong authoritarian society to control its centrifugal impulses and opted for a belief in the *tabula rasa* (blank slate), the idea that people are born with minds empty of psychic content and that the attainment of all knowledge is sensually perceived and imprinted, he was revealing himself a player in his own culture's repudiation of the ideology that led to Europe's destructive Wars of Religion, in this case the concept of "original sin." (We will discuss Hobbes and Locke in Chapter 13.) Late nineteenth century thinker Adolph Bastian disagreed with Locke and believed in the "psychic unity" of all humankind, an almost "value-free" return to Hobbesianism. To Bastian, fixed patterns of thought, called "mental universals" were common to human beings all over the world. Their differences were due to varied natural environments and the vagaries of cultural evolution. Patterning the cultural "regularities" on the order observed in nature and their sense of this order, anthropologists reasoned that the ideas and behaviors of a given group of people could be understood if the unconscious structures in their minds could be discovered. What prompted this need to plumb the mind? It was the shattering of democratic ideals in the trenches of World War I. The world community realized that "White Men" couldn't "civilize" themselves, much less the benighted savages in imperial domains. Citizen-soldiers returned to their homes with post-traumatic stress and nightmares. Munch's "Scream" displaced Comte's positivism in many minds. Yet, despite the political separation of state from church, men still had nightmares and still needed "priests." And they would find them. Freud and Jung would be the prophets of the new "salvation" wrought through psychology, and anthropology would follow suit in the new worldview.

Psychological anthropology is the sub-field of anthropology that looks at the relationships among cultures and phenomena such as personality, cognition, and emotions. Ruth Benedict and Margaret Mead were products of this generation and conducted their field researches accordingly. Mead focused on how culture affects the process of growing up from childhood to adulthood among various cultures, especially among the Admiralty Islands of the Pacific. Other anthropological responses to the war flowered, or re-flowered. **Neoevolutionism, promoted by White and Steward, refined the earlier evolutionism of Morgan.** Men like Adolf Hitler would gravitate toward this way of cultural thinking and re-work Social Darwinism from a notion of "survival of the fittest" in his nation suffering from Depression-era want to a notion of "destruction of the unfit," especially if they diluted the bloodlines of the "Master Race." Hitler was, in many ways, a product of his times. At the same time, from the ashes of the pre-war ideal of democracy, Communism would suffer a nasty birthing process in the Soviet Union.

Untouched by the ravages of World War I and returning to its traditional isolationism, the United States yet maintained the beacon of democratic ideals after Europe had dampened its light, even in traumatized France and Britain. World War II would follow and extinguish the flames of neoevolutionism with the defeat of Germany, Italy, and Japan. The ideals of the Soviet Union would themselves flower and compete with those of the United States in the aftermath and so would those of France, which had been traumatized again. Anthropological methods would mutate accordingly. After the war, France sought to regain its preeminence in its colonies and found disappointment. The anthropologist Claude Lévi-Strauss developed his anthropological methodology as a result of arriving late on the participant observation "train." As lamented in his book, "Tristes Tropiques" (1973), he had found not pristine cultures, but impoverished imitations of his own, set off here and there by the relics of a discarded past. Realizing that as a Westerner he couldn't truly penetrate the mindset of a pristine people whose conceptual universe was a "closed cell" and holistic, cyclical and non-progressive in nature, he began to perceive that it was yet possible to construct out of the particles and fragments of cultural debris a theoretical model of society.

Believing that the mind of man is, at bottom, everywhere the same, Lévi-Strauss concluded that primitive societies are at a deeper, psychological level, not alien at all. He sought to reconstruct the conceptual systems of primitive life, compare, collate, and sift assorted samples, and distill a universal grammar of the intellect, that level of "primitive thinking" ("*la pensee sauvage*") which is the immanent foundation of human thought everywhere.

From his observations, Lévi-Strauss developed structural anthropology. **Structural anthropology determined to analyze cultural phenomena in the forms of languages, myths, and kinship relationships to discover what ordered patterns, or structures, they seemed to display.** These, Lévi-Strauss suggested, could reveal the structure of the human mind. "In any society, the same

FIG. 7.7. Claude Lévi-Strauss.

minds that create myths also create the organizations of social relationships, the political systems, religious beliefs, magical rituals, pottery – in fact, everything cultural. Hence, the orderly patterns used to structure myths may be replicated in these other areas of culture." As in the aftermath of the trauma of the First World War, structural anthropology was a return to psychological anthropology in the aftermath of the trauma of the Second World War.

According to Lévi-Strauss, the first step in primitive thought is the acute and accurate observation of nature—its animals, plants, climate, seasons, heavenly bodies and holistic cycles—and then thinking deeply about them. To anthropologists, the process of observing, selecting, and interrelating sets of elements from various orders of phenomena and communicating them to a "closed cell" of preliterate people is called "operations."

"Savages," or oral-traditional people, do not condense their knowledge into abstract, formal theories as moderns do; instead, they construct a naturalistic "science of the concrete" by means of mental constructions that intelligibly resemble the "real" world (*imagines mundi*). Sense is made of the world by analogically structuring the invisible and underlying order of reality. Through binary opposition—juxtaposing various pairs of opposites—the primitive "social scientist" makes mental linkages in ways that reflect the invariant mechanics of the analogical human mind. The particular contrasts chosen are constrained by the environment, experience and selection values of a group. These "things" of cultural operations—objects, events, persons, relationships, time periods, etc.—that "naturally" typify something else and eventually become "rigidified" are called "symbols," as we have seen. In the cross-referencing of symbols, culture is born.

Structural anthropologists believe that human societies never create out of whole cloth, but reorient and recombine certain "stock themes" or "ideational structures" from a repertoire of ideas previously available to them. The governing notion of structuralism is that the universe of conceptual tools used by the savage is closed, but malleable. Myths are composed of building blocks called "mythemes" in a process Lévi-Strauss calls bricolage, again as we have seen. Like chips in a kaleidoscope, though finite in number but capable of variegated arrangement, it is the quality of relationships among primitive symbols and not their intrinsic, quantifiable properties that can be reshuffled and reintegrated in response to systemic stresses.

When confronted with the shattered kaleidoscopes of dead and dying societies due to Western cultural imperialism, Lévi-Strauss understood that the totems of these primitive peoples represented the social kinship structures of their clan systems. Moreover, he understood that the representations were metaphorical, not biological. That is, a series of natural symbols and a parallel series of cultural symbols had been subconsciously united in a logical "scientific" way. He sensed the connection between the referents of totems and the referents of language, which linguists had long demonstrated reconstituted deep binary structures from surface manifestations by combining sound with meaning. And the meaning that gave order to primitive reality was encoded in the dialectical linguistic symbols of myth. We shall examine the Haudenosaunee in this light in Chapter 11.

Though these symbols did not mean the same things to all peoples, or the same things to the same people at all times, various myths could be deconstructed, which despite superficial differences, revealed the invariant "structuring" mechanics of the mind. Preliterate peoples, in their "closed cells" of "scientific" thinking, are unaware of the operations of myths, but the structural anthropologist could fathom their underlying unity through a rational, scientific methodology. This is an etic approach.

What was necessary to uncover was the way cultural "zones of operations" were mythically presented by and to its participants. By analyzing the covert classifications found in the multiple versions of myths existing among different groups and languages and subtracting out mythical elements due to a group's experience and selection values, one could map out the structural order of myths, and hence, the unconscious operations of primitive thinking. What often appeared at first glance to be epiphenominal, afterwards led to the conclusion that social organizations and languages had been exchanged across myths. An **epiphenomenon** is a secondary phenomenon that occurs alongside or in parallel to a primary phenomenon. As Lévi-Strauss noted, the goal of structuralism, therefore, is to "map the human universe of selection values, totally reduced and arranged through comparison, which, within limits, are always capable of new operations."

One of the results of structuralist thinking, ironically, was to divest cultural institutions of cognitive human choice. Man, in fact, would become an "economic animal," and advocates of **cultural materialism** would propose that concrete, measurable things, such as the natural environment or technology, are far more responsible for specific aspects of culture than other factors. "How does a particular idea, institution, or custom help the people in a given society adapt more efficiently to their natural and social environments and their particular level of technological expertise?" the cultural materialist, Marvin Harris, would ask. Even more particularly, cultural ecologists would focus in on the natural environment as the primary materialist perspective influencing humans. **Cultural ecology** is an anthropological sub-field that assumes that people who reside in similar environments are likely to develop similar technologies, social structures, and political institutions. One advantage of the cultural materialist and cultural ecological methodologies is their diachronic approach, which studies societies and cultures as they shift through time. By balancing diachronic with synchronic methodologies, anthropological studies profit by encompassing far greater ranges and depths of cultural and social issues. These sub-fields are products of their times and reflect the elevation of Marxist ideology, with the rise in power of the Soviet Union, in the worldview of the Cold War era. Marx will be discussed more fully in Chapters 12 and 13; yet, his ideas pervade anthropology to this day.

To answer the Soviet Union's assaults on the hypocrisies of First World imperial democracies like Britain and France, which were busy re-establishing their hegemonies in their colonies after World War II, the post-war United States called on these allies to decolonize and liberate the peoples of these imperial domains. This would be done in a chaotic way, but at the same time, it set up the United States to become the moral, financial, and physical leader of the First World; from this role, ethnoscience was born in an effort to understand the cultures of the newly independent nations that came under the nurturing mantle of the United States. **Ethnoscience** is a theoretical method that tries to understand a culture from the point of view of the people being studied. It is an emic approach. And from this welter of intellectual and political activity, Blacks in the United States analyzed their sub-status conditions and questioned how segregation could still be enforced domestically while at the same time the government could call for independence of colonial peoples internationally. The Civil Rights era ensued, and with it, the emergence of the Feminist Movement, the Gay Movement, the Environmental Movement, etc. **Feminist anthropology** seeks to explain cultural life from the perspective of women.

As the Cold War dragged on and numerous peoples around the globe failed to gain the benefits of modern "progress," a new worldview in anthropology emerged. This worldview was termed postmodernism. **Postmodernism** questions the positivist promises of the scientific method itself. It is a rejection of the notion of absolute truth for a more subjective relative truth. Rather than seek rational and scientific laws with which to govern society, anthropologists should describe and interpret cultures and search for meaning through that endeavor. It is a rejection of a Platonic ideal for one subtly more Aristotelian. Interpretive anthropology was born from postmodern ideas. **Interpretive anthropology** holds that critical aspects of cultural systems are subjective factors such as values, ideas, and worldviews.

Interpretive anthropologist Clifford Geertz sees culture not as a set of concrete behavior patterns ensconced in customs and traditions, but rather as a set of control mechanisms or rules for the governing of behavior. As an organized medium for guiding the trafficking in significant symbols, culture represents the accumulated totality of such patterns. Although understanding the cataloging of the "layers of man" methodology of the functionalists and structural functionalists, as well as the "hunt for underlying universals" of the structuralists, Geertz decries to the former that the turning of culture into institutions is an escape, while to the latter he disparages, "don't lose surface realities to dig for turtles." For Geertz, culture is not an experimental science in search of a law, but an interpretive one in search of meaning. It is not a power, something to which social events, behaviors, institutions or processes can be causally attributed; it is a context, something within which they can be intelligibly, that is, thickly-described. Anthropological knowledge is a scholarly artifice and does not depict social "reality," hence, the methodological solution for the anthropologist is to look for systematic relationships, not substantive identities. Culture provides the link between what men and women are intrinsically capable of becoming and what they actually become. Individual expression takes place

FIG. 7.8. Marvin Harris, father of Cultural Materialism.

within a general idiom. The Geertzian anthropological methodology, as an interpretive science seeking extensively contextualized "meaning," rejected positivism's quest for laws and gravitated toward Michel Foucault's and Jacques Derrida's model of post-modernism, thereby influencing greatly many of the new cultural historians. To a new generation of Marxists, hegemony became the idea that an elite can establish its power only if it can exert a cultural domination over other social classes; material strength alone was no longer enough.

For these histories "in the ethnographic grain," economic and social relations are not prior to or determining of cultural ones; they are themselves fields of cultural practice and cultural production. But, if all meaning, even scientific law depends on cultural context, how can any causal explanation be derived? Geertzian anthropological history can only thickly-describe; it risks explaining nothing. If men and women are stripped of the ability to make meaningful choices, cultural historians will only be left with the defacing post-modernist tools of relativism and skepticism. Is there nothing then upon which to build? Applied anthropology rises to that challenge, as we shall see in Chapter 11.

KEY WORDS

American historicism
Cultural diffusion
Cultural ecology
Cultural materialism
Epiphenomenon
Ethnoscience
Evolutionism
Feminist anthropology
Functionalism
Interpretive anthropology

Organic Analogy
Neoevolutionism
Postmodernism
Psychological anthropology
Social Darwinism
Structural anthropology
Structural functionalism

IMAGE CREDITS

- Fig. 7.1: Copyright in the Public Domain.
- Fig. 7.3: Daniel Maclise / Copyright in the Public Domain.
- Fig. 7.4: Canadian Museum of Civilization / Copyright in the Public Domain.
- Fig. 7.5: Source: Library of the London School of Economics and Political Science (1930).
- Fig. 7.6: Copyright © 1972 by Rob C. Croes / Anefo, (CC BY-SA 3.0) at http://commons.wikimedia.org/wiki/File:Margaret_Mead_(1972).jpg.
- Fig. 7.7: Copyright © 2005 by Michel Ravassard / UNESCO, (CC BY 3.0) at http://commons.wikimedia.org/wiki/File:Levi-strauss_260.jpg.
- Fig. 7.8: Qoan / Wikimedia Commons / Copyright in the Public Domain.

CHAPTER EIGHT

BONDING HUMANS TOGETHER: FAMILY, KINSHIP, AND MARRIAGE

Without sharp fangs and claws to defend itself, the human species utilizes its intellectual and emotional mind to draw the various members of its groups together to live collectively for security, resource accumulation, and procreation. Culture determines how these needs are met in any particular environment. The basic cultural unit that gets these needs met is the family. A **family** is a social unit characterized by economic cooperation, the management of reproduction, the ensuing period of childrearing, and the living arrangements in time and space needed to accomplish these things. Functionalists, remember, study how parts of a culture contribute to the overall well-being of a society. The formation of families serves societies in three critical ways. First, families provide the stable framework within which sexual mating and production is regulated. Second, in order to maximize the chances of a group's survival, they regulate the sexual division of labor. Men usually do the "peripheral" work, while women do the "domestic" work. Third, the institution of marriage creates the network of family relationships that provide for the material, educational, and emotional needs of all of its members.

Why families come together is primarily determined by sex. **Sex** is the hormonally driven, and thus highly desirable, means by which humans reproduce. Sex is also a cultural "good" in its own right or according to some cultures, an "evil." (The Hua people of tribal New Guinea consider women to be evil creatures who sap the vital spiritual essence of a male through sex. Although Hua males reproduce with Hua females, it is a duty to propagate the tribe, not a pleasure. Pleasurable sex is restricted to other men and pubescent boys who must have their "vital essences" primed for reproduction through ritual fellatio with an elder.) Access to sex is less regulated among societies worldwide, including our own Western society, than is reproduction. Reproduction entails jobs, income, living quarters, mate support, child support, etc., in addition to hormonally-driven sex. The primary cultural institution through which these ends are met is marriage. **Marriage** is a formalized custom that unites partners in a family. Partners are generally adult males and adult females in most cultures, both today and through time. Deviations from this cultural norm are generally related to resource possession, as we shall see. The wealthier a society is, the more sexual freedom its members possess. Where resources are scarce, access to reproductive sex is highly regulated. Another mouth to feed cannot be tolerated where no food will be available to take care of an irresponsible act of passion. Marriage is a cultural universal designed to increase the efficiency of human groups in securing a sustainable life in the present and a sustainable future for a people's posterity. Let us examine these ideas in more detail.

The human creature possesses intrinsic and instinctive drives. A **drive** is a basic, inborn biological urge that motivates behavior. Sex is a drive. Cultures conceive standards of what is desirable and undesirable by its **values**. From their values, cultures determine their ethics and morals. **Ethics** are behaviors that do "good" to others or "bad" to others. In simple terms, they relate to how one treats the entire human species. Ethics are holistic. **Morals**, derived from the Roman phrase *mos maiorum* "the customs of the ancestors," are those rules that one's forebears have passed down from generation to generation. They are the rules of one's group. They are specific in scope. Ethical values and moral values often overlap, but they are not the same. For example, universal ethics posit that killing another human is "bad." It is not doing "good" to others. Morals, however, can justify killing for specific and culturally approved reasons. War is where the interface of ethics and morals often grind against each other. As we saw in past chapters, humans are enculturated into the wisdom of their ancestors in conservative tribal societies. Those right-brained societies live close to nature, and as a result, live in harmony with it. They do not expropriate more resources from it than are necessary and live close to the subsistence level. Hence, marriage is central to a people's continued existence and, therefore, too important to be left for the partners themselves to decide. Because of the dire consequences and resource transfers involved in marriage, those children who were born within the recognized societal norms were deemed **legitimate**. Legitimate children had access to the power, prestige, and resources of its society. **Illegitimate** children were those children conceived in unregulated reproductive activity and were thus denied access to socially sanctioned power, prestige, and resources. A **genitor** is the man that impregnates a woman who delivers a child. He may or may not support that child. Historically, a **traditional father** was both the man who impregnated his wife and maintained the household for the functional rearing of the children, while a **traditional mother** was the father's spouse, the deliverer of the children, and the primary maintainer of their nurturing.

Incidentally, most societies find means to care for illegitimate children. Orphans generally have their minimal needs met in orphanages, and in many agricultural societies such as historical Ireland, fosterage is practiced. **Fosterage** is the practice of adopting illegitimate children into a family and taking care of their basic needs until they can become viable workers in the fields. In typical fosterage cultures, and for most pre-industrial cultures for that matter, there was no period of childhood as a stage of growth wherein an adolescent had no social responsibilities. Historically, children were viewed by their families as loved, but unproductive consumers until they could start earning their keep with menial chores and progress to more demanding household chores with age. Hence, it should not be surprising that in an industrial society, children worked long and hard hours right beside the adults. Adoption has long been used by societies to increase family power, prestige, and love. **Adoption** is the legal practice of taking the child of other parents as one's own. In republican Rome, Julius Caesar adopted Octavian as his son, who later became his heir and the first emperor of Rome. The Haudenosaunee also often adopted people of different bloodlines into their social structures in order to replenish their stock of males and females in the clans. Today, many people adopt children, both locally and internationally, to increase their families for a variety of reasons.

As a result of these views on reproduction and child-rearing, many cultures view marriage as a sacred custom that entails the obligation of partners, not only to themselves, but also to their families, their peoples, and their environments to live responsibly and productively. If a holistic social consciousness is not part of the vision, cultures will not sanction the union of two partners. Therefore, many cultures engage in a practice called arranged marriage. An **arranged marriage** is when the selection of a spouse is outside of the control of the bride and groom, although they usually have a say in the process.

Marriage bonds people together through a set of familial relationships called **kinship**. Kinship determines both the property and the status one holds in a family unit. Kinship can be of three kinds. **Consanguinal kinship** is determined biologically through one's blood relatives. **Affinal kinship** is based upon marriage, not blood, such as the relatives of a spouse. **Fictive kinship** is a recognized relationship of others who, though related neither by blood nor marriage, perform the functions of a family unit. My mom's best friend "Aunt Margie" functioned in the role of fictive kinship in my life.

How is a mate determined? Generally, one chooses outside of one's group. This is called exogamy. **Exogamy** is marriage between people of different social or kinship groups. The Haudenosaunee must marry outside of their clans, as we shall see. Generally, exogamy increases the bonding among different social groups in a society that increases mutual alliances for protection and sustenance. **Endogamy** is marriage within a specified social or kinship group. For example, historically in India, people in different castes cannot marry outside of their caste.

There are several theories about how people choose their partners. One is the incest taboo. The **incest taboo** is the prohibition of sexual intimacy between people defined as close relatives. This is closely related to the **natural aversion theory**, which states that people possess an innate distaste for sexual relations among those who have grown up together. Again, this is closely related to the **inbreeding theory**, which prohibits sexual intimacy with close relatives because of the increased likelihood that deformities and diseases will be engendered in the offspring. All of these theories are probably linked by biology. Living creatures on this planet thrive within their niches and adapt to environmental changes through variation and genetic mixing. Genetic material exchanged through pheromones wafting through the air or saliva ingested through kissing send strong sexual signals to the brain. The brain then ferrets out "good" potential mates—those who have a better chance at producing viable and compatible offspring with your own genetics—from those "bad" potential mates—those whose genes may produce offspring predisposed to disease or dysfunction. Romantic love can get in the way of eon-old genetic selection of mates. Be careful. If it looks like a heavenly angel, but kisses like a dead fish, there may be a biological signal there.

Consanguinal marriages have produced traditional laws that wed not only man to woman, but patriarch to his land. Hence, in the Judeo-Christian/Western heritage, land passes through the males in a straight line of descent from father to son. Yet, among the Hebrews, one's heritage was traced through the bloodlines of the mother. **Lineality** is the ability of a member of a family to trace his or her line of descent back to a common ancestor. Since power is transferred through males in the Western heritage, the practice called **primogeniture**, that is, that the eldest son inherits all the family's wealth from his father, was established to keep the transfer of power stable through successive generations. To sustain the patriarchal inheritance through the male line, levirate is often practiced. Traced back to the Hebrew Bible, **levirate** is the practice of a younger brother marrying the widow of an older brother who has died without offspring. This practice keeps the blood, the resources, and the alliances of a group intact and stable. Primogeniture and levirate are designed to preserve patrilineal descent. **Patrilineal descent** is a form of descent in which people trace their primary kin relations through their fathers. In some nomadic or semi-nomadic societies in which males at the periphery are expendable and females are the "sacred" carriers of a family's blood, kinship relations are derived primarily through the mothers. This is called **matrilineal descent** and it should come as no surprise that sororate is often practiced among matrilineal groups. **Sororate** is the practice of a woman marrying the husband of her deceased sister. Sororate is practiced by the Native American Sioux. Finally, **cognatic descent** is a form of descent traced through both males and females.

It may come as a surprise to some that the form marriage takes is greatly related to issues such as time, space, resource need, and resource availability. Monogamy is one example. **Monogamy** is the practice of having only one spouse at a time, usually one adult male and one adult female, for the purpose of responsible procreation. This type of marriage is the norm for societies in which there are sufficient resources for a unit of land to sustain a recognized family through its generations. One man will provide the "peripheral" resources for one woman to maintain a "domestic" household in order for both to ensure the next generation will be successfully raised. Where resources are scarce, such as in Nepal in the Himalayas, it may take the labors of two or more men to glean enough resources to successfully nourish and provide for one child. The union of several men and one woman in a functional family unit is called **polyandry**. The opposite may also be true. There may not be enough people in a population to adequately exploit and defend a territory teeming with resources, so one man may marry several women to produce adequate numbers of children quickly to develop a territory's potential and security as quickly as possible. This type of marriage is called **polygyny**, or polygamy. This type of situation is exactly what the Mormons faced in Utah and partly explains why Utah is a much smaller state today than it was as a territory. To join the United States, the Mormons, whose numbers were small, had to sacrifice land in order to retain their culture.

The origins of some marriage customs may again surprise some. Remember, marriages are the responsible unions of two partners to provide for a variety of obligations. Good stewardship of resources is vital in a society living near the subsistence level. Yet, despite good stewardship, contingency, accidents, and death happen. Who will take care of one's offspring in an environment that offers only meager resources? Who will want to marry a widow who has several other mouths to feed and whose body shows the evidence of life with another man in such an environment? Hence, ideas of levirate and sororate make sense. They are forms of primitive "insurance policies" against calamity, as are ideas of gift exchange at weddings: bridewealth, dowry, bride service, and reciprocal exchange. **Bridewealth** is the transfer of goods from the groom's lineage to that of the bride's in order to legitimate the marriage. **Bride service** is work performed for, or services rendered to, the bride's family by the groom for a specified period of time in order to compensate the bride's family for the loss of work or services she had formerly provided them, and thus legitimize the marriage. A **dowry** is goods or money transferred from the bride's family to the groom or his family in order to provide for any children in the event of the death of the bride and the loss of her domestic support in the household of the groom, and thus legitimize the marriage. Among Turkish peoples, girls typically began sewing their dowry rug at the age of four, and it was not completed until she was of marriageable age, usually around the time of puberty. A rug designated the wealth and status of her family by the richness of the materials utilized in its making and earned the bride a

FIG. 8.1. A Turkish rug.

higher or lower social value. For the groom, typically, a rug was a necessity as a ground cover inside a tent for a people who were historically nomadic. Please see the accompanying diagram for a depiction of a Turkish rug. **Reciprocal exchange** is the equal exchange of gifts between the families of both the bride and groom to legitimize a marriage. This is what we typically do today in Western society. The father of the bride pays for the wedding to publicly demonstrate its legitimacy, and the father of the groom gives the biggest check as a gift, in order to get the "kids" on their way financially.

Kinship within a family structure is demonstrated in two directions. One's descent in a family is both vertical and horizontal. Recall the cosmogenic (x) within the chaotic (o) of tribal Native Americans that gives a sense of reassurance to the contingent anxiety of any individual within the group. Westerners will call this "ground-zero" center of self-identity within a kinship structure the **ego**. Yes, it is the same ego that Freud described. The **vertical function of kinship** is the binding of one's ego through past generations. The **horizontal function of kinship** is the binding of one's ego to living relatives in the present generation. Vertical kinship structures are related to lineality, while horizontal kinship structures are related to the concept of collaterality. **Collaterality** is the relationship of kinship relations in the present generation, for example, first cousins, second cousins, etc. The ego can situate itself in familial, status, and power structures via documents called **genealogies**.

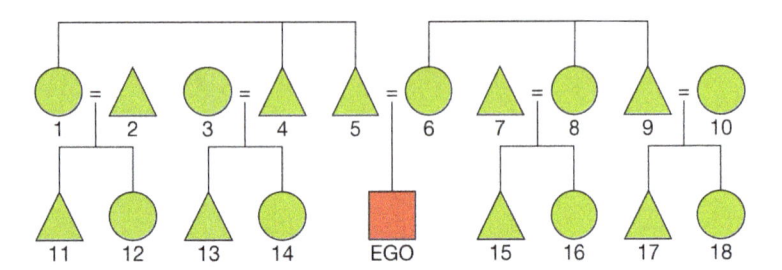

FIG. 8.2. The ego is situated in a genealogy that depicts vertical and horizontal kinship structures.

Families are also designated as nuclear and as extended. A **nuclear family** is the most basic family unit. It is traditionally composed of a husband—an adult male—a wife—an adult female—and their offspring. In the United States, a nuclear family aspires to the accumulation of sufficient resources to finance its own household in whatever part of the country it can afford, and will often move its household in order to increase access to increased resources. This is the traditional "American Dream." In the case of the American Dream, the bonds of collaterality and extended family kinship break down with distance. At the same time, angst increases in a nuclear family unit that is isolated from its familial support group. Most other families in the world, particularly the non-Western world, historically and today, live in extended families. An **extended family** includes in one household one or more nuclear families, and other relatives, often of older and/or younger generations. Extended lineal descent patterns form clans. A **clan** is a unilineal descent group that consists of members who claim a common ancestry back to a common ancestor. Where families reside is also determined by cultural values. **Patrilocality** is a residence pattern in which a married couple lives with or near the relatives of the husband's father. **Matrilocality** is a residence pattern in which a married couple lives with or near the relatives of the wife. **Neolocality** is a residence pattern in which a married couple establishes its own residence apart from the relatives of either spouse.

The values of modern family life are the result of modern societies having access to a superabundance of natural and social resources. For instance, high wage earners can often afford to marry one spouse, raise a family, divorce, marry another spouse, and raise a new family while still maintaining the support of the previous family. Some can afford to do this many times. This practice of marrying a succession of partners is called **serial monogamy**. **Divorce** is the legal and formal dissolution of a marriage. Here is where the boundaries of historical family patterns get fuzzy in the modern

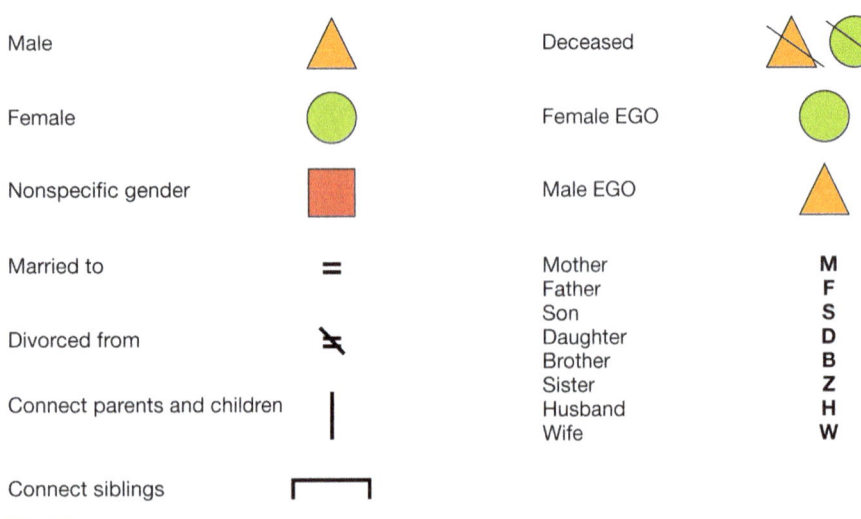

FIG. 8.3. Standard designations of individuals within a typical genealogy.

age. Today, with the resource-driven unraveling of nuclear and extended families as well as a rich governmental superstructure, fathers other than the genitor may raise children. Indeed, even the terms husband and wife, father and mother have given way to the neutral term partner. A **partner** is a person who has a committed relationship with, may or may not reside with, and may or may not have sexual activity with another person, and that relationship may or may not be legally sanctioned. However, resources are generally

Patrilineal Descent

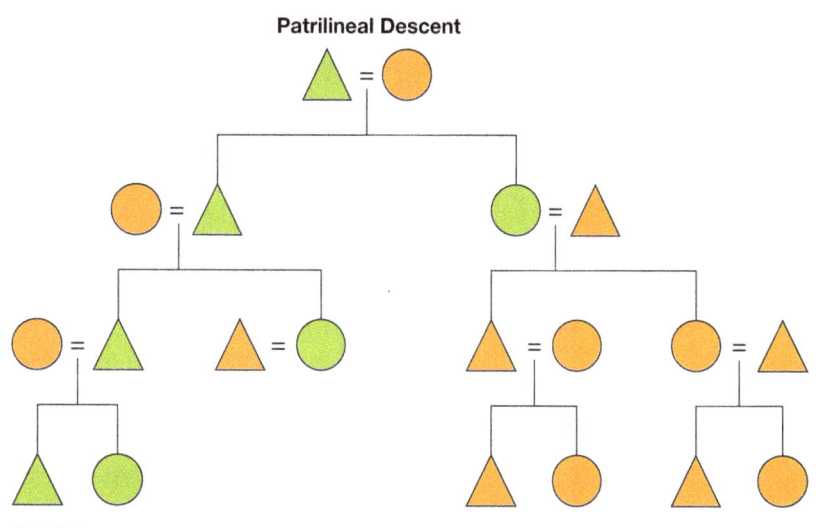

FIG. 8.4. A typical genealogy depicting patrilineal descent.

shared between partners. In a modern, secular society, legally sanctioned partnerships, heterosexual marriages, and homosexual marriages are commonplace. Gendered relationships will be discussed in the next chapter. Other forms of resource sharing and sexual relationships, whether legally sanctioned or not, include concubinage, sex trafficking, pedophilia, single parenthood, and surrogate parenthood. **Concubinage** is the cohabitation of persons not legally married. It predates the modern term partner, and usually refers to a man who bestows resources on a woman in exchange for sex. In a related way, when spouses had married for practical political and/or financial reasons, they often kept mistresses and lovers to satisfy a more sexual intimacy that was lacking in their lives. This practice was invariably frowned upon, but winked at because it "functionally" helped keep a society in stasis. **Sex trafficking** is an organized criminal activity in which human beings are treated as commodities to be controlled and exploited in sexual activities involuntarily. Because of its overpopulation, coupled with its lack of resources under Mao Zedong, China adopted a one-child policy. A **one-child policy** is a state policy that allows a couple to maintain only one child in its household. In an extremely patriarchal society like China, that child will usually only be a male. If a female is born prior to the birth of a male,

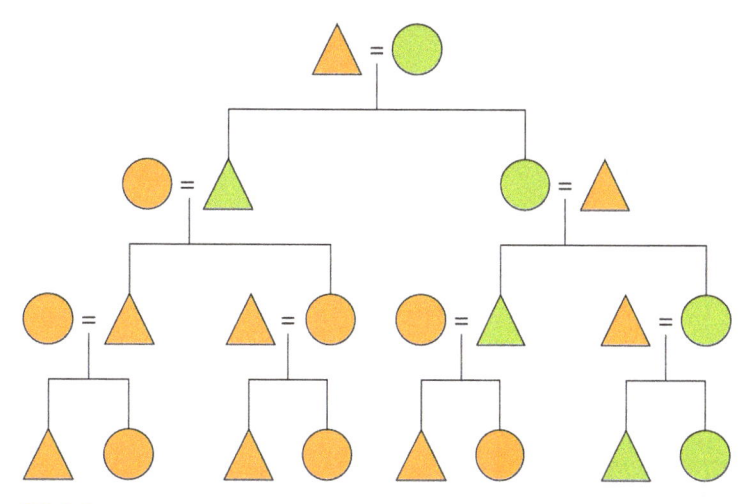

FIG. 8.5. A typical genealogy depicting matrilineal descent.

that female child will often be killed. This is called **female infanticide**. However, China changed its policy in 2015 and now allows all married couples to have two children. **Pedophilia** is adult sexual feelings and/or activities that involve children. **Single parenthood** is the social condition in which one parent only, who does not live with a spouse or a partner, has most or all of the responsibilities of raising one or more children. Both single women and single men can be single parents. Many single parents, including teens, who have had children out of wedlock, gain access to resources for the maintenance of a household by a resource-rich modern society that enables a utilitarian care for many of its non-working members through tax collection and social welfare. With the technological resources available today, an infertile woman may make a legal arrangement with another woman to carry a child for the infertile woman in exchange for payment. This is called **surrogate parenthood**.

Many of these modern cultural manifestations of family raise critical questions. Does society have a say in who is able to engage in reproductive activities? Should it? Is this an infringement upon freedom, that is, is a citizen entitled to the resources of the nation in making reproductive decisions? Do any members of a society have the right to seek resources for making a decision that they do not contribute towards, such as having a child out of wedlock? Does it "take a village to raise a child," metaphorically speaking? "Am I my brother's keeper," in a social context? The answers to these questions raise others. Who "owns" a mother's body—the mother, the father, the fetus? Can a man "own" a fetus? If so, will it be the man who has familial rights to a child, the genitor by blood, or the father by responsibility? For a woman, who has rights to a child—the surrogate by genetics and gestation or the mother by responsibility? These are serious questions worthy of deep thought. They will be touched on again in the following chapters.

KEY WORDS

Adoption
Affinal kinship
Arranged marriage
Bride service
Bridewealth
Clan
Cognatic descent
Collaterality
Concubinage
Consanguinal kinship
Divorce
Dowry
Drive
Ego
Endogamy
Ethics
Exogamy
Extended family
Family
Female infanticide
Fictive kinship
Fosterage
Genealogies
Genitor
Horizontal function of kinship
Illegitimate
Inbreeding theory
Incest taboo
Kinship
Legitimate
Lineality
Levirate
Marriage
Matrilocality
Matrilineal descent
Monogamy
Morals
Natural aversion theory
Neolocality
Nuclear family
One-child policy
Partner
Patrilocality
Patrilineal descent
Pedophilia
Polyandry
Polygyny
Primogeniture
Reciprocal exchange
Serial monogamy
Sex
Sex trafficking
Single parenthood
Sororate
Surrogate parenthood
Traditional father
Traditional mother
Values
Vertical function of kinship

IMAGE CREDIT

- Fig. 8.1: Copyright © 2014 by Nazmiyal Collection, (CC BY 3.0) at http://commons.wikimedia.org/wiki/File:Antique_Red_Turkish_Oushak_Carpet.jpg.

CHAPTER NINE

NATURE AND NURTURE: RACE, ETHNICITY, AND GENDER

Human beings and chimpanzees share approximately 96 percent of the same genes. Most people would not find this too surprising, since chimpanzees are the closest kin to our species on this planet. But, what might surprise many is that fruit flies share 60% of their genome with humans. Should it really be that shocking if all creatures share descent from a single organism that existed billions of years ago and branched and speciated repeatedly? If you have accepted the first two facts, then get ready for the next one. Humans share 25 percent of its genome with rice plants. Indeed, we do. There may be some deep truth to the adage that plants are stationary animals and animals are moving plants. Life it seems is one, big interwoven net of species that are mostly composed of the same stuff and communicate with one another through genetic and chemical transfers of information. For example, sharks do not eat pilot fish because the pilot fish and the shark have transferred communicative genetic material to each other that allow for a wonderful symbiotic relationship to prosper. The pilot fish eat the bits of shark kill that cling to the shark's teeth and skin and the cleansing action of the pilot fish keep the shark healthy. Countless examples of such homeostatic symbiotic relationships could be listed. To go even further in our pondering about the "mysteries" of life, consider how simple cellular organisms, called prokaryotes, have evolved independently of eukaryotes and may have nested within them in a symbiotic relationship early in the history of life on this planet, a symbiotic relationship that may have made multicellular life even possible. A **prokaryote** is a single-celled organism that lacks a membrane-bound nucleus and other membrane-bound organelles. A bacterium is a prokaryote. A **eukaryote** is an organism, including humans, whose cells have a well-defined membrane-bound nucleus and membrane-bound organelles. A popular theory states that prokaryotic cells nested within eukaryotic cells; in fact, the theory states that organelles called mitochondria are in fact ancient prokaryotic cells that furnish vast amounts of energy to eukaryotic cells, which, in turn, abundantly deliver the food sources needed by prokaryotes to them. Evidence for this theory lies in the fact that mitochondria possess their own DNA sequences that differ from the DNA of the nuclear genome. Why should we care? Well, we should for many reasons, but one is that all of our mitochondrial DNA is derived from the egg of our mother when we were conceived—our dad's mitochondrial DNA is jettisoned after dad's nuclear material from his sperm penetrates the egg—and mom's mitochondrial DNA carries markers all the way back to our first *Homo sapien*s ancestor, mitochondrial Eve. **Mitochondrial Eve** is a single East African female who lived between 200,000 and 300,000 years ago and to whom all human beings can trace their ancestry. And who mitochondrial Eve was dances on our notions of how culture is primarily determined. Is it biological or is it ideational? That is, does nature, our genetic inheritance, or nurture, the way we were enculturated as children, play the dominant role in determining cultural structures? This question was passionately debated during the Cold War years when much of the outcomes of political agendas depended upon which side was correct in the debate. Remember, the United States urged its imperial allies to decolonize their possessions in order to deny the Soviets leverage in the moral debate raging between the preachers of democracy and the zealots of communism; this catalyzed American Blacks, women, and gays to re-examine both biology and ideology in the milieu of Geertz's postmodern, deconstructive world. Although the dust has not yet settled on this debate, it feels safe enough to say that human culture is an ideational construction that must be erected upon an environmentally unique foundation that must support the biological needs of the human creature that dwells therein.

The human species is very tightly organized genetically, and the distinctions we use to differentiate human beings into groups are really very marginal in the holistic view of the gene pool. One such distinction is race. By definition, **a race** is a subgroup of the human population whose members share a greater number of genes and physical traits with one another than they do with members of other subgroups. Ironically, the abuses that have been perpetrated in the past via the early modern stages model of cultural development, which made some humans "superior" to others, are today seen as advantageous evolutionary adaptations that enabled our species to thrive in a wide variety of environments and climates. Anthropologists have given these observations names. **Thompson's rule** states that long noses on humans are better for arid and colder conditions because they contain more membranes and blood vessels in them to moisten the air and allow efficient gaseous transfer in the lungs. The opposite is true for the tropics, in which shorter and flatter noses allow for maximal gaseous exchange. **Bergman's rule** states that the longer, thinner bodies humans have in the tropics, such as the Maasai people of Kenya, contain more surface area to dispense body heat efficiently lest heat stroke should occur. The Inuit people of the arctic region, by contrast, have thicker, stockier bodies to hold heat in more efficiently. **Allen's rule** states that the relative size of protruding body parts increases with temperature, again to maximize the efficient shedding of heat. Rather than be a negative characteristic of the human species, these biological differences should be lauded as a triumph of our species' collective survival in a contingent world. Yet, sadly we choose to place judgments on one another because of these biological differences. One such judgment is called racism. **Racism** is the belief and practice that advocates the superiority of certain genetically-based groups and the inferiority of others. Prejudice is often practiced against peoples of different subgroups. **Prejudice** is a preconceived opinion that is not based upon reason or experience. Ironically, people confuse the term prejudice with discrimination. They are not the same thing; in fact, they are opposites. **Discrimination** is the ability to make rational and knowledgeable distinctions based on reason and experience. A wine connoisseur, for example, can discriminate between good wines and bad wines based on their qualities. Racism is often based on skin color. Skin color is based on the amount of melanin one possesses in the skin. **Melanin** is any kind of insoluble pigment that accounts for the dark color of skin, hair, fur, scales, feathers, etc. All humans, except those who exhibit albinism, an extremely deleterious condition, have melanin in their skins to protect them from harmful radiation. Blacks who live in the tropics have darker skins to protect them from more harmful radiation coming from space than do Caucasians who have less melanin in their skins to allow for sunlight to produce the vital vitamin D they would otherwise lack in northern climes. Skin color is really a "rainbow" spectrum of melanin pigmentation that has allowed our species to adapt wonderfully into many nuanced ecological niches on this planet. Racism is pure foolishness and really meaningless. Look at President Barack Obama, whose father is Kenyan and mother is Irish-American. What "race" is he? Humans can all interbreed successfully; hence, by definition, we are all the same species.

Another human distinction that has become blurred in its modern meaning is ethnicity. **Ethnicity** is the condition of belonging to a social group that has a common national or cultural tradition. Ethnicity is not race; it is not distinguished by skin color, although certain ethnicities are highly characterized by their skin colors. Rather, ethnicity is about the values, traditions, morals, and religions that one identifies with, and which defines one's ethnicity. For example, in pre-1990's Yugoslavia (the land of the Southern Slavs), six different national peoples existed in one nation-state. If one undressed them all and told them not to speak, it would be impossible to tell who belonged to which group because they all share the same race. But, put their ethnic clothing on them, listen to their languages, and observe their customs, they would become culturally distinct peoples. The ensuing ethnic cleansing tragedy was based on ethnic differences, not racial ones. **Ethnic cleansing** is the systematic and forced removal of ethnic groups from a given territory by oppression, rape, and torture to induce submission to a dominant ethnic group in order to ultimately achieve an ethnically homogeneous community. Ethnic cleansing is not about killing people; it is about maximizing the dominant group's control of available resources in a region through acculturative means. **Genocide**, on the other hand, is about killing people. It is the mass murder of an ethnic group of people in order to gain access to all of the resources a region has to offer without sharing them with other ethnic groups. Another social consequence of racism is segregation. **Segregation** is the enforced separation of different racial and/or ethnic groups in a country, community, or establishment. In South Africa, the former official policy of racial segregation was called **apartheid**.

Judging other groups and acting on those judgments often go hand-in-hand with stereotypes. A **stereotype** is a standardized mental picture held in common by members of a group that represents oversimplified ideas, opinions, and prejudices. Racism, prejudices, stereotypes, and discriminations have much to do with "rules"—those morals, ethics, norms, and values that humans conceive of to orient their egos in time and space as well as on land. Virtues are often made on the distinctions between "good" and bad." **Virtues** are the living of those principles in life that are in conformity to moral and ethical principles. **Good** is something that is morally right, like telling the truth. **Bad** is something that is morally wrong, like stealing cookies and blaming somebody else. Is it good or bad to point out to mom that your brother took the cookies and blamed it on somebody else? Would a Crip or a Blood agree with your answer? Virtues are culturally specific. Good and bad actions will have an impact on the way your life plays out during the course of your lifetime. To take these "rules" to a spiritual level, the rules of "good" and "bad" are called **righteousness** and **evil**. Righteousness is that set of rules that are in accord with pleasing deity. Evil is that set of rules that are displeasing to deity. Acting on righteousness in a way that is pleasing to deity is called godliness, while acting on evil in a way displeasing to deity is called sin. Godliness and sinfulness play out are in a life beyond this present life, or as some believe, an eternal life. These ways of categorizing rules and behaviors have, and have had, profound impacts on the ways we treat and interact with others. I will state that the way we interact with other peoples according to rules is primarily driven by access to resources. The more the availability of resources, the more the tolerance of others, and the more freedom is bestowed on individuals. Conversely, the more competition there is for resources, the more the drawing of distinctions there will be among peoples and the more justifications there will be in excluding the "out" group from the assets controlled by the "in" group. The way that the European Iberians, for instance, viewed and interacted with the indigenous peoples of the Americas brings together all of these layers of judgment and behavior. We will see more of Iberian-Native American interaction later.

How peoples can interact with other peoples in space and time can be highlighted by the evolution of the Hindu religion and society. A dark-skinned people dubbed the Harappans inhabited an area that would become India. We don't know their real names because we have not been able to crack their pictographic language. We have their artifacts depicting it, but as of yet, have not discovered a Harappan "Rosetta Stone." What happened to them was that a semi-nomadic light-skinned people who called themselves the Aryans—the "noble ones"—conquered their massive numbers with smaller, but rapidly moving numbers. The reason that the fewer Aryans could conquer the numerous Dravidians (the family group of the Harappans) was because the Aryans had domesticated the horse. They were people from the grassy steppes. It was they who introduced their God "Indra" to the region; this is where we get the name India. What the Aryans set up was a caste system based on color; the darker skinned Dravidians occupied the lower castes, while the lighter skinned Aryans controlled the leisurely and lucrative upper castes. A **caste** is a rigid form of social stratification in which membership is determined by birth and social mobility is prohibited. The word **varna** means "color" and is the original Hindu word for caste. But having conquered the Dravidians and establishing the overtly racist caste system, how could the Aryans hope to dominate the Dravidians? The answer was, as the answer always is with imperialism, acculturation, or as imperialists often say, the righteous evangelization of "truth." A new religion settled over the region that taught that if one performed one's duties well, no matter how humble the occupation, one would accrue good merit, called **dharma**. At the end of one's life, one's "good" actions and one's "bad" actions were weighed and the **reincarnation**, or rebirth of the self into another life form, whether "higher" on the chain toward righteous nirvana—the extinguishing of all ego—or "lower" toward a lesser human, or subhuman state, depended upon the sum of one's merits and determined the status of one's rebirth, or **karma**. Eventually, with the social mobility of people's spiritual selves through the centuries, people's bodies followed through marriage, and the bloodlines mixed. They mixed so much that the word for caste changed from "color" to "occupation," or **jati**. Henceforth, priests consorted with priests, rulers consorted with rulers, warriors with warriors, farmers with farmers, and so on. Aryan and Dravidian "racial" differences eventually yielded ethnic "Indian" unity.

Sex is another way humans are divided in some obvious and some not so obvious cultural ways. Throw gender into the mix and the plot thickens dramatically. Sex, remember, refers to the biological and physiological characteristics that define men, women, and intersexuals. In animals that exhibit sexual dimorphism, a number of individuals within a population will not differentiate sexually into bodies that are typically male or female. In humans, these individuals are called **intersexuals**. **Gender** refers to the socially constructed roles, behaviors, activities, and attributes that a given society considers appropriate for men, women, and intersexuals. Gender is also an abstract quality that is ascribed to people and things. For example, a human can be described as masculine or feminine. Masculine is that quality ascribed to action, power, and the accomplishments of material and imaginative projects. Feminine is that quality ascribed to nurturing, sensitivity, and passionate, artistic and spiritual projects. In Western cultures, men are traditionally expected be masculine and women are expected to be feminine. This ramification of human relations into masculine men and feminine women is derived from the Bible and is bounded by strict morality. Men are to be patriarchal and rule the family, albeit with wisdom and justice. Women are supposed to be submissive, dutiful, obedient, and caretaking. Many languages are ramified into masculine and feminine components. In Spanish, for example, a pencil is masculine—*el lapis*—and a pen is feminine—*la pluma*—for reasons I do not know. In many Native American cultures there are five recognized genders: masculine men, feminine men, masculine women, feminine women, and two-spirits. A **two-spirit** is an individual who has two identities occupying one body. They are equally male and female. Their dress is usually a mix of traditionally male and traditionally female articles, or they may dress as a man one day and as a woman another. Two-spirits are sensitive to the qualities possessed by both men and women and can address and counsel the needs of both. Two-spiritism is a charismatic gift bestowed upon an individual by the Creator, and as a functionalist would say, is assigned a traditional role of healer, counselor, and medicine person based upon an organically social need. There are no wasted people. Everyone has a function. This difference in gender identification among the interfacing cultures in the early modern era will lead to many clashes and much bricolage. In left-brained and rationalistic Western culture, the only two genders—masculine men and feminine women—were constructed for the primary purpose of procreation and the maintenance of inherited property that will be maintained both at the "active" periphery and in the "nurturing" domestic center. Native Americans lived more right-brained, holistic and communal lives, and therefore, persons who were more physically "alive" or more spiritually "alive" than others were accommodated for in their social structures. To westerners, two-spirits were seen as freaks, demons, deviants, perverts, corrupters, and sinners," and were treated as such. Western cultures are still quite uneasy with non-traditional gender identifications in the ever-expanding definition of "freedom."

FIG. 9.1. A two-spirit is quite welcome in the dance of warriors among the Sac and Fox peoples. A two-spirit could bring blessing, protection, and counsel to the warriors going into or coming from battle with all of its accompanying fears and traumas.

Traditional gender identification in the Western world is coupled with the ideas of traditional gender roles and heterosexuality. A **gender role** is an expected way of behavior based on a society's definition of masculine and feminine. Two particular roles are that of breadwinner and housewife. Traditionally, a **breadwinner** is the role that males assume for the economic and protective support of the family. This is an ideological extension of the peripheral duties of males in tribal societies. A **housewife** is the role that females assume for child-rearing and domestic duties within the household. This is an ideological extension of the central domestic duties of females in tribal societies. **Heterosexuality** is sexual attraction to and sexual activity with someone of the opposite sex. Where the two cultural groups, civilized and tribal, differ are the degrees of prestige attached to the relative gender roles. Tribal people certainly have strong values about gender and gender differences, but they see those roles in a complementary, not hierarchical way. That is, men, women, and intersexuals are different by charisma and personality, but they are equal in the society. A functionalist would agree. The Haudenosaunee see their gender roles as complements, as we shall see.

Western ideas of gender are based upon the notions of universal male dominance and patriarchy. **Universal male dominance** is the notion that men are more powerful than women and should be more influential than women in all societies. A **patriarchy** is a society dominated by males both through access to power and resources, as well as through bloodlines. The fact that there have been no matriarchies recorded in history should not be construed as an endorsement of patriarchy. A **matriarchy** is a society dominated by women. Gender structures, such as genderlects, may in fact be based upon sexual morphological differences. **Genderlects** are linguistic differences between individuals of different sexes and/or genders. Women have been described as engaging in "rapport" talk, that is, their conversations tend to be more sensitive, emotional, and nurturing than those of men. Remember, women have communication centers and emotional centers in both hemispheres of the brain and use 22,000 words to express themselves daily. Men tend to engage in "report" talk, that is, brief, direct communication. Their brains segregate to a high degree their emotional right hemispheres from their logical hemispheres, and they give their "bullet" discourses in 7,000 words daily. In traditional, complementary, tribal societies, the types of work that males, females, and intersexuals do is often a direct result of the physical, communicative, and emotional differences among them. Intersexuals as we have seen are often healers, counselors, and spiritualists. Men generally engage in "typical" male tasks, such as hunting, fishing, herding, mining, metallurgy, clearing land, waging war, working wood and stone, etc. These tend to be more peripheral roles. Women generally engage in foraging, preparing food, caring for children, making clothes, collecting fuel and water, and maintaining the household. These tend to be more central roles. Both men and women generally tend and harvest small domestic animals and crops, build shelters, make craft items, and conduct trade in markets. **Mechanization**, based on the Greek word *mechane* "to trick," in this case the ability of humans to "trick" nature via "progressive" technology—pulleys, hydraulics, etc.—will progressively blur traditional gender roles in the modern age, since anyone can pull a lever and press a button in order to move mountains. (Just look at some of the physiques of our highway pay-loader operators.) The steady progressiveness of mechanization in logical, left-brained cultures will result in a shift in the predominance of arguments that foster "nurture" as the dominant factor in social and cultural constructions and diminish the role of "nature." This is also partially a result of some of the negative consequences of universal male dominance. The encroachment of women into traditionally male dominated activities like working outside of the home for pay, that is, becoming a breadwinner, has resulted in the male backlash known as the double workload for women. **Double workload** is the situation in which employed married women, especially those with children, must care for the household and the children in addition to working for wages outside of the home. An opposite negative reaction to traditional patriarchy is the feminization of poverty. The **feminization of poverty** is the growing proportion of women that lead households in the modern world and are denied equal access to resources by males who own the access to power and resources in a patriarchal culture. In some Muslim and Hindu cultures, the practice of **purdah** keeps women in seclusion from the populations in general, and often requires that they wear clothing that conceals their bodies entirely. When males feel deeply threatened in their ego structures by a challenge upon their patriarchal prerogatives by women, they may react with deprivation, intimidation, domestic violence, and physical abuse. **Honor killing** is a euphemistic term that describes the practice in many Middle Eastern cultures of killing women whose families believe they have brought dishonor to them. All of these factors contribute toward promoting the Feminist Movement.

Despite strong pressures to turn back the clocks culturally, modern, democratic, liberal cultures continue to "progressively" push the concept of "freedom" to its inexorable, logical end. This entails acknowledging alternative forms of gender and sexuality, which by extension includes the democratic and secular recognition of legal homosexuality. **Homosexuality** is sexual attraction to and sexual activity with someone of the same sex. **Bisexuality** is sexual attraction to and sexual activity with both males and females. Another alternative lifestyle is tranvestism. **Transvestism** is the practice of a person who lives as a member of a different sex from his or her birth sex and can include dressing in the clothing of that different sex. Another alternative lifestyle is transexualism. A **transsexual** is a person who has undergone a sex change operation and lives and dresses accordingly. People who live alternative modern lifestyles often come into strong ideological, legal, and political conflicts with people of traditional ideologies; they fight over issues such as the legality of gay marriage

9.2A (LEFT) AND B (RIGHT). The people of Celtic Ireland gendered their landscape according to gender roles. The king married his "queen"/landscape by a ceremony that would today be considered non-traditional. The king mingled his potent seed in the presence of the "masculine" sun with a serum and placed it atop the sacred Liafail stone—a ritualized phallus—at the *omphallos* "navel" (of creation) at the Hill of Tara. This serum was then deposited in the earth in a barrow chamber that symbolized the labia, the vagina, and the womb of a woman, which was awaiting penetration of sunlight via the chamber. This, in turn, energized the serum sacredly and impregnated the Mother—Erin—in a propitiation to her for abundant harvests, herds, children, and wealth. Her "feminine" domain was also located on the sacred Hill of Tara and resided under the auspices of the moon. The Celtic word Tara is akin to the Hebrew word *torah*, which means "law." In Greek, a similar cognate is *ter*, which means "land."

with all of the exchanges of resources and services that that institution entails and the adoption of children, citing the psychological health of the child as the reason. Is marriage an institution that is for procreation of successive biological generations only? Can gay couples successfully adopt and perhaps through surrogate motherhood, engender and successfully rear functional members of the next generation? Recent studies are leaning toward a yes. Functional children respond in healthy ways to parents that balance masculine and feminine roles in a nurturing way more so than males and females who raise children in dysfunctional "gender roles."

Gender is typically associated with people and roles, but it is a much subtler and basic cultural term than that. I have mentioned how languages are gendered in a primal binary way by structuralists. Gender is typically projected onto time, space, things, places, and ideas in cultural constructions. Remember how the cave art in Chapter 4 depicted the gendered "horned" male deity of the periphery and the projected zaftig fertile mother-goddess of the center. These cultural projections are often codified into a people's mythology.

Mythical tales give ego centeredness to individuals in time, space, land and ideology in culturally-specific ways. Such tales include the cosmogenic myths of the Aztecs and the Maya, the tale of Maui of the Polynesians, the Jesus myth of the Christians, and the Haudenosaunee creation myth, as we shall see. Myths may or may not be true. They need only explain and be believed. All religions are based on basic mythical stories, even secular ones. Just look closely at them, as Socrates would have you do. I will deconstruct the myth called "Beowulf" and compare it to the modern "mythological" construction of Erik Erikson's stages theory. Beowulf is a "how-to" book for an Anglo-Saxon parent to raise a mature man from an immature boy. Erikson does the same for a gender-neutral secular modern.

Myths orient people to the metaphysical dimension, explain the origins and nature of the cosmos, validate social issues, and, on the psychological plane, address themselves to the innermost parts of the psyche. Mircea Eliade related the connection between the human psyche and the conceiving of myths when he wrote, "Man constructs according to an archetype." The Irish philosopher George Berkeley believed that archetypes are the images of things that exist in the mind of the Christian God and were used to create the world. Carl Jung, as we have seen, identified four main archetypes in the human psyche: the Self, the Shadow, the Anima, and the Animus. Let us examine the Shadow. The Shadow is:

> a part of the unconscious mind consisting of repressed weaknesses, shortcomings, and instincts. It may be, in part, one's link to more primitive animal instincts, which are superseded in early childhood by the conscious mind. It is the "dark side" of the ego, containing qualities that the ego does not identify with but possesses nonetheless. Actually, the shadow is amoral—neither good nor bad, just like animals. The shadow, in being instinctive and irrational, is prone to project: turning a personal inferiority into a perceived moral deficiency in someone else. These projections insulate and cripple individuals by forming an ever thicker fog of illusion between the ego and the real world. The shadow may appear in dreams and visions in various forms, often as a feared or despised person or being, and may act either as an adversary or as a servant. Many archetypes are story characters in myths. The hero is one of the main ones. He is the defeater of dragons; he represents the ego, who is engaged in fighting the shadow, in the form of dragons, demons, and other monsters.

According to Lévi-Strauss' structuralism, the oral-derived tales of the wandering tribes of Israel in their written form lie midway between the "tribal" mind of the Beowulf tale and the "civilized" mind of Erikson's paradigm. Edward Edinger has deconstructed the Old Testament prophetic book of Isaiah in terms of the psychic maturation of an alienated ego-Self relationship within one's own psyche and the mythical alienated relationship of the Nation of Israel itself with its God. The ego is symbolized by the public prostrations and punishments of Isaiah and the Self is Yahweh, the transcendent and inscrutable entity that subsumes and guides the nation.

> No, the hand of Yahweh is not too short to save, nor his ear too dull to hear. But iniquities have made a gulf between you and your God. (Isa. 59: 1-2)

Here, personified in beautiful imagery, is the "crisis" of the juvenile confronting his incipient maturation to adulthood. Reaping the consequences of its inflation, misjudgment, and hubris, the ego experiences an epiphany, which is followed by a change of attitude on the part of the Self. And with that change of attitude, one sees positive Self-images as opposed to negative Self-images. When the prostrate and mortified Isaiah—the grandiose, immature, and limitless ego—has made peace, becomes one with—the integrated, subliminal, and holistic realms of the unconscious levels of the mind—then the low places will have been made high, the high places will have been made low, and the highway to God will have been prepared in the wilderness. Only then will the holistic glory of Yahweh emerge within a healthy ego-Self axis. Healthy maturation, under the aegis of wise counsel, is the timeless message of the passage. It is part of the Hebrew mythological corpus.

The same process of psychic maturation in males is addressed in the modern Jungian analysis of Robert Moore and Douglas Gilette in their book "King, Warrior, Magician, Lover" (1990). In it, the psyche of all males is divided into "double quaternios." That is, there are two psychic phases in each man's life, the immature and the mature, each of which is composed of four interwoven archetypes. Immaturity is the timeless, healthy, and necessary developmental stage of every boy everywhere prior to his metamorphosing into a balanced, holistic, and productive mature adult male. An immature adult is the bugbear of salutary development, not an immature boy. The four archetypes of normal boys/immature males are: the Divine Child, the Precocious Child, the Oedipal Child, and the Hero. The numinous psychic qualities associated with these are: self-centeredness; curiosity; sensuousness and aesthetics; and individuality, respectively. All are grandiose and subject to no limitations, except from external mores that are imposed upon them, which are yielded to grudgingly. They are immature, adventurous, and experiential; yet all are tied in some way to mother. The Divine Child is born of a "pristine" and "perfect" mother, in a healthy boyish immaturity. His Precocious Child seeks nurturing approval, and his Oedipal Child desires not sexual intimacy with his physical mother, but a healthy leavening of emotional and "feminine" intimacy with his environment and those in it. The Hero is defined as follows:

> As is the case with the other immature masculine archetypes, the Hero is overly tied to the Mother. But the Hero has a driving need to overcome her. He is locked in mortal combat with the feminine, striving to conquer it and to assert his masculinity. In the medieval legends about heroes and damsels, we are seldom told what happens when the hero has slain the dragon, and married the princess…, because the Hero, as an archetype, doesn't know what to do with the Princess once he's won her. He doesn't know what to do when things return to normal. The Hero's downfall is that he doesn't know and is unable to acknowledge his limitations.

The Hero archetype, in the Hero Quest is the psychic catapult that will launch the immature boy into limited, sage, and mature masculinity, the second quaternion of the double quaternio. The corresponding archetypes to the Divine Child, the Precocious Child, the Oedipal Child, and the Hero archetypes of the initial quaternion are: the King, the Magician, the Lover, and the Warrior, respectively. The numinous psychic qualities associated with these are: the structuring, protecting, and blessing qualities of the "King"; the psychic, spiritual, and technical mastery associated with the "Magician"; the sensual, emotional, holistic, and empathetic qualities of the "Lover," and the disciplined, loyal, and proactive characteristics of the "warrior." The initial quaternion of the immature boy can be related to the ego and the second quaternion of the mature man to the Self in Edinger's analysis. We will remember all of this in the analysis of Erikson and Beowulf.

Every maturing male must embark upon a "Quest for Self-Development," that is, to die to the immature Self and become "born again" into the mature Self. The sequence of events unfolding in the life of the protagonist in the "typical" Quest myth are: a Divine Birth, a subsequent Alienation, Trials by Combat, a Damsel Rescue, a Dragon Fight, and the garnering of a Treasure hoard. These correspond to the developmental stages of "every" male from infancy to eldership gained by education, mentoring and experience. The Divine Birth, whether he is Moses of the Hebrew people or the Peacemaker of the Haudenosaunee, is that selfsame Divine Child, whose immature ego "is the center of the universe" unto which all things answer. The Alienation, again whether he is Moses in the reeds or Oedipus at the roadside, begins in the young boy's consciousness the first time he hears the word "No!" From then on, the adolescent will push against the limits to his grandiosity in his "constraining" domestic setting. Straining at the bit against the externally imposed values of his parents and society, the "Hero" nature of the boy fights back and tests these values in order to gain individuation and a Self-identity around the time of puberty. This is a true liminal process, usually catalyzed through a rite of passage. He will wage a series of "Trials by Combat," winning some and losing others, in order to discover his own charismatic gift and master it. Through this process he will learn his own limitations as well as his unique Self-worth. This is his first step into team-building and community. This sets him up for his confrontation with his own nurturing "feminine" nature. He must "Rescue" this "Damsel." He may fail in this several times, like Parcival in his quest for the Holy Grail, before he eventually asks the right question. This entails Self-sacrifice, not self-grandiosity, and leads to a man's mature adulthood. He has already mastered his trade, his "masculine" method of livelihood through his combats, and now must utilize his masculine expertise in his middle-aged years to nurture others, in a truly "feminine" sense, to nurture his wife, his family, and his community. Later, in his "empty nest" years, with an aging "warrior's" body, a confident "magician's" mastery, a stable "lover's" heart, and a "king's" sagacity, he experiences his "Renaissance" period when he is "born again" to the dusty and unlimited dreams of youth, which he now reclaims and tempers with the wisdom of his life's experiences. He sets out once again on a quest for worth, but this time his quest is "worthy." This time he confronts the Dragon, that creature whose sloughing of its skin has been a timeless symbol of "rebirth," both psychically and spiritually. This time Parcival asks the right question and gains the Grail. The prize of this fight is the treasure hoard that Beowulf only gains at the end of his days. It is a coming to terms with the paradoxes and conundrums of human existence and a gaining of inner wisdom that is evinced outwardly through a kindly nod and a knowing smile. It is the time of the Pearl of Great Price, the redeeming of the faithful stewards of the talents and the pounds, the sharing of one's garnered wisdom with the youth of one's community. It is the time of the elders, the grandfathers. It is the precious legacy that we leave to those who come after us. It is the true treasure of "Everyman."

Erik Erikson focused his research on the effects of society and culture on individual psychological development. Graduating from the Vienna Psychoanalytic Society in 1933, he transcended the Freudian focus on dysfunctional behavior to pursue the ways that the normal Self is able to function successfully. This is encapsulated in his eight-stage model of human development, shown in the accompanying chart. Notice in the chart that each stage, I-VIII, corresponds to a progressive range of ages from infancy to old age. Notice also that each stage corresponds to a psychological crisis, a catalogue of significant relations with others, psychological modalities, virtues, etc. The exact correspondence of these stages and corresponding characteristics are detailed in Erikson's book, "The Life Cycle Completed" (1997), and I will not delve into them very deeply here. I do want to point out, however, that Erikson's life cycles cosmology, although cast in the mores of the modern Western worldview of the sexless, genderless, secular, democratic individual, cannot escape the subliminal structuring inherent in the Quest myth of the Trial by Combat, the Damsel Rescue, and the Dragon Fight—Lévi-Strauss' dichotomy between the "masculine" left brain and the "feminine" right brain, and Jung's archetypal syzygy between the male persona and the anima. A **syzygy** is the balancing of paired masculine and feminine qualities in the human mind for a holistic, complete, and healthy outlook. Notice that stage I corresponds to the Divine Birth phase of the Quest until sometime in stage I when the encroachments of moral principles from the world outside of the child's unlimited ego begin to clip his wings and define socially acceptable limits. This ushers in the Alienation phase of the Quest, which comprises stages II and III. This "outside" mentoring can be done in a functional or a dysfunctional way and leads to several developmental crises: trust versus mistrust, autonomy versus shame, initiative versus guilt, etc. Herein is also waged the war between the ego and the shadow in the individual psyche of each child. In stages IV and V, the adolescent male becomes a pubescent teen and is developing his sense of technical mastery in a career; his competence, industry, and social place among his peers; and hones his sense of loyalty through tests while striving to determine his

Stage (age)	Psychosocial crisis	Significant relations	Psychosocial modalities	Psychosocial virtues	Maladaptations & malignancies
I (0-1) – infant	trust vs mistrust	mother	to get, to give in return	hope, faith	sensory distortion – withdrawal
II (2-3) – toddler	autonomy vs shame and doubt	parents	to hold on, to let go	will, determination	impulsivity – compulsion
III (3-6) – preschooler	initiative vs guilt	family	to go after, to play	purpose, courage	ruthlessness – inhibition
IV (7-12 or so) – school-age child	industry vs inferiority	neighborhood and school	to complete, to make things together	competence	narrow virtuosity – inertia
V (12-18 or so) – adolescence	ego-identity vs role-confusion	peer groups, role models	to be oneself, to share oneself	fidelity, loyalty	fanaticism – repudiation
VI (the 20s) – young adult	intimacy vs isolation	partners, friends	to lose and find oneself in a another	love	promiscuity – exclusivity
VII (late 20s to 50s) – middle adult	generativity vs self-absorption	household, workmates	to make be, to take care of	care	overextension – rejectivity
VIII (50s and beyond) – old adult	integrity vs despair	humankind or "my kind"	to be, through having been, to face not being	wisdom	presumption – despair

own ego-identity. This is his time of Trial by Combat, in which his "masculine" identity is molded within his male psyche in the process of holistic integration. In stages VI and VII, he is Rescuing the Damsel, during which his nurturing "feminine" identity within his male psyche is in the process of holistic integration. He is developing his sexuality, intimacy, and generativity as he loves and cares for others in an altruistic and cooperative way. Stage VIII is the Dragon Fight, the time of his Renaissance and eldership. In this time of wisdom he acts in the holistic fullness of his integrity and serves humankind, as "my kind," or ossifies in despair as an acerbic, stingy, and stodgy curmudgeon.

Let us now examine briefly the myth of Beowulf. As a pre-literate oral tale of the tribal Anglo-Saxons that has been captured in writing by their literate descendants, the tale is a "how-to" scheme of development that wise elders would broadcast to huddled assemblages of their young listeners who are seeking wise mentorship. In this analysis, I will utilize Seamus Heaney's translation of Beowulf (2000). Again, I will trace the stages of the Quest myth through relevant passages of the Beowulf tale. In my redaction I will be mixing family heritages, but the cycles that play out for the development of each "hero" in the repetitive, mnemonic cycles inherent in this genre are the same.

> So the Spear-Danes in days gone by and the kings who ruled them had courage and greatness. There was Shield Sheafson, scourge of many tribes beyond the whale-road who had to yield to him. That was one good king.

Here are presented the credentials for an Anglo-Saxon "hero's" birth, the Divine Birth of the Everyman Quest, Erikson's stage I, and the "sacred" birth of every human boy.

> Afterwards a boy-child was born to Shield, who was cast away when he was a child and launched out over the waves.

This is the Alienation phase of a young boy in terms that an Anglo-Saxon youth could understand, as terrible and as awesome as Oedipus' abandonment was to any ancient Athenian, or Moses' abandonment and salvific training was to any Israelite. It is also correspondent with Erikson's stages II and III. This alienation and the psychic conflict between the ego and the shadow is exemplified in the monster Grendel when he wreaks havoc in the heretofore ordered realm of the Danish "King" Hrothgar:

> Merciless Grendel, malignant by nature, he never showed remorse. He ruled in defiance of right. All were endangered by that dark death-shadow. He would never parley or make peace with any Dane.

FIG. 9.3. Grendel, the "masculine" monster to a man's ego.

This is the archetypal call at the salient stage in life when the collective unconscious musters its inherited imagery to guide the boy through his liminal fears and angst into manhood. This metamorphosis of immaturity into maturity is inherent in the character Beowulf, the vassal of Hygelac, king of the neighboring Geats.

> When he heard about Grendel, Hygelac's vassal announced his plan: to sail the swan's road and search out that king, the famous prince who needed defenders. Nobody tried to keep him from going.

Here Beowulf embarks upon his Quest for integrated masculinity within his psyche by seeking the Trial by Combat that will abet the transformation of his immature "Hero" archetype into that of the mature "King."

> I can calm the turmoil and terror in his mind. Beowulf is my name. Now I mean to be a match for Grendel, settle the outcome in single combat.

In full public view he confronts his monstrous, shadowy enemy and masters him. The accolades and rewards he garners are appropriate, in an Anglo-Saxon social milieu, to the masculine mastery of a vocation in any other society, one that will enable him to make his way in the world:

> You have made yourself immortal by your glorious action.

This event corresponds to Erikson's stages IV and V. Feasts are held and largesse is dispensed, but all is not well in the mead-hall. Houses are always symbolic of one's psychic life in a Jungian sense. The male's mind is not fully integrated. He has only mastered his outward, public, masculine mind. The damsel must yet be rescued, the feminine mind integrated:

> Grendel's mother brooded on her wrongs. She sallied forth on a savage journey, grief-racked and ravenous.

FIG. 9.4. Beowulf, the hero, seeking maturity.

She wreaks havoc in Heorot just as her son Grendel had done before her. She retreats after each attack to her den at the bottom of a murky swamp.

> And the swamp bottom has never been sounded by the sons of men.

This is feminine space, Erikson's stages VI and VII, where men do not like to tread. The return to the womb for sacred transformation, for full, mature integration of the feminine mind with the masculine mind is alien to the immature male mind. Beowulf begins to understand this and plans for the nurturing of his men in the event of his death:

> If this combat kills me, take care of my young company, my comrades in arms.

That he does not fully understand the nature of the fight he is in becomes evident when he observes:

> the hag in all her terrible strength, then heaved his war-sword and swung his arm, but here at last the fabulous powers of that heirloom failed.

FIG. 9.5. Grendel's mother, the "feminine" monster to a man's ego.

Beowulf was fighting the right fight, but with the wrong weapons. He was trying to "conquer" the feminine mind with the tools that integrated the masculine mind. It will not work. He must become as the feminine is in order to integrate the feminine. That entails a different approach with a different arsenal. And in the end, he only partially succeeds. His feminine mind, like that of most men, is only partly integrated as he takes on the full responsibilities of adulthood. He will still put more importance on the peripheral aspirations of his mind than on the central, humble ones. His syzygy will be lopsided. As king for a span of 50 years, he will make mistakes that will eventually garner him timeless wisdom, albeit through bitter experience.

> He suffered in the end for having plagued his people for so long: his life lost happiness.
> So learn from this and understand true values. I who tell you have wintered into wisdom.

In old age, the shadow, the adversary/servant of Beowulf's unconscious nagged heavily at him once again, and proffered a rebirth, a renaissance. A dragon had been awakened from a barrow and the land of the king was once again being ravaged. Beowulf, in his last hurrah, confronts his final foe.

He slays the beast, but not before being mortally wounded. But, he does gain the treasure hoard that eluded him with the incomplete integration of the psychic fight with Grendel's mother.

> I want to examine that ancient gold; my going will be easier for having seen the treasure, a less troubled letting-go of the life and lordship I have long maintained. I give thanks that I behold this treasure here in front of me that I have been allowed to leave my people so well-endowed on the day I die.

At the end of his life, Beowulf finally integrates his mind, and gains the wisdom of transcending the grasping after external self-rewards he so long hungered for, and exchanged them for the selfless rewards inherent in true nurturing and stewardship. Beowulf gains his "treasure" by dispensing it freely. And that is his legacy. At his funeral, he is buried with the dragon:

FIG. 9.6. Hitler's mother.

> Beside him lies the bane of his life. The living nation, keeping weary vigil, holding a wake for the loved and the loathed.

In the end, the ego and the shadow were united and the holism of the Self revealed.

This analysis shows how different cultures attempt to bring about the holistic functional development of their generations. Without the guidance of functional parents, dysfunctions can be imprinted into offspring, and myths address these pitfalls. Adolf Hitler was the son of an aggressive, abusive, over-drinking, and male dominating father, and he quailed under the affections of an overly doting, dysfunctional mother. He became an insecure "momma's boy" as result, imbued with the cold-heartedness that often accompanies an emotion-squashing father. At the height of his power in Nazi Germany, in the company of sycophants, he saw a picture of the Medusa in a museum and reverted to his traumatized childhood and quailed, "Those are the eyes of my mother!" What more perfect image of a dysfunctional man than the "Medusa-as-mother" that can turn a man's heart to stone! And only a man with a heart of stone could perpetrate the Holocaust as a moral "good."

FIG. 9.7. Medusa image that Hitler saw.

KEY WORDS

Allen's rule
Apartheid
Bad
Bergman's rule
Bisexuality
Breadwinner
Caste
Dharma
Discrimination
Double workload
Ethnic cleansing
Ethnicity
Eukaryote
Evil
Feminization of poverty
Gender
Genderlects
Gender Role
Genocide
Good
Heterosexuality
Homosexuality
Honor killing
Housewife
Intersexuals
Jati
Karma
Matriarchy
Mechanization
Melanin
Mitochondrial Eve
Myths
Patriarchy
Prejudice
Prokaryote
Purdah
Race
Racism
Reincarnation
Righteousness
Segregation
Stereotype
Syzygy
Thompson's rule
Transsexual
Transvestism
Two-spirit
Universal male dominance
Varna
Virtues

IMAGE CREDITS

- Fig. 9.1: George Catlin / Copyright in the Public Domain.
- Fig. 9.2a: Copyright © 2005 by Verdasuno / Wikimedia Commons, (CC BY-SA 3.0) at http://en.wikipedia.org/wiki/File:Tara_stone.jpg.
- Fig. 9.2b: Copyright © 2011 by Anthony Foster, (CC BY-SA 2.0) at https://commons.wikimedia.org/wiki/File:The-mound-of-hostages.jpg.
- Fig. 9.3: J. R. Skelton / Copyright in the Public Domain.
- Fig. 9.4: J. R. Skelton / Copyright in the Public Domain.
- Fig. 9.5: J. R. Skelton / Copyright in the Public Domain.
- Fig. 9.6: Copyright in the Public Domain.
- Fig. 9.7: Franz Stuck / Copyright in the Public Domain.

CHAPTER TEN

SOCIAL STRUCTURE, ART, AND RELIGION

Social structure is what glues a society or community together. A **society** is a group of people who reside within a specific territory and share a common culture. The organic analogy of the functionalists compares a society to the body of an organism, in which all of the organs and systems work together as equally valid elements in a composite whole. But, not all elements are the same or equal. What then makes a people "the same?" The word community is derived from the Roman prefix *cum* "with" and *unum* "oneness." A **community** is a group of people who share tasks and goals. The ancient Celtic peoples used the word *tuath* as their word for community. It actually means more than that. *Tuath* means the entire country itself, the land. It also means all the people who inhabit that land. Finally, it means the tribe within the people within the land that one's ego identifies with. Celts lived not only in relation to one another, but collectively in relation to the natural environment. Community is really a very small word for a very big idea. Christians have long identified themselves as "the community of believers" or "the church." A church is not a building; rather, it is derived from the Greek prefix *ek* "out of" and *lesia* "cut," as in a lesion, or "cut/called out." Christians, therefore, are those individuals called out from the profane world of human morals into a spiritual realm of deity's morals only by the invitation of the Holy Spirit. Notice, the church is by definition a "closed" community until supernatural forces open the door to others, not the community itself. In Buddhism, the word *sangha* is the community of believers and is considered one of the three sacred refuges for followers of the Buddha's path. The "Buddha's Way" is not a closed community; it is open and available to all by the volition of each individual. Communities are held together through values and virtues. Again among the Celts, the cardinal virtues were hospitality, honor, and sovereignty. Sovereignty means power, but in addition to the sovereignty inherent in the power given to the kingdom and the tribe, Celts believed sovereignty meant freedom. Each Celt, like an early Socratic, must live a life that became ever more virtuous through the gaining of knowledge and experience to forge wisdom. It is really the quest that we explored in the analysis of Beowulf and Erikson, and it is the psychic basis upon which social structures are erected, as Lévi Strauss explored. And what is the true quality of sovereignty/freedom? Is it not in hospitality, that is, is it not in bestowing generously your bounty to others that the land itself has so generously bestowed upon you? This is the moral lesson of the Beowulf tale, as we shall see.

In an organic model of society, social structures are stratified; that is, they are inherently unequal. They can be complementary and have equal status or hierarchical and have unequal status. A **hierarchy** is a system or organization in which people or groups are ranked one above the other according to status or authority. There are three categories for measuring social status: wealth, power, and prestige. **Wealth** is the material objects that have value in a society. **Power** is the capacity to produce intended effects for oneself, others, situations, and the environment. **Prestige** is the social honor or respect valued within a society. Patriarchies pass prestige and power over land and wealth down through the male line, as we have seen. Primogeniture is designed to pass power, prestige, and wealth down through the eldest male in order to utilize the environmental resources available in a plot of land to their maximum and, if all is conducted virtuously, efficient advantages. A pitfall of primogeniture in a hierarchical society is that the firstborn son gets everything and is the "physical" expression of the family. In Europe, the second son entered an ecclesiastical profession, profited from the resources of land, and was the "supernatural" expression of the family. Boys number three, etc., inherited no resources, especially in noble families, and were dependent upon the hospitality and generosity of their elder brethren for their sustenance. These younger sons often became the conquistadors embarking upon quixotic quests, in order to gain power, prestige, and wealth for themselves in foreign lands. Religion would justify these enterprises, as we shall see. Primogeniture is designed to ease the transition of power, wealth, and prestige from generation to generation. An alternative to primogeniture is **partible inheritance**. Partible inheritance is the practice of dividing one's patrimony equally among all of the surviving children, usually sons, of a family. A pitfall of partible inheritance is that it puts increasing pressure on the land to produce more as it becomes divided up into smaller and smaller family parcels with each succeeding generation, until the carrying capacity of the land is exceeded, productivity plummets, and people fight and die until the ability of the land to support human social structures once again becomes feasible. Racial and ethnic differences between the Hutu and the Tutsi were offered as excuses to commit genocide in Rwanda; but, the real catalyst for the tragedy was the erosion of the land due to excessive deforestation driven by overpopulation. **Carrying capacity** is the maximum number of people a society can support given the available resources.

There are different ways for people within societies to achieve status. **Ascribed status** is the status an individual has by virtue of birth. People born into historic Hindu India possessed ascribed status via the caste system. **Achieved status** is the status an individual acquires during the course of his or her lifetime. Persons pursuing the "American Dream" gain achieved status. There is no social mobility in a society with ascribed status; there is in one that values achieved status. The smallest unit of social organization is called a band. A **band** usually consists of a few dozen to a few hundred individuals who are united by kinship. The social structure of a band is called an egalitarian society. An **egalitarian society** is a society that recognizes few differences in wealth, prestige, and power. The next level of social organization is called a ranked society. A **ranked society** is a society in which people have unequal access to prestige and status, but equal access to wealth and power. **Tribal societies** are examples of ranked societies. Tribal societies are small-scale societies that are composed of autonomous political units, usually based on clans, which share common languages and cultures. Tribal societies are often based on chiefdoms. A **chiefdom** is a form of tribal organization that achieves integration through the offices of chiefs, an office that is usually acquired through merit, at least initially. The early Germanic people are an example of a ranked society based on chiefs. Resources were meager and shared, but leaders were often chosen by their merit and leadership could always be revoked by the group. This notion has been dubbed the social contract, based on the concept of "*primus inter pares*, or the "first among equals." The leaders of the Enlightenment in Europe would invoke the social contract to dispute the idea of "divine right monarchy" via rebellion and revolution, as we shall see. **Pan-tribal societies** are those tribal societies that have unified in a larger political and social unit that cuts across kinship lines. The Haudenosaunee Confederation is an example of a pan-tribal society. The next level of social organization is called a stratified society. A **stratified society** is a society that is organized with considerable variations in the sharing of wealth, power, and prestige.

FIG. 10.1. The Hadza of Tanzania are organized as an egalitarian society. They are a hunting and gathering society, and though the number of roles for men and women are few, they are highly gendered.

Unequal access to power, wealth, and prestige in a stratified society is based on class. A **class** is a ranked group within a stratified society that is characterized by achieved status and considerable social mobility. Traditional Western civilization is based upon class distinctions and can accommodate a wealthy businessman leaving a champagne brunch and passing a "street person" begging for money as a normal everyday occurrence. A class society can also accommodate lower "class" individuals dispossessed by a natural calamity, such as a hurricane or flood, living in shelters for extended periods of time, while an inept CEO of a large corporation can be discharged with an inordinately lucrative severance package that is not based upon merit. Stratified societies are usually organized into bodies called states. A **state** is a type of political structure that is hierarchical, bureaucratic, centralized, and has a monopoly on the legitimate use of force to implement its policies. States are often "glued together" by the concept of nationhood. A **nation** is a group of people who share a common identity, culture, and history. The combination of the political institution of the state with the kinship structures of the nation is called a **nation-state**. **Nationalism** is the secular religion that dispels supernatural allegiances for a community and substitutes human ones instead. We will examine this further in Chapters 12 and 13.

Communities, societies, and states maintain social order through social control based upon social norms. A **social control** is a mechanism found in a society that functions to encourage people to follow the social norms. **Social norms** are expected forms of behavior. Obedience is expected in a society to its social norms and laws. A **law** is a cultural rule that regulates social behavior and maintains social order. **Deviance** is the violation of a social norm. Some deviance is expected in the normal maturation of an immature person into a mature one, but that deviance is constrained within tolerable limits and does not harm others. The hero quest is often an act of tolerated deviance. A **crime** is a form of deviance that is not tolerated. It is doing harm to a person or property that society considers unlawful. **Sanctions** are the means a society uses to enforce compliance with the rules and norms of a society. There are both positive sanctions and negative sanctions. **Positive sanctions** are means of social control for enforcing social norms through rewards. Honorary degrees, bonus checks, and gold stars in kindergarten are all examples of positive sanctions. **Negative sanctions** are punishments for violating the norms of a society. Detention, prison time, and capital punishment are all examples of negative sanctions. Social control is a function of the logical left brain, while social expression is a function of the creative right brain. Art and religion bridge the two functions of the brain in "gluing" societies together.

Art is the conscious use of skill and creative imagination in the production of aesthetic objects. **Aesthetics** is a branch of philosophy dealing with the nature of the beautiful and with judgments concerning beauty. Art is intended to be transformational. **Transformation** is the quality of an artistic process that converts a mental image into a concrete work. Concrete works of art can be either graphic or plastic. **Graphic arts** are forms of art that include painting and drawing on various two-dimensional surfaces. The male horned deity in the cave painting in Chapter 4 is an example of graphic arts. **Plastic arts** are forms of art that involve molding certain forms in three-dimensional space, such as sculpture. The bas-relief of the Mother Goddess in Chapter 4 is an example of plastic arts. Film is an interesting blend of graphic and plastic arts, especially 3-D films. Religion, remember, are the rules that bind a society together. They can be physical rules and/or supernatural rules. Physical rules can be accommodated within folk culture as well as rationalistic science. It is worth noting that anthropologists posit four means by which people and communities can teach and heal themselves. They are storytelling, music, dance, and meditation. The first three are communal and fit an individual ego into the group's identity. The last is introspective and fits the ego into the Self. I will weave together all these ways of learning and healing with art and religion to demonstrate how they are utilized to embed social norms, even as those norms change diachronically (0ver time) via progress and bricolage to maintain social control and social order. Cultural evolution and syncretistic religions are the result. **Syncretism** is the fusion of diverse religious beliefs and practices into a new whole.

People story-tell through folklore. **Folklore** is the collection of unwritten arts, such as myth, legend, proverbs, jokes, and folktales that make up a culture's traditions. **Legends** are stories aimed at explaining local customs, which may or may not be based on fact. **Folktales** are stories that are instructive, entertaining, and mainly secular. The study of the relationship between music and other aspects of culture is called **ethnomusicology**. Music has often been called the "universal language." In some ways this is true because all cultures use similar ranges and pitches of sounds to induce the same moods in the brain. Everywhere from an aboriginal campfire in Australia to a honky-tonk in Nashville, Tennessee, a pitch that descends from high to low will induce sadness. Listen to the pitches of any heart-break/torch song. And pitches that start low and peak high will induce gladness, like one of my favorite feel-good dance songs, "Walking on Sunshine" by Katrina and the Waves. Dance is often inter-related with music. **Dance** is purposeful and intentionally rhythmic nonverbal movements that are culturally patterned and have aesthetic value. Being grounded in the three communal aspects of aesthetic culture leads us to the last, introspective one, meditation and religion. Religion is, by definition a communal event, but it must lead to a state of metaphysical, supernatural, or spiritual inner "space" in order to bring stasis and/or healing to the Self.

To Geertz, "savages" live in a world composed entirely of mystical encounters, but faced with the uncomfortable suspicion that there is no real order at all, humans are driven in their bafflement to embrace gods, deities, spirits, and totems. Religious authorities, such as shamans and priests, formulate an order of existence out of a complex of metaphysical symbols and prescribe religious action/social behavior for a people.

The **ethos**—moral evaluative elements—and the **worldview**—cognitive existential aspects—of a culture shape the spiritual consciousness of a people. The world as lived and the world as imagined can be consecrated—made the same—through ritual. This is an essential element of all religions. Religion, then, is partly an attempt to conserve the fund of general cultural meanings in terms of which each individual interprets his experience and organizes his conduct. These meanings are stored in symbols such as the cross, the crescent, or the feathered serpent, and are dramatized in rituals and related in myths.

Anthropologist Erik Schwimmer reduces religion to the human struggle to dominate nature and other humans and sees the food quest and social conflicts as the raw materials that are transformed into religion. He also understands that religions serve to explain the uncontrollable forces in nature. Functionalists tend to focus on ritual as the physically integrating role of religion, whereas structuralists focus on myth as its mentally integrating role. Schwimmer favors those anthropologists who unite the two, and says, "myth sets out the original ideal state of affairs and after presenting a set of inherent contradictions poses resolutions leading to dynamic present time. Rite, on the other hand, starting from the imperfect present, attempts to achieve the ideal conditions set out in original mythic time." A rite is a prescribed form or manner governing the words or actions of a ceremony. The dynamic duality between myth and ritual and the notion of original time permeated the worldview of the Greek rationalists; Plato will espouse an ideational reality, which corresponds to structural myth and Aristotle, an empirical reality, which corresponds to functional ritual. As states develop, religious structures often take the form of metaphysical doctrines transcending the forces of nature. Here, Schwimmer notes, "structural analysis must be supplemented by a more generalized semiotic analysis that takes full account of complex economic and political factors, as well as those basic truths encoded in classical myths, which nonetheless continue to have a general underlying validity." Semiotics is the study of signs, sign systems, and the way meaning is derived from them. A sign is something that serves to indicate the presence or existence of something.

All religions recognize, in one way or another, the ideas of sacred "feminine" space in the center, wherein lie the agoras, temples, and communal areas of human groups—the hearth—that will be defended and protected at the shadowy and threatening liminal borders of the numinous "masculine" periphery by the sacred, often ecstatic, and if need be, sacrificial warriors. In this schema, societies worldwide will found their mores upon a holistic complementarity of the ideas of "feminine" communion and "masculine" sacrifice. There are two types of religious experience, ecstasy and piaculum. **Ecstasy** is a type of religious experience, wherein the practitioner invites a god or spirit into him or herself to achieve a highly desirable altered state of consciousness. **Piaculum** is a type of religious experience wherein the practitioner follows rules and rituals to keep the presence of deity away from him or herself, generally through fear of intimacy with spirituality.

All religions, whether Hinduism or quantum mechanics, also recognize that there is a fundamental vital essence to all life and the inter-penetrating cosmos in which we all live, think, and act. Some people, such as scientists, call it energy; some, such as Buddhists, call it a force; and some, such as animists, call it spirit. **Animism** is the belief that spiritual beings exist and that spirits also reside in plants, inanimate objects, and natural phenomena. **Animatism**, by extension, is the belief in a generalized, impersonal power over which people have some measure of control. This leads to the idea of magic. **Magic** is a system of supernatural beliefs that involves the manipulation of supernatural forces for the purpose of manifesting willful change in human activities and natural phenomena. Magic can be of two types—imitative or contagious. **Imitative magic** is based on the idea that correct performance of a ritualized procedure resembles and produces the desired result. The use of symbolic dolls in Voodoo or the fashioning of a body part that is diseased as a votive offering among the Celts are examples of imitative magic. **Contagious magic** is a form of magic based on the idea that something that has contacted something or someone will absorb its energy and will continue to influence that person or environment even after separation of space and time. Hence, many cultures believe there are some places continuously holier than others, like Mt. Sinai or Mount Fuji; and other places that are more sinister, like haunted houses. Shaka of the Zulu would exterminate all members of a family of someone condemned of witchcraft, based on a belief in contagious magic. **Witchcraft** is the systematic practice of practicing magic and sorcery. **Sorcery** is the practice of ritualized magic to influence the lives of others, either for "good" or "bad." A *sangoma* is the Zulu word that would be translated into English as witch (doctor) or sorcerer.

FIG. 10.2. A Zulu sangoma.

Perhaps when scientists atomize atoms into their most fundamental state, they will have re-discovered what many peoples call spirit by English-speakers, mana by Pacific Islanders, or the Tao by Asians. **Mana** is an impersonal supernatural force that is believed to confer power, strength, and success. The **Tao** is the

SOCIAL STRUCTURE, ART, AND RELIGION 115

spontaneous creativity and regular alternation of natural forces in Chinese philosophy. These alternating and creative forces are called yin and yang. Yin and yang are inherent in every "thing," and every "non-thing." **Yin** is the feminine passive principle in nature in Chinese cosmology that interacts with yang in the creation and maintenance of all things. **Yang** is the masculine active principle in nature. The interface between the principles of yin and yang is the **Golden Mean**. It is within the interface of the Golden Mean that the Taoist makes his or her moral choices. Truth and behavior are relative to

FIGS. 10.3A (LEFT) AND B (RIGHT). Notice in the diagram how the interface of "good" and "bad" in the Taoist culture is a sliding curve that is dependent upon the situation, and how in the West, there is absolute "good" and absolute "bad" that can only be integrated and assuaged by a third "special" element. Only the hero, in a Jungian sense, can transcend the earthly realm to bring back the wisdom of the heavenly realm in order to aid mortals. Only the hero can bridge the gap between the values of the "good" heavenly realm, and the "bad," that is, sinful earthly realm. Heroes can include priests, prophets, angels, messiahs, saviors, Mahdis, and in a secular society, superheroes, such as Superman and Spiderman.

a given situation in the Taoist philosophy; they are not an "absolute" moral and behavior like the "black" and "white" choices of the Western ideologies – Judaism, Christianity, and Islam. That is because there is no god in Taoism, just a force. A person who doesn't believe in "God" is called an **atheist**. Atheists do have religions, that is, they live by secular morals and ethics. Just ask atheists if they have a religion. If they go berserk, you will have not only identified, but also offended their religion, wherein the first commandment is "there is no god" and the second is "I have no religion." On the other hand, people who believe in a god are called **theists**. Theists have religions and get offended by people who say there is no God. There are two types of theists: polytheists and monotheists. Polytheists believe in more than one god. **Polytheism** is an extension of animism, except that the spiritual entities involved have been **anthropomorphized**, that is, they have the shapes, motives, and behaviors of humans in addition to their spiritual, magical qualities. The Greek pantheon of gods and goddesses are an example of a polytheistic religion. **Monotheism** is the belief in only one God. Judaism, Christianity, and Islam are monotheistic religions with a male, salvific God. This is a cultural construction that serves the same psychic need for spiritually religious Westerners to individuate

FIG. 10.4. The Trimurti of the Hindus is another depiction of the three-in-one trinitarian God in three different *avatars* (manifestations): Brahma, the Creator; Vishnu, the Preserver; and Shiva, the Destroyer.

FIG. 10.5. The holy meteorite within the Kaaba.

their egos in much the same way that the Beowulf myth did for Anglo-Saxons. That is, that the masculine and the feminine elements combine holistically to bring stasis to the Self for each ego. In the Western patriarchal system, the mores of patriarchy have become anthropomorphized into the paternal deity of order and power, and the notions of redemption and salvation integrate the nurturing feminine ideals for the three great monotheisms. Notice in the accompanying diagram the basic symbols of the trinitarian Westerners, in this case, a Celtic *triskele*—a three-in-one Trinitarian symbol—and the yin/yang duality of the Chinese Taoists.

Other forms of supernatural belief systems include ancestor worship, ghost invocation, and ghost vengeance. **Ancestor worship** is the worship of deceased relatives, that is, those members of one's descent group that now live and "function" in a supernatural realm. **Ghost invocation** is the practice of making contact with the spirit of a departed person. **Ghost vengeance** is the punishment of immoral people by the empowered spirits of departed humans.

All supernaturally based religions are called cults. The word cult is derived from the Latin root *cultus* "to plant." A **cult** is basically an organized form of religious organization that "cult"ivates and plants ideas into the minds of its members. The word culture itself is derived from this idea. There are four types of supernatural cults: individualistic cults, shamanistic cults, communal cults, and ecclesiastical cults. An **individualistic cult** is a cultural structure that fosters each individual member to develop his or her own supernatural experiences and beliefs. Societies that embrace individualistic cults often practice vision quests. A **vision quest** is a ritual that involves bodily mortification, such as fasting, the intention of which is to communicate with helpful spirits through trances and visions in order to gain knowledge, power, and protection. Individualistic cults often involve totems. A **totem** is a spirit being, sacred object, or symbol that serves as an emblem of a group of people, such as a family, clan, or tribe. Crazy Horse, the powerful warrior of the Sioux peoples, communed with his totem spirits via a vision quest and was given the sacred thunderbolt totem with which to adorn his body for guidance and protection. Within the Kaaba in Mecca, the *omphallos* of Islam, lies enshrouded a holy meteorite. This meteorite can be considered a totem. Ironically, what totems are to some people can be idols to other people. Cultural contexts make all the difference.

FIG. 10.6. This new Maasai man has just been "born again," that is, he has crossed the transitional boundary from boyhood into manhood via a communally recognized rite of passage. Note that he is adorned with the totems and symbols of his communal cult.

SOCIAL STRUCTURE, ART, AND RELIGION   117

A **shamanistic cult** is a type of religious organization in which shamans intervene with spirits on behalf of their people. A **shaman** is a charismatic spiritualist gifted with supernatural powers from birth or by otherworldly calling. One does not choose to become a shaman, but a shaman can certainly be trained by a mentor. A **communal cult** is a type of religious organization in which groups of ordinary people conduct religious ceremonies for the well-being of the total community. Communal cults often practice rites of passage. A **rite of passage** is a ceremony that celebrates the transition of a person form one station in life to another, such as that from adolescence to adulthood at puberty. Communal cults also practice rites of solidarity. *Bar* and *bat mitzvahs* in Judaism are examples of rites of passage. A **rite of solidarity** is a ceremony that enhances social integration among groups of people. Annual holy days are examples of rites of solidarity.

FIG. 10.7. This image/idol of an airplane was inspired by that generation of Pacific Islander that witnessed the combat of Japanese and American warplanes during World War II.

All three types of supernatural cults described are oral based and hence, right-brained cultural constructs. An **ecclesiastical cult** is a form of highly complex and hierarchical religious organization that is based upon a book. Hence, it is the form of supernatural worship constructed by literate, logical, and left-brained societies. Incidentally, ecclesiastical cults can incorporate the qualities of the other three forms of cult in their practices. For example, "speaking in tongues" is a form of individualistic spiritual endeavor. "Laying on of hands" can be categorized as a shamanic practice.

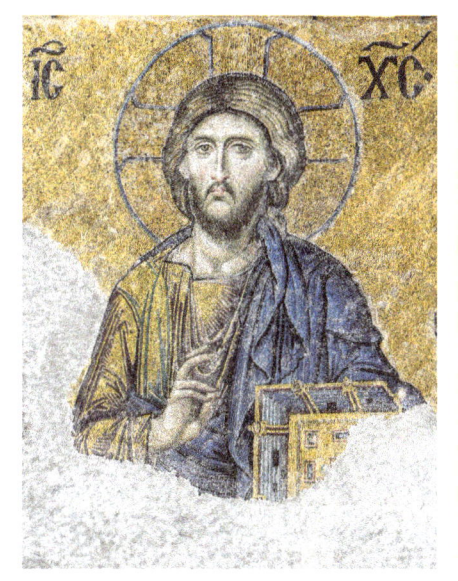

FIGS. 10.8A AND 10.8B. Byzantine art.

FIGS. 10.9. The Creation of Adam.

Circumcision among the Jews and Communion and Confirmation among the Roman Catholics are examples of communal cult practices. Ecclesiastical cults tend to be progressive, that is, they are future oriented. They are constructed to evangelize, either overtly or subliminally, the non-believers and thus either please deity and/or proselytize for deity. Evangelization for deity will often go hand-in-hand with overt military expansion for deity, either through crusade (for Christians,) *jihad* (for Muslims,) or empire (for secularists.) These cultural manifestations also go hand in hand often with millenarian movements for Christians and Mahdist movements for Muslims. A **millenarian movement** is a social movement by repressed people who are looking forward to better times in the future. A **Mahdist movement** is a revitalization movement by Muslims looking forward to a *Mahdi*, or Muslim "savior," to restore traditional virtues and bring material blessings. A **revitalization movement** is a religious movement designed to restore morality within a society in order to please deity who will reward the faithful, and the society, with blessings. A final expression of cult is a cargo cult. A **cargo cult** is revitalization movement found among Pacific Islanders who have come into contact with more technologically advanced cultures and benefitted materially from that contact before the technologically advanced culture departs. Cargo cults yearn for the "Second Coming" of the advanced cultures replete with material blessings. Cargo cult religions have inspired the modern-day "ancient astronaut" theorists to propose that extraterrestrials from outer space have come, still come, and will continue to come and interact with humans on this planet, and perhaps also in space and on the moon. Evidence exists for this theory. As with most other theories, proof is yet to be made manifest.

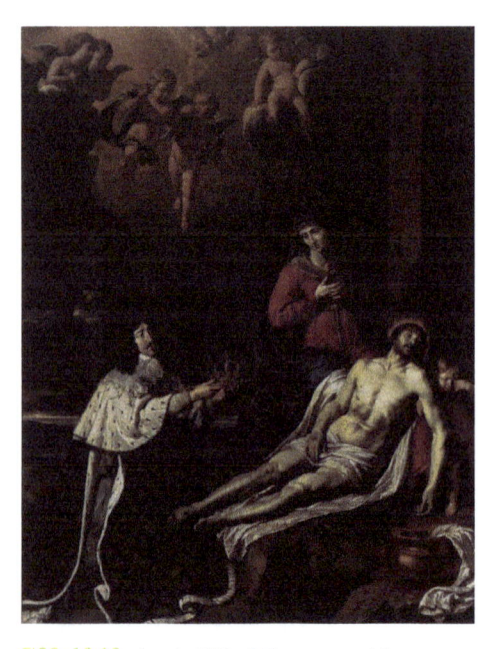

FIGS. 10.10. Louis XIII of France combines evangelization and conquest in this painting to justify religious colonialism.

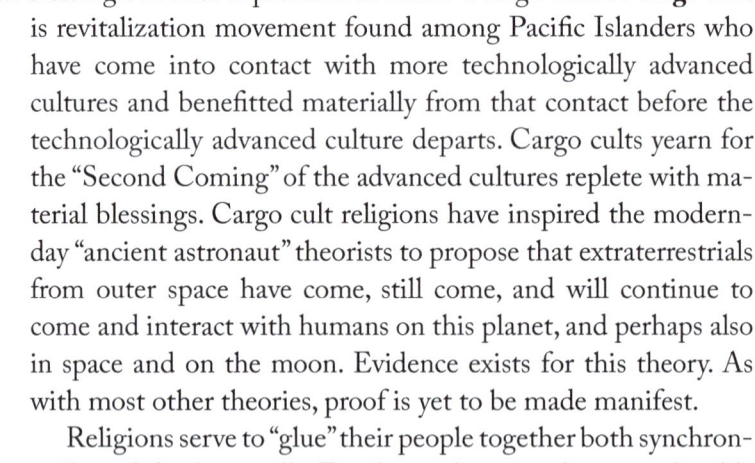

Religions serve to "glue" their people together both synchronically and diachronically. For that to happen, they must be able to adapt to changing conditions and changing times. Science is able to do this masterfully, although there are a few fundamentalists among the cadres of the faithful that resist change, which is the cardinal virtue of science. Religions that have become ossified in stone or on page have a bigger challenge, yet they manage. The next few diagrams will illustrate how art supplies the transformational energy needed for religious ideas to transmogrify through time in order to meet the contingent needs of egos orienting themselves within contemporary and evolving cultural constructs. Remember how the "sacrificial" component of masculinity was demonstrated at the periphery by a horned deity and the "communion" component was depicted by the feminine Mother Goddess image in the cave art in Chapter 4. These ideas and dual religious constructs will survive into logical Byzantine Christianity. In the accompanying images, notice how the integrated masculine and feminine trinitarian male God has split into the feminine Mother (of) God and her "incestual" consort—the Son/Father. Also notice how the logic "logos" (of the book) of the Son/Father is depicted by the adult Jesus on the left and as a "homunculus," that is, as a little adult fully capable of arguing law with the Pharisees, on the right.

During the Renaissance, when humanistic values began displacing supernatural ones, the relationship between "God" and "man" began to change. Notice Michelangelo's famous painting

FIGS. 10.11. The modern Madonna and Child.

depicting the creation of Adam in the Sistine Chapel, which shows how nearly equal Adam and God are in the phi-ratio construction of human anatomies. Recall also in Chapter 3, the new mathematical analysis of the scientific Vitruvian Man by Leonardo da Vinci at the same time. During the seventeenth century Age of Colonialism, notice how the sacrificial element of Christ and the communal role of the Virgin Mary have been customized to prop up the conquest of Quebec, Canada by Louis XIII of France, who offers his crown—the symbol of political and spiritual evangelization—and the scepter—a mace—which is a weapon utilized to bludgeon the "them" group into submission by the "us" group.

Today, in our modern, multicultural, global world, a Caucasian Mary will never do. Neither will a Christ-child who is a homunculus. Children are allowed to be children today, thanks to Erikson, and Middle Eastern heroes must be Middle Eastern. Hence, our modern semitic Madonna and Child are depicted in the final diagram.

KEY WORDS

Achieved status
Aesthetics
Ancestor worship
Animatism
Anthropomorphized
Art
Ascribed status
Atheist
Band
Cargo cult
Carrying capacity
Chiefdom
Class
Communal cult
Community
Contagious magic
Crime
Cult
Dance
Deviance
Ecclesiastical cult
Ecstasy
Egalitarian society
Ethnomusicology
Ethos
Folklore
Folktales
Ghost invocation
Ghost vengeance
Golden Mean
Graphic arts
Hierarchy
Imitative magic

Individualistic cult
Law
Legends
Magic
Mahdist movement
Mana
Millenarian movement
Monotheism
Nation
Nationalism
Nation-state
Negative sanctions
Pan-tribal society
Partible inheritance
Piaculum
Plastic arts
Polytheism
Positive sanctions
Power
Prestige
Ranked society
Revitalization movement
Rite
Rite of passage
Rite of solidarity
Sanctions
Semiotics
Shaman
Shamanistic cult
Sign
Social control
Social norms
Society
Sorcery

State
Stratified society
Syncretism
Tao
Theists
Totem
Transformation
Tribal societies

Vision quest
Wealth
Witchcraft
Worldview
Yang
Yin

IMAGE CREDITS

- Fig. 10.1: Copyright © 2008 by Woodlouse / Flickr, (CC BY-SA 2.0) at http://commons.wikimedia.org/wiki/File:Hadzabe_Hunters.jpg.
- Fig. 10.2: Copyright © 2011 by Mycelium101 / Wikimedia Commons, (CC BY-SA 3.0) at http://en.wikipedia.org/wiki/File:Sangoma_Dancing_in_Celebration_of_his_Ancestors.jpg.
- Fig. 10.3a: AnonMoos / Wikimedia Commons / Copyright in the Public Domain.
- Fig. 10.3b: Sarang / Wikimedia Commons / Copyright in the Public Domain.
- Fig. 10.4: Copyright © 2014 by Michael Gunther, (CC BY-SA 4.0) at http://commons.wikimedia.org/wiki/File:Trimurti_Wat_Phu_0519.jpg.
- Fig. 10.5: Rashid Al-Din / Copyright in the Public Domain.
- Fig. 10.6: Copyright © 2004 by Ferdinand Reus, (CC BY-SA 2.0) at http://en.wikipedia.org/wiki/File:Young_Maasai_Warrior.jpg.
- Fig. 10.7: Copyright © 2007 by Raymond Ostertag, (CC BY-SA 3.0) at https://en.wikipedia.org/wiki/File:Nasca_Astronaut_2007_08.jpg.
- Fig. 10.8a: Photo by Myrabella / Wikimedia Commons / Copyright in the Public Domain.
- Fig. 10.8b: Copyright in the Public Domain.
- Fig. 10.9: Michelangelo Buonarroti / Copyright in the Public Domain.
- Fig. 10.10: Philippe de Champaigne / Copyright in the Public Domain.
- Fig. 10.11: Pompeo Batoni / Copyright in the Public Domain.

CHAPTER ELEVEN

AN ETHNOLOGICAL CASE STUDY AND APPLIED ANTHROPOLOGY

I recently worked on an archeological dig in the western portion of New York State that had been petitioned for by the Clan Mothers of the Cayuga Nation of the Haudenosaunee (Iroquois) Confederation, through their chiefs, because the site had revealed to the spiritual leaders of the Cayuga that it was ready to tell its story. I felt quite honored and humbled that I was chosen to be part of this team of excavators who would perform "surgery" on the living remains of Sky Woman—the pregnant primordial female deity who fell from the heavens to land upon the back of a vast turtle, and through her sacrifice, provide the firmament upon which the communal Haudenosaunee society and culture would be grounded, literally. From the bodies of Sky Woman and her offspring would spring the staple plants: corn, beans, squash, strawberries, and tobacco. She, the site, had to be treated reverentially, and I was more than happy to do so. This would be an emic approach. The fact that the site was referred to as "she" was a reflection of how the environment was gendered in Haudenosaunee cosmology. This chapter will show how ethnographic field work and ethnological scholarship can describe the worldview and culture of the Haudenosaunee. With

FIGS. 11.1A The pregnant Sky Woman fell to earth to land on the back of a giant sea turtle to dispense her fertility to it to create.

FIGS. 11.1B Turtle Island—the land from which humans would be created.

this case study, we will explore how this information can be utilized to try to solve contemporary problems via applied anthropology.

Historically, the geographical landscape of the Haudenosaunee has been culturally demarcated into two "places"—"the Woods," the "place" for men; and "the Clearing," the "place" for women.

The site that we excavated was part of "the Clearing," and our surgery was often done under the watchful eyes of the clan mothers. The Haudenosaunee are a people who have strong gender roles woven into the fabric of their society and history, a truism for which they are not only unapologetic, but also, and for generations now, have been struggling to keep unpolluted from the cultural mores of the westernized peoples that have encroached upon and continue to encroach upon them. Their longhouses are still adorned with the totem symbols of the Clan Mothers of the respective nations, and the men must still leave the

FIGS. 11.2. The Woods, the "untamed" place for men.

longhouses of their mothers and migrate to the longhouses of their wives after marriage. It is a matrilineal society. Gender consciousness is part of what it means to be Haudenosaunee; oppression, a term which is all-too-often associated with the concept of "gender roles," is not. Like all cultural symbols, the name Haudenosaunee—meaning "the Peoples of the Longhouse"—relates in a symbolic way the geographical alliance of the six nations of the Haudenosaunee from east to west with the physical compartmentalized structure of the longhouse, which is likewise aligned from east to west. These domiciles "in the Clearing" are the domains of the women. "The Woods" are the domain of men. These geographical/cultural "spaces" will be examined later, as will the gender roles dominant in each one.

The Peoples of the Longhouse are a confederation of originally five, and later, six nations—the Seneca, the Cayuga, the Onondaga, the Oneida, the Mohawk, and the Tuscarora—that have their origins in the vicissitudes of hunter-gatherer societies. They claim that their confederacy extends back over 1,000 years to the time of their legendary hero Hiawatha, who helped found the confederacy and codified its institution in a specific belt of wampum. **Wampum is a coded text composed in an intelligible sequence of white and purple clamshell beads.** Wampum is used as a mnemonic device. In fact, the invention of wampum is attributed to Hiawatha. This is vital to understanding and dating the origins of the Haudenosaunee Confederacy, because the belts have been assiduously and reverently passed on from generation to generation, as is customary with oral traditional people.

According to the Peacemaker epic, the separate nations of the Seneca, Cayuga, Onondaga, Oneida, and Mohawk were at constant war with one another, so much so that the social structures of the several nations were unraveling. Seeing this, the Creator took pity and sent among them a visionary, a man named Deganawidah and known as the Peacemaker, a man born of a virgin in Huron territory to the north of Lake Ontario. He sailed across the lake in a white stone canoe, which he carved himself, and came among the warring nations who refused his message until a woman named Jikonsaseh, a woman of Good Mind at the Seneca village of Ganondagan became the first convert to his teachings. Thereafter, the Peacemaker came upon the dwelling of Hiawatha in the middle

FIGS. 11.3. The Clearing, the "domesticated" place for women (to grow corn and supervise the community).

of a forest. Hiawatha was himself a warrior, but had fled from such a life after the death of his wife and daughters in these destructive wars and was utterly inconsolable. It was in trying to bring peace to his troubled mind that he invented wampum belts, which from that time on signified Iroquois unity and policy. The Peacemaker climbed to the roof of Hiawatha's dwelling and peered down through the smoke hole. Upon seeing such a radiant and peaceful face in the reflection of his water bowl, Hiawatha was converted to the Peacemaker's message. This was a fortunate union because the prophet Deganawidah found in Hiawatha a powerful spokesman. Together, their mission was to unite the five tribes in a confederacy that would forever prohibit the ravages of blood feud, and for the next 25 years, they preached the message sent by the Creator. That message was the Great Law of Peace, that is, that the principles of Peace, Equity, Justice, and the Good Mind must be cultivated among humans. Clan by clan, chiefs and people were persuaded, but unity was most resisted by the inveterate enemy of Hiawatha and the Peacemaker, the shaman Tadodaho. Eventually the collective triune powers of Hiawatha, the Peacemaker, and Jikonsaseh were able to overcome Tadodaho. And because Tadodaho had allowed Hiawatha to comb evil snakes out of his hair, which opened his mind to reason and effectively removed the last obstacle to the formation of the Iroquois Confederacy, he was accorded primacy among the 50 chiefs of the Five Nations that would comprise the Grand Council. Because of the powerful spiritual qualities associated with it, the name Tadodaho became a hereditary title that is passed on to those who convene the Grand Council to this day. Likewise, Deganawidah said to Jikonsaseh, "Because you were the first to accept the Good News of Peace and Power, you will be known as the Mother of Nations." And so, the message of the Creator was spread by the Peacemaker, Hiawatha, and Jikonsaseh: "There are many nations, each with its own council fire, yet they shall live together as one household in peace. They shall be the Haudenosaunee, the People of the Longhouse. They shall have one mind and live under one law. Thinking shall replace killing, and there shall be one common wealth." This message constituted a social revolution among the Iroquois. Henceforth, instead of a patrilineal family descent from the fathers, Haudenosaunee families traced their ancestries from their mothers and each clan was headed by a Clan Mother. It became the custom that women name the chiefs and only a man of Good Mind could become chief.

Here we have an elegant tale that unites all of the elements of Haudenosaunee origins in a balanced worldview, a worldview that is inherently gendered. Tadodaho, the evil, snake-crowned shaman is the personification of the dangerous and male-dominated hunter-gatherer periphery of the distict, pre-confederation Iroquoian tribes. The liminality of such an existence is mollified when humans learned how to domesticate corn. The advent of agriculture provided more security to the contingent existence of humanity and effected a revolution in the human mind. Corn cultivation, having travelled northward from Meso-America about 1,000 years ago, is central to the Haudenosaunee sense of survival and identity. This is evident in such aphorisms as, "Our people come out of the ground," and "The law is in the corn." The name Jikonsaseh has been translated as "little corn tassel." Metaphor and simile are devices used to make the relationships between humans and nature understandable to a mind living in communion with nature.

FIGS. 11.4. Originally, the Haudenosaunee were five independent tribes.

FIGS. 11.5A. The Creator sent Deganawidah to heal the wounds of the independent tribes and forge among them a peaceful confederation, FIG. 11.5B. Deganawidah converted some through signs, like paddling in a white stone canoe. Deganawidah's first converts, the warrior Hiawatha, and the woman, Jikonsaseh.

The fact that nature and humans are so intimately linked is intrinsic to the mindset of the Haudenosaunee people. The land itself is their story; and not only their story, it is their very being. In the restructuring of rival Iroquoian tribes into a confederacy, and a patrilineal society into a matrilineal one, the tales reflect a gender-driven harmonization of Haudenosaunee cosmology. As in Dumézil's schema, the elements of the masculine and the feminine are harmonized in a trinitarian way; the "roles" of masculine and feminine "speaker" are realized in Tadodaho, the newly enfranchised chief (masculine) and the Peacemaker as the shaman (feminine); the "fighter" in Hiawatha the warrior (masculine); and the "worker" in Jikonsaseh, the fruitful Good Mother (feminine). And this harmonization of gendered structural castes is played out in the socialization of physical space,

FIGS. 11.6. The last major player in the formation of the Haudenosaunee Confederation to be converted by Deganawidah, here in the company of Hiawatha, was Tadadaho.

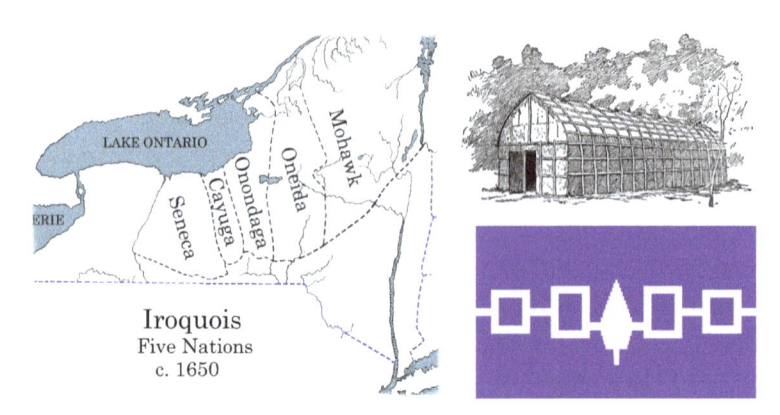

FIGS. 11.7A. A map of the traditional Haudenosaunee landscape, FIG. 11.7B. A traditional Haudenosaunee longhouse and the symbol of the Haudenosaunee Confederation.

both in "the Clearing"—the space for women—and "the Woods"—the space for men. The preceding analysis is an example of the etic approach. Language and culture shifted accordingly, in a way commensurate with the hypothesis of Sapir and Whorf. "Wathonwisas," which means "to sway like corn in the wind," is a term describing the way women dance in traditional ceremonies. Men dance more frantically, like "beasts in the woods." With the domestication of the physical landscape at the dawn of agriculture came a domestication of

FIGS. 11.8A AND 11.8B. The peripheral woods and an effigy of the deity "Broken Nose." His face has been obscured in deference to Haudenosaunee sensitivities.

the Iroquoian mental landscape as well, and the cultural seeds around which the new confederacy nucleated were those firmly grounded in the archetypes of gender.

Notice in the accompanying diagram how the pan-tribal Confederation of the Iroquois tribes on the map corresponds to the symbolic construction of a Haudenosaunee longhouse, and correlates with the abstract "*E Pluribus Unum*" quality of the Haudenosaunee symbol and flag. It is easy to see from these cultural and geographic structures how a Haudenosaunee ego orients itself holistically to the land, the kin, and the culture.

As stated often before, the Haudenosaunee have constructed their society according to the symbolic representations of the periphery and the center, the masculine and the feminine. The woods are undomesticated and wild and the peripheral deity that the men honor there has been translated as "Broken Nose." This is the realm where men "sacrifice" their lives to protect their people, the "in" group residing in the center.

In the sacred center, Clan Mothers act as the legislative body of Haudenosaunee government. Fully cognizant of the needs of the clans inhabiting each longhouse, the Clan Mothers, as women, possess the logical and emotional centers in both hemispheres of their brains, which enable them to promote the policies that would most efficiently serve their people's needs. Chiefs, who act as the executive branch of government, utilize those brains that separate, to a greater degree, logic and emotion to realize those legislative decisions made in the center at the chaotic zone beyond the periphery.

It should come as no surprise to learn that even Haudenosaunee cosmogeny is anthropomorphized and gendered. In their Thanksgiving Prayer, Grandfather Sun and Grandmother Moon are honored.

FIGS. 11.9. A "sacrificial" warrior at the periphery.

FIGS. 11.10A AND 11.10B. Corn, the staple crop of the Haudenosaunee, and the corn transmogrified as a deity.

FIG. 11.11. The sacred and domestic "center," the "place of women."

FIGS. 11.12. Haudenosaunee Chief and Clan Mother.

FIGS. 11.13. In the Haudenosaunee Thanksgiving Prayer, Grandfather Sun is honored.

FIGS. 11.14. In the Haudenosaunee Thanksgiving Prayer, Grandmother Moon is honored.

We now send our greetings and our thanks to our eldest Brother, the Sun. Each day without fail he travels the sky from east to west, bringing the light of a new day. He is the source of all the fires of life. With one mind, we send our greetings and our thanks to our Brother, the Sun.

We put our minds together to give thanks to our oldest Grandmother, the Moon, who lights the night-time sky. She is the leader of woman all over the world, and she governs the movement of the ocean tides. By her changing face we measure time, and it is the Moon who watches over the arrival of children here on Earth. With one mind, we send our greetings and our thanks to our Grandmother, the Moon.

It is now time to return to some of the methods used to put together this ethnographic and ethnological study of the Haudenosaunee people. One method used was the ethnographic interview. Ethnographic interviews can be either unstructured or structured. An **unstructured interview** is an interview used in fieldwork that asks interviewees to answer broad, open-ended questions. A **structured interview** is an interview used in fieldwork that asks interviewees to answer a set of short, specific questions. In conducting interviews, an ethnographer must avoid the obtrusive effect as much as possible. The **obtrusive effect** is the presence of the researcher in the interview that causes people to behave differently than they would if the researcher was not present, often trying to "read" the researcher to give him or her the information the informant thinks the interviewer wants.

Here is a sample of interviews used in this case study.

Peter Jemison, a leader of the Seneca Nation, said, "Everything within the Clearing is the domain of the women: the gardens, they are the ones who farm, the houses, and all of the things in the Clearing. Everything outside of the Clearing, that is the domain of men: the hunting, the fishing, the trapping, the trading, the travel for diplomatic reasons, and the protection of the site and the town."

Cheyenne Williams, a mother of the Cayuga Nation stated, "My role as a Cayuga Wolf, because wolves live in dens, is to take care of all of the others. That's our role as the wolf, to take care of all of our clans and our nation. The way that I was raised, we were always told it takes a nation to raise a child. So when I look at a child, I don't look at them as that's my cousin, that's my friend's sister, that's my friend's brother, this is my son, this is my daughter. They're all my children, because I am a mother in the Cayuga Wolf Nation."

Allen Kettle, a protector among the Bear Clan of the Cayuga Nation, said, "The Bear Clan's been in our society for a long time because we're matrilineal and it came from the First Mother, which is the Earth, and it has been told from generation to generation that everything comes from the mother. My grandmother, her grandmother, and her grandmother were all Bear Clan, so it comes right through the mother. I'm Bear Clan and they're Bear Clan."

In collecting ethnographic data an anthropologist must gain **topical expertise** on the culture and environment of the people he or she is studying. Topical expertise is gained through ethnography, which entails participation observation. **Participant observation** is a fieldwork method in which the ethnographer lives with the people under study and observes their everyday activities. This entails choosing appropriate informants from which to accurately study a culture. An **informant** is a person who provides information about his or her culture to the ethnographic researcher. The ethnographer then analyzes the collected data

FIGS. 11.15. How difficult it is to be "unobtrusive" as a researcher.

FIGS. 11.16. Peter Jemison.

FIGS. 11.17. Cheyenne Williams.

FIGS. 11.18. Alan Kettle.

via quantitative and qualitative methods. **Quantitative data** is data that is counted and interpreted through statistical analyses. **Qualitative data** is data obtained through interviews, participant observation notes, and relevant documents.

The preceding case study of the Haudenosaunee was utilized for the sub-field of anthropology called applied anthropology. **Applied anthropology** is the application of anthropological knowledge, theory, and methods to the solution of social problems. **Problem oriented research** focuses in on a particular social problem and utilizes anthropological methodologies in trying to solve them. Another type of research methodology is called participatory action research. **Participatory action research** is a method of research whereby the anthropologist and the community work together to understand the conditions that produce the community's problems in order to try to solve those problems. Sometimes, despite their best intentions, anthropologists can experience feelings of revulsion, fear, and disorientation when immersed among a people whose values seem "alien" to their own. This condition is called culture shock. **Culture shock** is a psychological disorientation experienced when an anthropologist attempts to understand and help a people whose culture is radically different than his or her own.

Working with the Haudenosaunee involves problem oriented research. The relationship between the Haudenosaunee and the United States has been both long and intimate as well as cordial and troubled. A **confederacy** is a political entity uniting one or more independent nations in a loose political structure. The Haudenosaunee Confederacy is just such an entity. That means that not all nations have to follow the same policy as others. During the American Revolution, some Haudenosaunee backed the Americans and some the British. After the war, the British fomented various Native American groups to stir up trouble for the new American nation. The American nation dispossessed Native Americans from their lands. In the midst of this diplomatic quagmire, George Washington signed a federal treaty with the Haudenosaunee; part of the terms required the United States pay to the Haudenosaunee Confederacy a few thousand dollars annually as tribute, which it still does to this day. The trouble really began when New York State authorized land speculators to strong-arm land sales with the Haudenosaunee, disregarding the sovereign-nation status of the Haudenosausee that was recognized by the federal government, an illegal act. After two centuries of legal wrangling and ethnic insensitivity, New York State awarded several hundred million dollars in restitution to the Haudenosaunee, which was later overturned by the Supreme Court of the United States, an ironic turn of events. These land grant court cases have been supplanted by the land trusteeship court cases with New York State, in which the Haudenosaunee hope to gain access to lands under the tutelage of New York State in order to cultivate their crops in the traditional fashion.

Gaining evidence to support the Haudenosaunee oral traditions, which claim they confederated in the tenth century, would help their case. Hence, the archeological dig mentioned earlier. Without documents, only artifacts in the ground could corroborate the "story" of the oral tales. How? Haudenosaunee traditions maintain that palisaded walls that had protected villages disappeared after the ratification of the Confederacy, and if no palisades were discovered, credence would be given to the oral tales. Also, the Haudenosaunee believe that Hiawatha invented wampum at the time of the Confederacy's foundation and if wampum beads were found, that, too, would help corroborate the oral tales. Again, the symbolic longhouse architecture of the Haudenosaunee did not precede the Confederation. It was conceived as a response to confederation, and if a longhouse could be excavated, the oral tales would again be supported. In fact, all of the parameters for a tenth century confederation were confirmed during the excavation, along with others not mentioned. Seven wampum beads were found, some purple and some white. A longhouse was unearthed and no palisade was found.

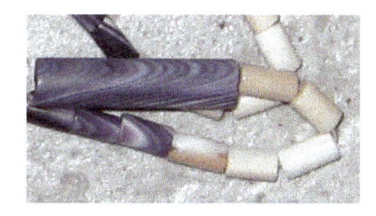

FIGS. 11.19. Wampum beads.

This evidence was used to refute the historical revisionist argument of state lawyers, who maintained that the Haudenosaunee didn't confederate until after contact with the Europeans, and hence, both sides had at least equal claims to the land. **Historical revisionism is the re-writing of history diachronically to reflect the opinions and interests of the current generation.** At the time of this writing, the land trust issue is still in the court system.

FIGS. 11.20. Fire pit in a longhouse.

KEY WORDS

Applied anthropology
Confederacy
Culture shock
Historical revisionism
Informant
Obtrusive effect
Participant observation
Problem oriented research

Qualitative data
Quantitative data
Participatory action research
Structured interview
Topical expertise
Unstructured interview
Wampum

IMAGE CREDITS

- Fig. 11.1a: J.L. Blessing / Copyright in the Public Domain.
- Fig. 11.1b: Copyright © 2007 by Thierry Caro, (CC BY-SA 3.0) at https://en.wikipedia.org/wiki/File:Lepidochelys-olivacea-K%C3%A9lonia-1.JPG.
- Fig, 11.2: Samuel de Champlain / Copyright in the Public Domain.
- Fig. 11.3: Paranoid / Wikimedia Commons / Copyright in the Public Domain.
- Fig. 11.4: Theodor de Bry / Copyright in the Public Domain.
- Fig. 11.5a: Gustave Hensel Studio / Copyright in the Public Domain.
- Fig. 11.5b: Copyright © 2005 by Pollinator / Wikimedia Commons, (CC BY-SA 3.0) at https://commons.wikimedia.org/wiki/File:Cornsilk_7091.jpg.
- Fig. 11.6: Hartley Burr Alexander / Copyright in the Public Domain.
- Fig. 11.7a: R. A. Nonenmacher / Copyright in the Public Domain.
- Fig. 11.7b: Wilbur F. Gordy / Copyright in the Public Domain.
- Fig. 11.7c: Copyright in the Public Domain.
- Fig. 11.8a: Copyright © 2007 by Snežana Trifunović, (CC BY-SA 3.0) at https://en.wikipedia.org/wiki/File:Biogradska_suma.jpg.
- Fig. 11.8b: Copyright in the Public Domain.
- Fig. 11.9: Copyright in the Public Domain.
- Fig. 11.10a: USDA / Copyright in the Public Domain.
- Fig. 11.10b: Copyright © 2010 by John Morgan, (CC BY 2.0) at https://commons.wikimedia.org/wiki/File:Corn_husk_doll.jpg.
- Fig. 11.11a: Copyright in the Public Domain.
- Fig. 11.11b: Copyright in the Public Domain.
- Fig. 11.12a: F. Bartoli / Copyright in the Public Domain.
- Fig. 11.12b: Copyright © 2006 by Eastonatti / Wikimedia Commons, (CC BY-SA 3.0) at https://commons.wikimedia.org/wiki/File:Rose_Doctor.JPG.
- Fig. 11.13: Copyright © 2012 by Kreuzschnabel / Wikimedia Commons, (CC BY-SA 3.0) at https://commons.wikimedia.org/wiki/File:Sun-in-the-sky.jpg.
- Fig. 11.14: Copyright © 2010 by Michael Gil, (CC BY 2.0) at https://www.flickr.com/photos/13907834@N00/4476783975.
- Fig. 11.15: Stanisław Ignacy Witkiewicz / Copyright in the Public Domain.
- Fig. 11.19: Uyvsdi / Copyright in the Public Domain.
- Fig. 11.20: Copyright © by Tina Stavenhagen-Helgren. Reprinted with permission.

CHAPTER TWELVE

ECONOMIES AND GOVERNMENT

In the book "People in Culture" (1980), Rossi and others reflect the idea that "the integration of the material and immaterial aspects of culture is especially strong in preliterate societies, where people do not experience the role fragmentation typical of modern western life." Adhering to the Marxist orientation that "modes of production" influence economic and social formation, Rossi and others equate the processes of production with the social modes of appropriating nature. They also believe that symbolization is the essence of human thought and here they see the value of culture as providing a ground of organized understanding for human beings to be able to function together.

Although primitive humans, as "feisty primates," viewed the earth as their primary means of production, work was never deemed a purely economic activity. Nature is mysterious as well as sacred. The hidden causes and invisible forces that control nature and make it prosperous must be bent to human needs. To these primitives, magic is indispensable to guarantee the harvest. In such pre-capitalist societies, work is always a multiple act, simultaneously economic, political, and religious. By analogizing nature with society, a double effect is produced in the primitive mind; nature becomes anthropomorphized and humans "supernaturalized." Both nature and society are sacred. Men are "cult-masters" of plants and animals and do not kill without reason. Economic surplus is an alien idea.

Rossi and others build their economic/religious model on that of Geertz. Culture patterns are programmed mental traits and humans depend upon symbols to be decisive for their creative abilities. Humans can adapt themselves to anything their imaginations can cope with, but they cannot deal with chaos, the "uncanny." Chaos threatens the "interpretability" of man: his analytic abilities, his power of endurance and his moral insight. The contingencies of life challenge his ability to meet challenges. Religion, therefore, is not intended to alleviate suffering; rather, it makes suffering sufferable. Economics and politics are intended to make suffering livable.

Radcliffe-Brown's claim that all societies have a political organization which maintains the social order within a territorial framework through exercised coercion, is also indirectly stating that functionalism and structural functionalism can provide only a provisionally stable anthropological "snapshot" of any society synchronically. Necessarily implying a dynamic social milieu, **political functions**—the strategies and activities directed toward the resolution of conflicts over basic resources—are fundamentally related to kinship ties. Rites of passage, whether via Piaget's cognitive theory, which develops a child's rational thought or Erikson's psychosocial theory, which channels and develops a child's libidinal energy, determine the role or status that an individual will eventually play in his or her society. The "political society" that emerges will, by its nature, be a stratified society. In a state, the obvious material differences among the classes are but shadowy survivals of earlier pre-state distinctions based on endowed functional "gifts." A shaman was gifted spiritually, a warrior imbued with wits and prowess, and a leader with officiating "charisma." Out of a sense of awe for the leader, as deity himself or deity's representative on earth, the mystery of kingship was erected. A king's sovereignty over his land and people was a sacred trust; his selection had been divined and the measure of his stewardship was the prosperity of his people. In times of stress, a king was expected to "sacrifice" himself to propitiate any offended sensibilities of divine sovereignty and restore cosmic harmony.

Despite all of the mental ideologies used to buttress societies, people live in the physical here and now. They must control this "physical" space via economics and governments. Although **economics** is understood to be the academic discipline that studies systems of production, distribution, and consumption of assets, usually in the industrialized world, and is typically studied by economists, the anthropologist studies economic anthropology. **Economic anthropology** is that sub-field of anthropology that studies systems of production, distribution, and consumption of assets wherever they occur, but focuses particularly on the non-industrialized world. An **asset** is any commodity that brings value and profit to its owner, and can be sold, traded, or bequeathed. Assets can include: material objects, such as gems, money, titles, deeds, etc.; resources, such as land, livestock, crops, gas, oil, water, and even air; and people, whether one's own nationals who can be taxed or slaves who can be exploited; and information, whether on paper or in cyber space. A **government** is an organization or agency through which a political unit exercises authority and performs functions and which is usually determined by the distribution of power within it. **Authority** is the power to give commands, take action, and make binding decisions. A government is consolidated by political integration. **Political integration** is the process that brings individuals together under the auspices of a single governmental system. Let's look at how economics and governments buttress one another.

As we have seen, the carrying capacity of a landscape is its ability to support the maximum number of people given the available resources of the land. Originally, humans gathered a wide variety of available foods. This is called **broad-spectrum collecting**. But very quickly, humans began to figure out ways to use their territories to the maximum caloric potential that can support the most desirable animals and plants that can support humans. This is called the **optimal foraging theory**. Tribal peoples have been called hunters and gatherers, or foragers. Simply speaking, they chase food. Plants know where the water is and grow there; so do animals. Humans simply have to track these food sources to thrive. With such a subsistence economy, tribal cultures usually retain a high degree of awe and respect for the "miraculous" growth of the foods they consume, miraculously. **Subsistence** is the minimum resource needs for a group of people to survive. Subsistence foragers are usually quite healthy; in fact, they are much healthier per person than are the denizens of a modern, industrialized economy. The drawback is that the bulk of their waking hours are consumed with drawing subsistence from nature. Tribal peoples, remember, are categorized as right-brained people. The governmental structure followed by foraging peoples has generally been

ECONOMIES AND GOVERNMENT   137

called the voluntaristic theory of political integration. The **voluntaristic theory of political integration** states that government arose because people chose to collectivize their sovereignties in order to maximize the benefits that each individual would receive.

Tribal peoples developed a primitive farming technique called horticulture. **Horticulture** is small-scale crop cultivation characterized by simple technology, such as sticks and hoes that put holes or furrows into the soil into which seeds are deposited. The seeds are watered by rain. Some societies practice **swidden** or slash-and-burn horticulture. **Swidden horticulture** is the process by which nutrients are put into the soil in order to nourish crops by burning the wild vegetation that exists in a landscape prior to planting. Tribal peoples also often practice animal husbandry over domesticated animals via pastoralism. **Pastoralism** is a method of obtaining food where the environment cannot support horticulture, but where animals can scrounge. There are two types of pastoralism, nomadism and transhumance. **Nomadism** is periodic migration of human populations as they follow plants and animals in the search for food. **Transhumance** is the seasonal movement of some men, known as shepherds, who move livestock to different pastures, while the bulk of the population remain in permanent settlements. Pastoralists must often learn how to share resources, such as watering holes for their herds, in regions where several groups of people migrate.

Tribal peoples construct rites that conform to the economic and political functions of their communities. For instance, the Bantu peoples of southern Africa conduct circumcision rituals, literally as flesh sacrifices to deity, for both males and females attaining puberty. A boy "dies" during the ceremony, for whom the women lament, is "re-born" as a man, and is awarded the shield and spear with which he will assume his peripheral duties. A girl will be ceremoniously enwrapped in a robe that resembles an egg, signifying her duty as a sacred

FIG. 12.1. The Ju/'hoansi of southern Africa are a very healthy foraging people.

FIG. 12.2. Pastoralists in Africa sharing a watering hole.

FIG. 12.3. Bantu boys during their circumcision ritual.

FIG. 12.4. Bantu girls during their circumcision ritual.

vessel for her people's kinship and continued existence. Tribal peoples often structure their societies around age organizations. An **age organization** is a type of social organization wherein people of roughly the same age pass through different levels of society together, from youth through age. An **age set** is one such group in the chronically ascending hierarchy. Shaka utilized circumcision ceremonies to gather annual age sets for his military machine. Each age set would constitute a new regiment.

What changes human attitudes towards land, nature, and spirit is the Neolithic Revolution. The **Neolithic Revolution** is the stage in human cultural evolution characterized by the transition from hunting and gathering to the domestication of plants and animals. This transition was facilitated by the second greatest invention in history, writing. Writing turned right-brained story-tellers into left-brained, logical thinkers who desiccated the spirit out of nature and instituted progress. Animals and plants were no longer "brothers"; they became assets. And the domestication of living assets was tended by a mind and a body that no longer reverenced nature, but dominated it to the point where rivers could be diverted to feed the domesticated plants and animals via irrigation and enable humans to remain sedentary in water-fed cities, where writing became a leisurely art that documented all facets of civilized life. These ideas are called the **hydraulic theory of political integration**. If one looks at a map of England and follows the Thames River from its mouth in the southeast to its source in the foothills in the central Pennine Mountains, one can discern why certain towns and cities are situated in their locations. The clue can be found in their names.

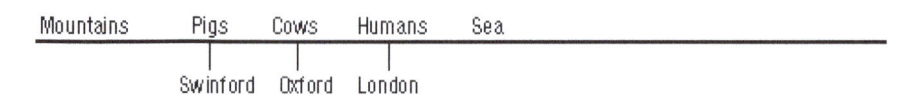

Mountains	Pigs	Cows	Humans	Sea
	Swinford	Oxford	London	

FIG. 12.5. Where would Catford be?

Communities settled at places where humans and animals could cross, or ford, rivers by keeping their heads above the level of the water and ease migrations.

Tribal people chase food and civilized people chase water. Hydraulic civilizations competed for the best lands in a region, since the best lands offered the optimal conditions for foraging and gave leaders the most people with which to secure those lands for the use of the "us" group, as well as the opportunity to dominate the "them" groups that inhabited neighboring lands that were less optimal. The **coercive theory of political integration** describes this type of governmental formation. The coercive theory of political integration states that governments came into existence as a direct result of conflict and warfare. Settled lands had boundaries to be defended and borders to be expanded. Evangelization and imperialism would go hand in hand with the coercive theory of political integration. Governmental officials would often act as intermediaries. An **intermediary** is someone who helps settle disputes among individuals or families in a society. And people would often swear oaths in political and judicial processes. An **oath** is a declaration to attest to the truth of what a person says. With the development of hydraulic civilizations came the concept of property and property rights. **Property rights** are the concept that the individual, not the community, owns assets.

Using irrigation in hydraulic civilizations vastly increased the amount of food people could produce via agriculture. **Agriculture** is an intensive form of crop cultivation using fertilizers to add nutrients to soils and irrigation to water fields. Agriculture is the most extensive form of food production on the planet. Terraces are often used among civilized peoples to increase their arable lands in areas where farming would otherwise prove impracticable. In fact, terracing, as monumental architecture, is a hallmark of civilization. So are aqueducts. Industrialized agriculture uses chemical fertilizers, pesticides, and heavy machinery to maximize yields. Industrial agriculture utilizes roughly 1 percent of the population of the United States, thus freeing up 99 percent of the people to conduct other "civilized" and some not so "civilized" activities. Playing video games and golfing may be considered civilized activities. To maximize profits, many farmers plant only one type of crop in vast fields. This type of farming is called **monocultivation**. A major pitfall of monocultivation is that once a pest invades a monocultivated field, there is virtually no way of stopping its ravages. Hence, in the modern world there is a constant competition between scientists to devise ever more lethal pesticides against those pests that mutate immunities to the former pesticides.

Economies are based on the principles of production, distribution, and consumption. **Production** is the process whereby resources are obtained from the natural environment and fashioned to become consumable goods. Food production has already been discussed, but consumable products, such as tools, weapons, utensils, furniture, clothing, and leisure items, have not. Primal societies fashion handmade products, such as shaping wood, knapping stones, tanning hides, etc. It is both labor intensive and the number of products is limited. As societies progress to civilizations, there is a division of labor. **Division of labor** is the splitting up of various productive tasks among specialized crafts people. Europe, during the Middle Ages, constructed a triune society according to the model of Dumézil. Because of the hit-and-run nature of attacks from the pagan Vikings from the North, the pagan horsemen from the East, and the civilized Muslims from the South, monarchs decentralized their power in a hierarchical system called feudalism. **Feudalism** is a form of governmental structure in which power and resources, usually in the form of land grants, are shared among political leaders at increasingly local levels in order to ward off sudden incursions. This is done in exchange for oaths of loyalty and taxes to the lord above in the hierarchy, all the way up to the king. But, because feudalism was such a ramified system of governance, all local communities had to be self-sufficient. Power and resources were distributed among three classes: the leaders, both lord and churchmen; the warriors, or knights; and the workers. In the early Dark Ages, traumatized former Roman citizens surrendered their personal liberties to become serfs on the land of a lord in exchange for protection. A **serf** is a feudal laborer bound to the soil and the will of his or her lord. Feudal communities produced their own food and most of the implements needed for daily living. These feudal communities were called manors. **Manorialism** was a decentralized system of mutually self-sufficient communities that provided for its own sustenance, organization, and defense. Some limited trade brought other consumable items to a manor in exchange for food or money. Most serfs, in fact, most people in history, never travelled more than five miles from the village in which they were born. The calamity of the Little Ice Age, which decreased the food supply, which lowered people's immunity responses, triggered the Black Death, which wiped out the serf population by nearly one half. This tragedy was bartered by serfs into the increased status of **peasant**, the station that allowed the land laborer to receive wages for his labor and migrate in search of better pay. With the development of intensive agriculture and the increase in relative power and security of Europe with the rest of the world, farming became increasingly more mechanical, which allowed more peasants to migrate to the cities in search of wage-paying employment. With industrialization, which accelerated this process, new social classes developed in the cities, the bourgeoisie and the proletariat. **Industrialization** is the use of sophisticated technology to satisfy the needs of society by transforming raw materials into manufactured goods. The **bourgeoisie** are the owners of the means of production in an industrialized society. The **proletariat** is the wage-earning working class in an industrialized society. Karl Marx will pick up this development in the next chapter.

Distribution is the apportioning of resources and products within a community or network of communities. And distribution entails reciprocity. **Reciprocity** is a mode of distribution in which goods and services of approximately equal value are exchanged among parties. The simplest form of reciprocity is called barter. **Barter** is the direct exchange of commodities between people. Pastoral tribal societies often exchange livestock, such as cows, sheep, goats, camels, etc. as a currency in trading products and cementing social relationships, such as marriage, or social obligations, such as paying tribute or taxes. **Tribute** is the practice of giving goods to a central authority, usually a chief, who in turn redistributes those goods among the people. **Redistribution** is a mode of distribution in which goods and services are given to a central governmental authority, which assesses, stores, and distributes those goods back to the donors according to a social plan. Chiefs often redistribute surplus goods that would otherwise spoil and are usually dispensed in a communal feast, such as a potlatch. A **potlatch** is a competitive giveaway of consumables through a communal feast among Northwestern Native Americans. Potlatches bring increased prestige and social status to the distributers.

Since bartering heavy commodities or vast quantities of products is inefficient, exchange media, such as standardized currencies and money, eased the trade of goods and services among people and communities. A **standardized currency** is a medium of exchange that has well-defined and understood value. Gold, silver, paper, oil, grain, gems, and people in the form of hostages, slaves, and indentured servants can act as media of exchange. Even sand acts as a medium of exchange in many cultures, although it is actually reconstituted sand. Pearls are reconstituted sand solidified within the confines of an oyster. Kula rings among the Trobriand Islanders are composed of shells that are formed by the sandy secretions of mollusks. Cowrie shells perform the same function among the Bantu and clam shells among the Haudenosaunee. And even among us moderns, sand is traded in the form of excited electrons that emit bits of photoelectric light in machines that register numbers. The fiber optics that conduct that light are composed of glass, which is composed of sand. The United States has built a "holy place" to sand in California—Silicon Valley. Silicon is the main element in sand. The funny thing about sand is that it is durable stuff, yet it can just as easily blow away. Having said that, market exchange is a mode of distribution in which goods and services are bought and sold and their value is determined by the principle of supply and demand. This is the basis of capitalism. **Capitalism** is an economic system characterized by private or corporate ownership of capital goods, by investments that are determined by private decision rather than by state control, and by prices, production, and the distribution of goods that are determined mainly by competition in a free market.

FIG. 12.6. Notice the potlatch poles among the totem poles of this Northwest Native American village. These are signifiers of prestige among powerful families within the community. Another ring is added to the top of a pole after each potlatch, gaining more prestige and status for the family.

Consumption is the utilization of economic goods in the satisfaction of social wants and needs. Markets, malls, sidewalk vendors, tourist traps, lemonade stands, insurance companies, mail and internet purveyors, all involve consumption of products through distribution. Satisfying social wants and needs can be a culturally- driven phenomenon. In order to drive the Soviet Union into financial collapse during the Cold War, the Eisenhower administration made it a policy of the United States to become a society of consumers, rather than the thrifty "Puritans" the bulk of Americans had been before World War II. He succeeded. And today, every nation on the globe wants to have its own "American Dream" for its citizens, at least the rich ones. We will examine these "modern" facets of culture and their consequences in the next chapter.

KEY WORDS

Age organization
Age set
Agriculture
Asset
Authority
Barter
Bourgeoisie
Broad-spectrum collecting
Capitalism
Coercive theory of political integration
Consumption
Distribution
Division of labor
Economics
Feudalism
Government
Horticulture
Hydraulic theory of political integration
Industrialization
Intermediary
Manorialism
Monocultivation

Neolithic Revolution
Nomadism
Oath
Optimal foraging theory
Pastoralism
Peasant
Political functions
Political integration
Potlatch
Production
Proletariat
Property rights
Reciprocity
Redistribution
Serf
Standardized currency
Subsistence
Swidden horticulture
Transhumance
Tribute
Voluntaristic theory of political integration

IMAGE CREDITS

- Fig. 12.1: Copyright © 2008 by Andreas Lederer, (CC BY 2.0) at https://commons.wikimedia.org/wiki/File:Hadazbe_returning_from_hunt.jpg.
- Fig. 12.2: Copyright © 2013 by Abdirahman Jama, (CC BY 2.0) at http://commons.wikimedia.org/wiki/File:Muhumed_watching_his_cattle_drink_water_at_a_in_Dhobley_(11400244664).jpg.
- Fig. 12.3: Copyright © 2005 by Steve Evans, (CC BY 2.0) at https://commons.wikimedia.org/wiki/File:Initiation_ritual_of_boys_in_Malawi.jpg.
- Fig. 12.4: Copyright © 2004 by Louisa Kasdon, (CC BY 3.0) at https://commons.wikimedia.org/wiki/File:Samburu_female_circumcision_ceremony,_Kenya.jpg.
- Fig. 12.6: George M. Dawson / Copyright in the Public Domain.

CHAPTER THIRTEEN

THE MODERN WORLD

In the 3,700 years since the advent of the alphabet began nuancing the evolution of the left-brained Western culture, many subliminal mental constructs have become interwoven to produce the modern world. One thing that shifts with the onset of left-brained literacy is the development of an offensive and evangelical warrior code from a defensive and protective one. This reflects a subliminal but profound shift in one's mindset from a closed "us-versus-them" tribal ethnocentrism to the adherence of a "chosen people" to a monotheistic deity's plan of universal pollution cleansing. Incidentally, this is true of both Christian and Muslim alike. The states of these various cultures are called galactic polities. A **galactic polity** is a type of state that rules primarily through spiritually-oriented religious authorities and cosmologies.

In Europe, ancient Greek history spanned the transformation of its various regional cultures from tribal and oral ones to ones that were oral-derived, urban, and literate. From an early modern European linear and progressive point of view, they were evolving from "inferior" cultural mores toward "superior" ones. As a result, ancient Greece bequeathed to Western civilization an ideological oxymoron, a legacy of equality and democracy for state citizens and enslavement for barbarian others. How this happened is intimately related to the geography of Greece. Greece is roughly the size of the state of Louisiana and is divided up by numerous crisscrossing mountain ridges that resulted in dozens of little bowl-shaped valleys that supported independent city-states. As were most societies of the Mediterranean, the typical Greek city-state was divided into the trinitarian model of Indo-Europe as we have seen several times now. The noble warrior class alone could afford the accoutrements of war—spears, shields, helmets, greaves, chariots, horses, and drivers—to wage the type of conflicts recorded by Homer in The Iliad. What made Greece unique, however, was the constricted nature of its city-states. In the center of each city-state was the acropolis where the business of government was conducted and where the wheat fields were located. Bread was the staple foodstuff for all the people of the polis, the noble class and under-classes alike. The center must be defended at all costs. The problem for heroic noble warfare was that the lucrative wine and oil crops derived from grape vines and olive trees grew only on the peripheral slopes of the bowl-shaped valleys, where the noble estates were located, and which were the most vulnerable lands to attack from neighbors. What eventually evolved in Greece was the sharing of military risk when nobles stepped down from their chariots, traded in their horses, drivers, and chariots for more spears, shields, and helmets with which to equip men from the underclasses who came in from the fields and shared bloodletting equally in the ranks of the hoplite infantry armies. These were the armies that Greece was famous for, and which defeated

FIG. 13.1. A Greek hoplite army.

FIG. 13.2. Adolf Hitler propagandized himself as a "World Restorer," that is, as a messiah come to save the German people in his new religion—Nazism. The Nazi slogan, "Germany is Life!" reflects the syncretistic nature of his new religion, a perversion of Darwin's new theory of evolution that justifies the "Master Race's" annihilation of "less fit" and insidiously dangerous races.

the expansive Persian Empire. This martial equality fostered political equality and the ideal of democracy was born. **Democracy** is a type of political system that involves popular participation in the political process. The Macedonian Alexander the Great was the man who would transform defensive Greek warfare into an offensive and expansive one. From him would derive the Western "cult of the offensive," and the "battle of annihilation." Rome would take these Greek and Macedonian martial developments and modify them into the legion, which we saw in Chapter 1.

As a result of its traumatic and martial birth, Rome gave to the Western mentality not only its triumphant ideal of republican governance, but also its concomitant ideology of *imperium*, "the god given right to rule others." The civic expansionism of the left-brained ancient Mediterranean world was justified by an ironically enviable acculturation of barbarian "others" to Hellenistic culture and the beneficent privileges of the Pax Romana that were dangled before provincials in the linear progression of civilization. In an effort to rejuvenate popular adulation of the flagging Pax Romana, the Roman imperial government embraced Christianity, a left-brained "religion of the book," the tenets of which were enticingly more compatible with a centralizing ideology of progressive *imperium* than with the parochial cosmogeny inherent in the old tribal pantheon of Palatine Rome. In a process of psychic transformation, devotion to the Roman Empire would come to mean devotion to the aspirations of the universal, that is, "catholic" will of the savior-god. In the salvific ideology of the Roman Catholic Church, "making disciples of all nations" equated with successful imperialism; in its application, the propagation of the gospel would be spearheaded, literally, by the cast of the javelin. The successful onslaught of the Germanic barbarians re-leavened Roman Catholic Western Europe with dollops of right-brained paganism to create a medieval cultural heritage that was a curious mix of western and pre-western influences. The Holy Roman Empire was its offspring and its chivalric code launched sacrificial martial artists on evangelical hero-quests and crusades. Christ remained the hero of Europe's urban centers; but, in more pagan areas old myths were resurrected and shape-shifted to meet current needs. Artio, the totemic bear-god of primeval Europe became King Arthur, the messianic *Restitutor Orbis*, the World Restorer, who would re-awaken in a time of national emergency and herald in a new age of British greatness. Revered leaders also conformed posthumously to the dictates of the hero archetype; in legend, both Charlemagne and the emperor Barbarossa would become "world restorers." Indeed, even in the twentieth-century, Adolph Hitler, in a time of reactionary anti-liberalism, would cast his gaze back to a Teutonic "golden age" and see himself as a messianic "world restorer" of the German people. All of this has been seen in past chapters, and will be seen again later in the chapter.

FIG. 13.3. The Master Race.

The re-birth of Europe's classical heritage and the invention of the printing press accelerated the pace of the West's "rite of passage" into a left-brained civilization. The rekindling of an analytical scientific spirit would abet the technological achievements necessary to propel European power overseas. The Reformation was an unforeseen, but understandable consequence of this evolution as a growing literate population shed its obsolete, paganized religion and supplanted it with a more timely and urbane one. Martin Luther was instrumental in this. By fostering the teaching of literacy to the young in schools, the power of left-brained thinking was applied to the scriptures in vernacular languages that eventually split spirit from progress and bequeathed to the Western worldview its new religious ideals of the progress of rational science and popular ideas about democracy. The **vernacular** is the language spoken by the ordinary people in a country or region. Mass literacy and the use of the vernacular tongue diluted the Christian "glue" that united Europe, and the struggle between the Catholics and Protestants that resulted in the Wars of Religion separated "church" and "state," and elevated secular nationalism as the glue that held European countries together. Galactic polities would give way to radial polities. A **radial polity** is a state that rules through government and military officials who have centralized control over the assets of a land.

Despite the progressive, secularizing tendencies that were transforming the Western worldview, one could argue that until the late nineteenth century, the left-brained transformation of the European mind never seeped too deeply into any but the relatively small numbers of literate bureaucrats and bourgeois elitists. In that sense, the much-heralded Renaissance and Reformation would be little more than cultural epiphenomena in their days, the quixotic days of the Ages of Exploration, Discovery, and Colonialism. On the other hand, another could argue that in those days, Europeans sailed to distant shores with full-blown left-brained, secularized, and Machiavellian mentalities, seeking nothing loftier in purpose than foisting a Marxist world systems domination on vulnerable societies around the globe and crassly exploiting them. Perhaps the truth lies somewhere in between. It would be in Ireland, its first overseas colony, that England would develop its concepts of **conquest**, the thinly-garrisoned extension of the motherland's physical power, which was always diluted by recidivistic re-Gaelicization; and **domination**, the overt proscription of native folkways, enforced acculturation of English mores, and establishment of plantations—imported communities of loyal and utilitarian settlers.

Although the brutal mechanics of amphibious imperialism were refined by the Spanish during the conquest of the Canary Islands and the subjugation of the Guanches living there, the unrealistic and chimerical "messianic imperialism" of Golden Age Spain had been tempered in the crucible of the *Reconquista*, the bitter and interminable religious fighting against the Muslims over the Iberian Peninsula. When Columbus sailed westward seeking trade with the Orient and stumbled across a "new world" after a hero quest fraught with numinous "otherworldly" trials, he christened his first landfall "*San Salvador*," Holy Savior, and raised a cross to re-cosmicize the wild and chaotic land before him. In his last voyage, he discovered an Eden-like mainland watered by the four primeval rivers, sheltered by a three-lobed island he named "*trinidad*" in honor of the trinity, and bounded on either side by the roiling waters of "la *boca del sierpe*," the "serpent's mouth," and "*la boca del drago*," the "dragon's mouth," both symbolic of the waters of the primordial abyss. These were manifestations of a mindset that was by no means either entirely desacralized or rationalized. When England's Queen Elizabeth I ascended an insecure throne, she sought survival by donning the overt trappings of Britain's virgin goddess of sovereignty, and she succeeded. Likewise, when Great Britain dispatched her "knights of empire" overseas to take on the evangelical "White Man's Burden," British Prime Minister Benjamin Disraeli affectionately dubbed Queen Victoria "the fairy" in a deliberate allusion to her as a "mother-goddess" cast in the likeness of Elizabeth, poet Edmund Spenser's "faerie queene," under whose "serge skirts" the heathen, the ignorant, and the wayward of the Empire might seek sanctuary and reform themselves.

Western motives during the Age of Imperialism betray a mix of left-brained rational materialism and right-brained evangelical sacrifice at one and the same time, albeit in uneven manifestations across a broad ideological and political spectrum. It is little appreciated today how unmodern were many of the cultural symbols that buoyed the social constructs of the West in the Early Modern age; yet, what resulted in the Columbian Exchange was a result of that mindset in contact with "other" peoples, ideas, and landscapes. The **Columbian Exchange** was the widespread transfer of animals, plants, culture, humans, diseases, technologies, and ideas between the Americas and Afro-Eurasia in the fifteenth and sixteenth centuries. The conquistadors did not recast the New World in a new image; they recast the New World in an old image, the Indo-European world of Dumézil. The conquistadors who conquered Ireland and later moved across to the colonies in North America were "poor" noblemen from western England and the Welsh Marches who were looking to establish estates and plantations of their own to achieve status among their peers. The same was true for the conquistadors of Spain from the "poor" region of Extremadura. The polity that was shipped across the Atlantic put governors and churchmen in charge of "those who speak" and conquistadors as noblemen in charge of "those who fight"; however, what was not shipped across on the tiny galleons were "those who worked." The labor force of the conquistadors would come from the "inferior" native peoples that civilized, hence, "superior" European people conquered. Unfortunately for native and conquistador alike, microbes also crossed the Atlantic and virtually annihilated the native peoples and left the Old World-cum-New World trinitarian scheme with all of its achieved status in a shambles. Black tribesmen and women, who were Old World peoples and shared the same immunities to diseases as Europeans and Asians, would be kidnapped as the new work force to support the upper classes in the newly transplanted trinitarian polities.

The form of economics that the Old World polities set up in the New World was called mercantilism. **Mercantilism** is a system in which the government regulates the economy of a state to secure economic growth, a positive balance of trade, and the accumulation of wealth, usually gold and silver. It is a progressive system of ever-increasing wealth, and was an early form of the globalization of capitalism. Mercantile economics is a **"zero-sum" game**. That means that there is only a fixed amount of resources, or assets, available on or in the planet, and whoever has more of these resource/assets than another has more wealth, power, and prestige. Gold and silver was sought because Imperial China was at the time, and for most of history had been, the longest continuous civilization on the planet and the economic engine of world trade. China was the Middle Kingdom of all those other peoples who radiated from her and to her. There was no other kingdom, people, or culture more "superior." This ethnocentric idea was one of the reasons why China's empire was

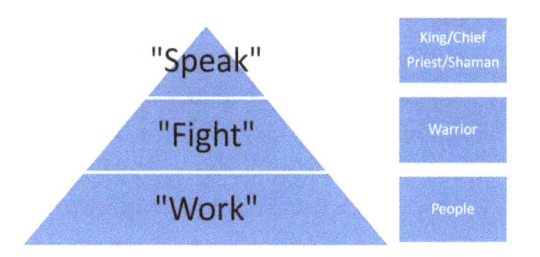

FIGS. 13.4A (LEFT) AND 13.4B (RIGHT). The Old World polity transplanted to the New World. In this case, those who "speak" and those who "fight" would be the conquistadors; those who "work" would be the indigenous peoples.

FIG. 13.5. The flagship of the Chinese mariner Zheng. He built 100 years before the much smaller flagship—the Santa Maria—of the great Spanish mariner, Columbus. However, the Santa Maria was seven times smaller.

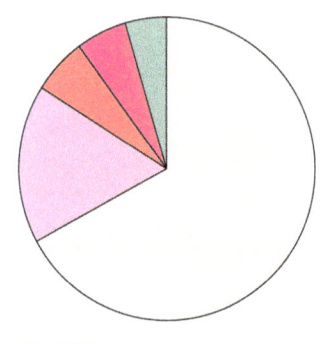

FIG. 13.6. Mercantile chart of resources as a "zero-sum" game.

not one that was expansive territorially, but was very expansive economically. The Chinese Empire was the vortex that sucked in all of the resources of Asia, Africa, Europe, and newly "discovered" North and South America to itself. The rigidly hierarchical Confucian dynasties of Chinese history had mastered the techniques of high temperature furnaces and for over a millennium had produced, through art and science, steel, porcelain, bronze, paper, silk, and more recently, gunpowder, which all the less technologically advanced societies that came into contact with China coveted. The only thing that China needed from her inferiors was gold and silver. And her inferiors were willing to kowtow to pay this specie for her valued goods. To **kowtow** is to bow down and humble oneself before the Chinese Emperor in an overt posture of submission. That would soon change.

As Europe embraced its logical, progressive mentality inherited from the Renaissance, and accrued the technology of gunpowder from China, it utilized this wedding of mind and material to dominate the landscapes, first of Europe, and later, after the "progressive" mentality of the conquistadors spilled overseas, the tribal areas of Africa and the Americas. Once Europe became hopelessly divided religiously between Catholic and Protestant nations, massive amounts of resources were needed to supply these technological wars among Europeans. Colonialism was the result. **Colonialism** is the political, economic, and socio-cultural domination of a territory and its people by a foreign nation. England desired raw materials from its colonies to finance its investment in industrialization. **Industrialization** is the use of sophisticated technology to satisfy the needs of society by transforming raw materials into material goods. Spain did not industrialize. It chose the mercantile accrual of gold and silver from its colonies to dominate the first world trade network form Iberia to the Americas, to the Philippines, and on to China.

As late as the seventeenth century in England, much of the awe associating god and king would inspire the absolutist philosophy of Thomas Hobbes, who called men brutish and self-seeking. This mentality was a vestige of the biblical notion of "original sin." Geertz believes that the point at which a political system begins to free itself from

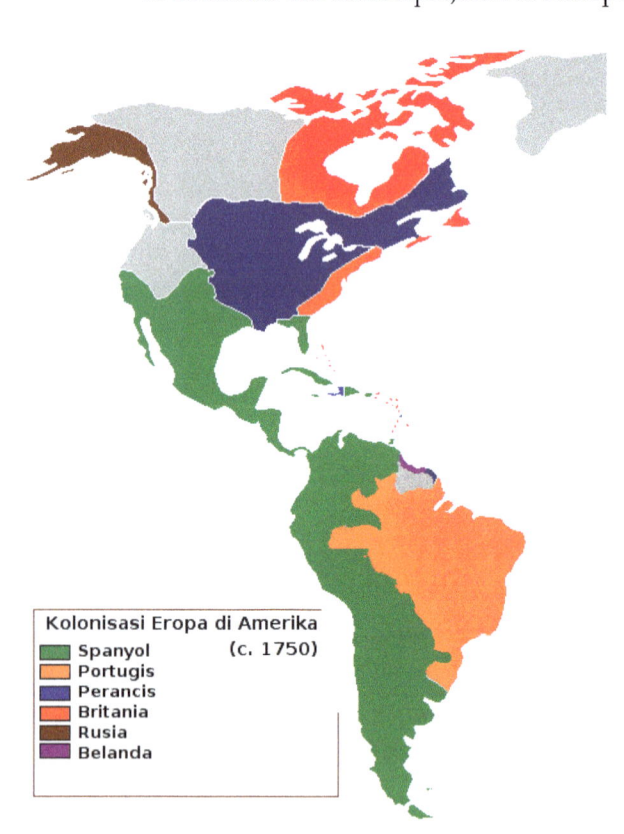

FIG. 13.7. Colonization in the New World as part of the mercantile "zero-sum" game.

the immediate governance of received tradition, or the direct and detailed guidance of religious or philosophical canons, is when formal "modern" ideologies tend first to emerge and take hold. The French Revolution became the greatest incubator of extremist ideologies in history, not because of inherently greater stresses, but because through it the central organizing principle of political life—the "divine right of kings"—was destroyed. That result was a product of the Enlightenment in Europe. The **Enlightenment** was a European intellectual movement of the late seventeenth and eighteenth centuries that emphasized reason and individualism as the prime buttresses of society rather than orthodox tradition. The Enlightenment was the gateway to democracy. This was the mentality of John Locke, who elevated the freedom of the individual to make rational choices for him or herself, and who denied that humans are born with "original sin," and therefore disposed to evil and brutishness. Instead, he posited that humans are born with a **tabula rasa**—a "blank slate"—that is, a mind that is imprinted with information through the five physical senses, not spirit. Hence, to imprint this blank mind with "good" cultural values rather than "bad" ones will increase the power and happiness not only of the individual, but also the community and the nation. It is a modern, left-brained, progressive notion. This new, "modern" ideology allows the individual to invoke the social contract, that is, that government and its sovereign power are derived from the people and not from a supernatural entity, and that the ideals of any government precede "the people." Thus, only "the people" can make and break a government. This allows for both rebellion and revolution. A **rebellion** is an attempt within a society to disrupt the existing political organization and redistribute the power and resources without overthrowing it. A **revolution** is an attempt to overthrow the existing form of government, the modes of production and distribution, and the allocation of social status, in order to establish a new one. From these ideas was born the notion of the nation-state as a government "of the people," that group of nationals who are connected via a jumbled "glue" of ethnicity, race, religion, kinship, and freedom. **Civil rights** would be those freedoms that accrued to an individual by birth or naturalization into a nation-state. These individuals would be called citizens, and ideally, all citizens would be free and equal in a democracy. All of this was part of the mantras of the religion called positivism; yet, despite this ideal of cultural "good," the seemingly oxymoronic social truth of early modern nation-states was that within a nation, citizens could be free and equal and possess non-citizens as slaves with no civil rights. A **slave** was an asset that contributed to the wealth of a nation, but may or may not be considered "human" for political reasons and the power that personhood allows for. In a search for greater access to resources and assets, European nation-states began to share power between democratic bodies and monarchs, at first in France and Great Britain. This went hand in hand with Europe's imperial expansion into Africa and Asia in search of assets for the technological arms race back in Europe when steel navies and advanced artillery replaced wooden ships and horse artillery. Great Britain's rebellious stepchild, the United States of America, was the first to experiment with the great ideal of democratic government without a king. This process of the gradual democratization of nation-states received a rude interruption when the clash over worldwide access to assets exploded. That clash was World War I.

Before looking at the consequences of World War, let's examine the religions that would replace Christianity as the "glue" of European identity. After Europe began expanding beyond its borders in the early modern period, the need for a warrior class diminished; yet, this warrior class desired to retain its aristocratic power and status and resisted the attempts of the monarchs to curb its power and to centralize the feudalized governmental system. To accomplish their centralizing ends, monarchs sold freedoms to peasants who migrated to cities and set up commercial enterprises. This became the new bourgeoisie class. In time, mechanization allowed more crops to be grown with less people, which, in turn, allowed more peasants to migrate to the cities to work now for the enfranchised bourgeoisie. This new lower working class was the proletariat. The bourgeoisie became the ever-expanding "middle class" that corroded the power of aristocrat and king alike. Gunpowder gave the bourgeois class the power to make the warrior class obsolete, and the French Revolution removed the nobility from the board. The French Revolution also excised the notion of divine right monarchy and the supernatural prestige that accrued to it. The modern citizen now wore the hats of all of the classes of Dumézil: he could now vote, and was hence a "king." He had religious freedom; he was his own "priest." He was already a worker, and with gunpowder, he became his own warrior. Thus was born the "equal" modern citizen, whose aspirations to economic and political progress paved the way for the American Dream in the United States.

Karl Marx lived in Germany when Bismarck militarized the German state behind the "kingly" Kaiser in 1870 in order to unite it to prevent the hitherto disorganized German polities from being exploited by their centralizing neighbors to the West. Germany embarked upon a massive program of industrialization to rival the power of the British Empire without granting creeping democracy to its working class. Marx foresaw disaster here. As a student of the German Romantic philosopher Hegel, who saw "God" not as the deity whose vocation it was to create and nurture "His Children," the Christians, but rather as a creator whose job description was simply that, creating, not raising children. Humans were just another of deity's "art projects," no more, no less. Hegel's deity created according to the dialectical method. The **dialectical method** is the conception of an idea as a thesis and analyzing it; then, analyzing all things that this idea is not, the antithesis; and finally, deriving new truth, the synthesis, as a conclusion in the process. This synthesis becomes the new thesis in the next exploratory syllogism of deity making physically "actual" its spiritual "potential." And on and on it goes, progressively, until deity figures itself out, totally. Marx looked at the inequalities of power, prestige, and wealth in the newly united and industrializing Germany—the Second Reich—and, as a secularist, dropped the supernatural element from Hegel's dialectical method and re-directed it towards the physical socio-economic element. He called this new process material dialectics. **Material dialectics** analyzed the flow of power, prestige, and wealth in European history and came to a startling conclusion. Let's look at his method. As his first thesis, he examined when power was the most unequally divided among Europeans in the Ancient period. Slaves, at the bottom of the social order, dialectically drew power from their Greek and Roman masters and synthesized a new relationship in the Medieval period, when lords had to yield power to peasants in a new dialectical relationship that synthesized the bourgeois class, which, in turn, shared power dialectically with the proletariat. This stage in the dialectical scheme was roughly 1850, Marx's generation, when Great Britain and Germany were locked in their deadly industrial arms race. Marx predicted that the exploited workers would rise up against the bourgeoisie in Germany, not England, which had begun the process of power sharing through creeping democracy. Marx saw the steady accrual of power by the people whose role was that of the "antithesis" in each dialectical relationship, and the erosion of power by the people whose role was that of the thesis in each relationship, and predicted, as a social prophet, that the two axes of gaining in power and erosion in power would intersect in a social culmination of bourgeoisie and proletariat he called communism. Under the "synthesis" of communism there would be total equality of people, and hence, no need for governments and governmental mechanisms to enforce inequality. **Communism** is a "utopian" theory of social organization based on redistributing the modes of production and the holding of all property in common, with the actual ownership being ascribed to the community.

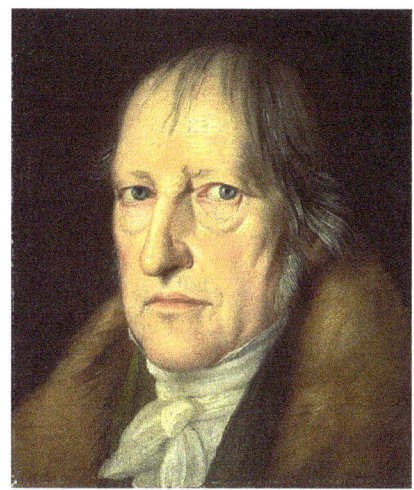

FIG. 13.8A. Hegel.

FIG. 13.8B. Marx.

Ancient World	Medieval World	1850	Future
Master			
	Lord		
		Bourgeoisie	
			Communism
		Proletariat	
	Peasant		
Slave			

FIG. 13.8C. Diagram showing Marx's dialectical reasoning.

The accompanying diagram should help in demonstrating Marx's dialectical reasoning:

Marx's material dialectics fostered two political approaches toward the utopian ideal of communism in the world of unequal citizens—rich bourgeoisie and poor proletarians—in the 1850s, that of the Mensheviks and that of the Bolsheviks. **Mensheviks** are those Communists who believe that Marx's dialectical material process is following a natural progression and should be allowed to evolve according to its own pace. **Bolsheviks** are those Communists who say, "Why wait? Let's foment a revolution to hasten the process and ease the suffering of the poor by a century or so."

FIG. 13.9. The Kensingtons at Laventie.

Marx chose the latter, which would have the literate Communists "unite the workers" and direct their energies in overthrowing the democratic system of inequality and redistribute the modes of economic production equally via a temporary system of socialism. Socialism, in turn, would operate a "top-down" command economy until communism is deliberately engineered, at which time the Socialist leaders would give up their temporary powers "and all would live happily ever after." A **command economy** is an economy in which production, investment, prices, and incomes are determined centrally by a government. **Socialism** is an economic system situated between capitalism and communism that advocates the collective ownership of the means of production and distribution of goods, which is temporarily administered by a literate government. World War I would catalyze the competition among these competing political ideologies.

World War I traumatized Europe's faith in its governmental and social institutions. Mechanization "tricked" humanity with its left-brained technological advances and replaced it with massive right-brained trauma as a consequence. Freud recognized the "discontents" of left-brained life in a civilization. Right-brained art reflected this.

During World War I, art was still depicted "scientifically," that is, it was governed by the ideas of perspective and rationalism in a logical and rational manner, at least initially. Notice in Figure 13.10—"The Kensingtons at Laventic"—how the traumas of industrialized warfare are beginning to tear at the idea of positivism. Very soon, these same "rationally-depicted" positivistic notions would be depicted "irrationally." Art captured this visceral transformation of Europe away from its positivistic roots and toward anti-liberal ones. In his painting "Guernica," Pablo Picasso portrayed the right-brained images of emotion as a left-brained, "black-and white" newspaper. This painting hallmarked the onset of the Postmodern age. **Postmodernism** is a viewpoint that is skeptical of "modern" scientific and philosophical perspectives. Adolf Hitler reacted against the modern, liberal world by installing his Fascist Nazi Party in Germany in order to return to a German Golden Age. **Fascism** is a way of organizing a society in which a government ruled by a dictator controls the lives of the people, and in which people have no power to disagree with the government. Fascism puts the state first; that is, that the state is an abstract idea of the political

FIG. 13.10. "Irrational" World War I art.

union of generations of biological humans, organized into races, not the individual lives of those races. Hitler would have Germany "live," even if he had to kill every German to do it. Italy and Japan also developed fascistic governments.

The agrarian economy of Russia collapsed under the industrial weight of World War I, the world's first "modern" war, and was replaced by a socialistic revolution led by Lenin. Ironically, the Russian Revolution, which supposedly set up the world's first "Communist" state was, in reality, a nationalistic defense by Russian patriots against an invasion of the Allied powers. It was not a worker's revolution, and instead of Communism, it installed a socialistic command economic state that never yielded power. Britain and France, as we have seen, went into collective depression over the "bloody nose" that World War I gave to positivism. Only the isolationist United States heralded Liberalism, until the Depression launched all nations into a "Darwinian" and "Hobbesian" all-against-all struggle for assets and power in World War II. **Liberalism** is a political philosophy based on belief in progress, the essential goodness of the human race, the autonomy of the individual, and the protection of civil rights under an elected government.

FIG. 13.11. Using a perversion of bushido—the warrior code of the samurai—Japan developed a fascist ideology to gain assets from China by treating the Chinese as inferior "sub-humans."

Because of its inordinate wealth and power, the United States was able to supply itself as well as all of its allies and engineer victory for the resurrected ideal of liberalism in World War II. That war ended the appeal of atrocity in the name of national interest in Japan and Germany, and expanded the civil rights of citizens within a nation to human rights for all members of our species. **Human rights** are the basic freedoms to which all humans are entitled that include: the right to life and liberty, freedom of thought and expression, and equality before the law. Only the United States and the Soviet Union were left strong enough at the end of the war to compete in the evangelization of the globalized world. **Globalization** is the worldwide impact of industrialization and its socioeconomic, political, and cultural consequences on the world. The United Nations (UN) was that worldwide political body developed at the close of the

FIG. 13.12. Pablo Picasso's "Guernica."

war that is intended to represent all nations in one political body that can guarantee all humans their rights and minimize global conflicts. This struggle between American Liberalism and Soviet Communism would divide the world into three camps. The **First World** was that sector of the global economy composed of modern, industrialized capitalist societies. The **Second World** was that sector of the global economy composed of industrialized socialist societies. The **Third World** was that sector of the global economy composed of non-industrialized and non-aligned societies. During the Cold War that followed the development of atomic weaponry by the Soviets, Third World nations were wooed, quasi-religiously, by both the First World and the Second World. It was at this time that the Eisenhower administration added "In God We Trust" to American coinage to counterpoise the "*E Pluribus Unum*" idea of the American civil religion. **American civil religion** is Robert Bellah's sociological theory that postulates a nonsectarian religious faith exists in the United States with sacred symbols drawn from national history. Pol Pot would exterminate 2 million of 8 million Cambodians during his reign of terror with the Khmer Rouge in the 1970s over an inflexibly conservative form of the Communist religion. The United States would posit modernization theory as part of its missionary work during the Cold War. **Modernization theory** states there is a linear and progressive way for pre-capitalist societies to modernize industrially in such a way as to lead directly to positive social and political change via a "take-off" stage of development that is followed by a "capitalist" stage of development. Just imitate the United States in all ways in the globalized world and you, too, can have the American Dream. Spain had accrued its take-off capital in Bolivia and Mexico, and Great Britain had in India; during the Cold War, the United States evangelized proffered "take-off" bounty to its disciples via the Truman Doctrine and the Marshall Plan. This is really the old wine of Tylor and Morgan's evolutionary theory dusted off and trundled out in the twentieth century. The Soviet Union countered by condemning this notion as dependency theory. **Dependency theory** is the idea that modernization theory is actually a form of neo-colonialism, packaged as a model of development for under-developed nations, but is actually intended to enrich and empower the imperial industrialized nations. In response to this dependency theory of the Soviets, Eisenhower leaned heavily on his First World Allies, Great Britain and France, to break up their empires. **Decolonization** is the process through which colonies become independent from an imperial nation and join the UN. Great Britain heeded in 1948, and the national rivalries in the Asian sub-continent, South Africa, and the Middle East ensued. France refused, and decades of conflict in Indochina followed.

Decolonization in Africa and Asia fomented the Civil Rights Movement in the United States when Blacks, living under "Jim Crow" segregation policies in the South, wondered aloud how the government could embrace freedom for Blacks internationally, while allowing it to be denied domestically. From the Civil Rights Movement would develop the Feminist Movement, the Gender Movement, the Green Movement, etc. The idea of "freedom" would be attenuated more and more abstractly to question, in a postmodern way, all facets of rights and responsibilities. Does government exist to give resources to people without contributions from them, or to protect people from having access to accruing resources through labor denied them for prejudicial reasons?

Is same-sex marriage moral? Who controls the life of a fetus—the woman, the man, the fetus, the society? Does a fetus have a life? Should taxation be administered as a strict percentage of income, or does a higher income entitle one to pay less taxes? Ultimately, all of the answers to these questions will be justified by "religion," and that religion will be resource driven.

Other issues that living in the modern/postmodern world have engendered include the very premises of capitalism itself. Does the planet have a finite amount of resources that can be recycled progressively to avoid the extinction of capitalism, either by the loss of profit, due to the diminishing returns on increasingly scarce resources, or by the environmental devastation wrought by those societies on the resources themselves, as well as on the biological viability of the societies extracting them? The boons and the banes of globalization are upon us. We can feed more people than ever before through industrial monocultivation; while at the same time, pests are mutating resistances to pesticides that have the potential to wipe out the inviting monocultivated fields and infect the biological hosts, which include humans, upon which they feed. Will medicine forestall the microbes, or will human rights get in the way of common sense? Will more food feed more mouths and give us all greater opportunities, or will it make some of us obese and let some of us starve? Perhaps we need to tune up the ideas that "bind" us, that is, our modern religions. By the way, the Bolshevik Marx has had a resurrection in recent years. He has recanted and become a Menshevik, that is, neo-Marxists say he was correct all along as a scholar of dialectical materialism, but wrong as a religious zealot. Capitalistic democracies were still too strong in his day to yield power to his Communist-inspired revolutions, and they failed. The Soviet Union collapsed and George W. Bush hailed the New World Order had arrived. If that meant that the First World won, the final chapter on that book has yet to be written. Neo-Marxists see now that Marx was too myopic. Capitalism had to expand to include the collective wealthy elites of the economies of the whole world—the **core**—in a crassly exploitative manner before that

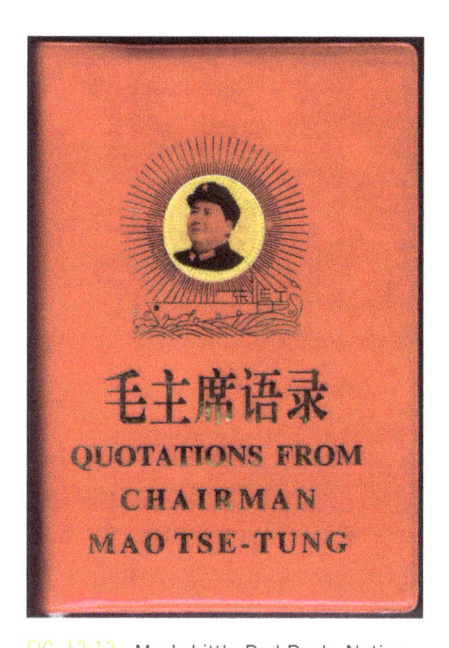

FIG. 13.13. Mao's Little Red Book. Notice that this book subliminally nuances the reader toward the "cult" of Mao. Though posing as a Communist leader (via the red color of the book), Mao is also portrayed as a Confucian emperor, a leader of the Chinese people who possesses the "Mandate of Heaven."

FIG. 13.14. Modern Chinese Army.

FIG. 13.15. A modern terrorist group.

bubble would finally burst and the collective "workers of the whole world"—the "**periphery**"—would revolt and redistribute the modes of production on a global scale. This would occur at a time when capitalism lay depleted of resources and politically impotent, and usher in the "golden age" of Communism according to the natural law that had been guiding it all along. This neo-Marxist idea would be called **world systems theory**.

In the welter of twentieth century ideas, religions would be evangelized at the pulpit, in this case, the UN; but, resources would be accrued on the battlefield. China is rapidly destroying its environment and the environments of its neighbors in a headlong rush towards Confucian/Communist/capitalism, whatever that is? Its previous one-child policy, promulgated under the aegis of Chairman Mao, who pontificated his own brand of Communism from his own bible, also known as "the Little Red Book," has ensured that millions of Chinese men are looking for women and may use guns to get them as well as the resources to maintain them.

Non-industrialized peoples do not have the resources to build big armies. What will they do to resist the implications of the world systems theory? They will try diplomacy, but if that fails, they will wage war. **War** is an organized, extremely violent, and often prolonged conflict carried out by states or non-state actors that is designed to gain resources, prevent domination, and/or right "wrongs." Remember, the nature of warfare is economic, political, and military. Any society fields combatants based on ideology, technology, and resources. Technological progress increasingly allowed human beings to administer lethal force upon others extrasomatically, while at the same time allowing the warrior a greater and greater degree of safety. Fists gave way to stones, stones to knives, spears, and shields; these gave way to guns, shells, and fleets of bombs, and on to atomic and nuclear weapons. Ultimately, war is a means to impose one's will upon the enemy and attain one's ends. The Romans discovered the best way to gain one's ends is to threaten to use force with a military that is able to deliver it, and thus overawe the resistance of enemies. Terrorists have rediscovered this Roman idea. They know that the television camera is the most powerful weapon on the modern battlefield. By committing an atrocity and hiding "among the people," terrorists lance the notion of nationality and self-determination in its liberal "heart," and use this atrocity to get its "eight-second sound bite" out to world opinion at almost no cost. Modern technology has so inundated the modern audience with stimulation that our brains begin to wander from any focused

FIG. 13.16. Camels, the age-old "ships of the desert" have retaken their roles in the Aral sea region from the rusting Soviet "ships of the desert."

topic in eight seconds. Industrial nations, whose medias pander to the television camera and its "If it bleeds, it leads; if it thinks, it stinks" mantra concerning the worthiness of news coverage must likewise shrink their messages to "eight-second sound bites," despite a plethora of resources. What an equalizer! But, is the method of self-determination utilized by terrorists ethical and moral? Is a "smart" bomb? A nuke? A spear? A fist? Where does one draw the line in the sand concerning moral murder? And if one can, what is the religion, that is, what set of rules allows you to do that?

Economically, is a multinational corporation, which makes the rich richer, the middle class shrink, and the poor poorer, ethical and moral? Is economic growth at any environmental cost moral and ethical? The shrinkage of the Aral Sea due to exploitation for cotton crops by the Soviet Union in its religious competition with the United States should be a salutary lesson.

One of the dangers that progress threatens the human race with was posited by Robert Malthus in the eighteenth century. He reasoned that human population rates tend to grow at an exponential rate relative to the arithmetic—linear—rate of food production, and that if the vector of population growth exceeds that of the food supply, then the future of any people and civilization will reach a "tipping-point" and collapse in a catastrophe of famine, starvation, and disease until the food supply and population growth again are restored to a harmonious level. This phenomenon is known as a Malthusian collapse. We, as creatures with ideas and power, must guard ourselves against such an eventuality.

Having presented lots of information, and given many examples of what cultural anthropology means, I now leave it to you, the student, to assess what has been presented to you, sift through it, and apply it meaningfully to your lives, the lives of your families, the lives of others and their families, and the planet as a holistic and inter-connected whole. This is the true purpose of education, not just getting a job. Education, by the way, is derived from the Latin word (you didn't think I'd let you go without one more of these) *educatio*—*ducatio* (to lead) and *e* (out). It means how an individual gains wisdom by garnering as much information and knowledge in one's lifetime as one can, and through experience, synthesize wisdom, in order to enrich one's own life inwardly and outwardly as well as enrich the lives of others. Education is the privilege to engage in that process of leading out from within and influencing the universe extrasomatically. It is the process of wedding left-brained "progress" and right-brained "conscience." Be well educated, and have fun doing it.

KEY WORDS

American civil religion
Bolsheviks
Civil rights
Colonialism
Columbian Exchange
Command economy
Communism
Conquest
Core
Decolonization
Democracy
Dependency theory
Dialectical method
Domination
Enlightenment
Fascism
First World
Galactic polity
Globalization
Human rights
Industrialization
Kowtow
Liberalism
Malthusian collapse
Material dialectics
Mensheviks
Mercantilism
Modernization theory
Periphery
Postmodernism
Radial polity
Rebellion
Revolution
Second World
Socialism
Slave
Tabula rasa
Third World
United Nations
Vernacular
War
World systems theory
"Zero-sum" game

IMAGE CREDITS

- Fig. 13.1: EDSITEment! / Copyright in the Public Domain.
- Fig. 13.2: Copyright © 1938 by Bundesarchiv, Bild 137-004055, (CC BY-SA 3.0 DE) at https://en.wikipedia.org/wiki/File:Bundesarchiv_Bild_137-004055,_Eger,_Besuch_Adolf_Hitlers.jpg.
- Fig. 13.3: Copyright © 1939 by Arno Breker, (CC BY-SA 3.0) at https://en.wikipedia.org/wiki/File:ArnoBrekerDiePartei.jpg.
- Fig. 13.4b: John Gabriel Stedman / Copyright in the Public Domain.
- Fig. 13.5: Copyright © 2011 by Vmenkov / Wikimedia Commons, (CC BY-SA 3.0) at https://commons.wikimedia.org/wiki/File:Nanjing_Treasure_Boat_-_P1070978.JPG.
- Fig. 13.7: Arkwatem / Wikimedia Commons / Copyright in the Public Domain.
- Fig. 13.8a: Jakob Schlesinger / Copyright in the Public Domain.
- Fig. 13.8b: John Jabez Edwin Mayall / Copyright in the Public Domain.
- Fig. 13.9: Eric Kennington / Copyright in the Public Domain.
- Fig. 13.10: M.A. Kempf / Copyright in the Public Domain.
- Fig. 13.11: Copyright in the Public Domain.
- Fig. 13.12: Copyright © 2009 by Papamanila / Wikimedia Commons, (CC BY-SA 3.0) at http://commons.wikimedia.org/wiki/File:Mural_del_Gernika.jpg.
- Fig. 13.14: Copyright © 2015 by Kremlin.ru, (CC BY 3.0) at https://en.wikipedia.org/wiki/File:Парад_в_честь_70-летия_Великой_Победы_-_40.jpg.
- Fig. 13.15: Copyright in the Public Domain.
- Fig. 13.16: Copyright © 2008 by Arian Zwegers, (CC BY 2.0) at https://commons.wikimedia.org/wiki/File:Moynaq,_Aral_Sea_(6226842732).jpg.

BIBLIOGRAPHY

Abdullah, A. and Packenham, T. Dreamers of Empire. Freeport, New York: Books for Libraries Press, 1968.

Akenson, D. God's Peoples. Ithaca: Cornell University Press, 1992.

Alexander, J. "The Making of the Age of Chivalry." History Today. (37: November 1987): 3–11.

Allen, J. Judah's Sceptre and Joseph's Birthright. Merrimac, Massachusetts: Destiny Publishers, 1917.

Appleby, J. et. al. Telling the Truth About History. New York: W. W. Norton and Co., 1994.

Altridge, D. et. al., eds. Post-Structuralism and the Question of History. Cambridge: Cambridge University Press, 1987.

Ashe, G. King Arthur: The Dream of a Golden Age. London: Thames and Hudson, 1990.

Bailey, S. Prohibitions and Restraints in War. London: Oxford University Press, 1972.

Ballis, W. The Legal Position of War. New York: Garland Publishing, Inc., 1973.

Baring, A. and Cashford J. The Myth of the Goddess. New York: Aranka, 1977.

Bartlett, T. and Jeffrey K., eds. A Military History of Ireland. New York: Cambridge University Press, 1996.

Basso, K. Wisdom Sits in Places. Albuquerque, New Mexico: University of New Mexico Press, 1996.

Bean, R. "War and the Birth of the Nation State." Journal of Economic History. (33: 1973): 203–21.

Begley, S. Brain Assymetry. Newsweek: March 19, 2007

Ben-Jochannan, Y. Africa: Mother of Western Civilization. Baltimore, Maryland: Black Classic Press, 1971.

Bettini, M. Anthropology and Roman Culture. Baltimore: Johns Hopkins University Press, 1991.

Blackburn, J. The White Men. London: Orbis Publishing, 1979.

Boak, A. and Sinnigen, W. A History of Rome to A. D. 565. New York: MacMillan Publishing Company, Inc., 1965.

Boase, R. The Troubadour Revival. Boston: Routledge and Kegan Paul, 1978.

Bolton, W. Alcuin and Beowulf. New Brunswick, New Jersey: Rutgers University Press, 1978.

Bowser, B. et. al., eds. Toward the Multicultural University. Westport, Connecticut: Praeger, 1995.

Braudel, F. The Mediterranean and the Mediterranean World in the Age of Philip II, v. I–II. New York: Harper Colophon Books, 1972.

British Broadcasting Corporation. Ideas and Beliefs of the Victorians. London: Sylvan Press, 1949.

Bryce, J. The Holy Roman Empire. New York: The Macmillan Company, 1911.

Bucholz, A. "Hans Delbruck and Modern Military History." Historian. (55: Spring 1993): 517–26.

Cahill, T. How the Irish Saved Civilization. New York: Anchor Books, 1995.

Cambrensis, G. The English Conquest of Ireland. New York: Haskell House Publishers, Ltd., 1969.

Campbell, J. The Hero With a Thousand Faces. New York: Meriden Books, 1962.

Campbell, J. Historical Atlas of World Mythology: Vol. I: The Way of the Animal Powers. New York: Harper and Row Publishers, Inc., 1988.

Campbell, J. Historical Atlas of World Mythology: Vol. II : Mythologies of the Great Hunt. New York: Harper and Row Publishers, Inc. 1988.

Canny, N. The Elizabethan Conquest of Ireland. New York: Barnes and Noble Books, 1976.

Cantor, N. The Civilization of the Middle Ages. New York: Harper Perennial, 1994.

Capellanus, A. The Art of Courtly Love. New York: Columbia University Press, 1960.

Capt, E. The Scottish Declaration of Independence. Muskogee, Oklahoma: Hoffman Publishing, 1983.

Carlyle, T. Oliver Cromwell's Letters and Speeches, v. III. Boston: Dana Estes and Company, Centennial reprint.

Chadwick, O. The Secularization of the European Mind in the Nineteenth Century. New York: Cambridge University Press, 1981.

Chaliand, G. The Art of War in World History. Berkeley: University of California Press, 1994.

Chambers, J. "The New Military History: Myth and Reality." Journal of Military History. (July 1991): 395-406.

Cheney, D. Spenser's Image of Nature. New Haven: Yale University Press, 1967.

Chickering, H. Beowulf. New York: Anchor Books, 1977.

Chirot, D. "The Rise of the West." American Sociological Review. (50: 1985).

Chirot, D. Social Change in the Modern Era. New York: Harcourt, Brace Janovich, Inc., 1986.

Chretien de Troyes. Arthurian Romances. London: Everyman, 1987.

Chrimes, S. Henry VII. Berkley: University of California Press, 1972.

Christianson, P. Reformers and Babylon. Toronto: University of Toronto Press, 1978.

Chudoba, B. Spain and the Empire. New York: Octagon Books, 1969.

Cohen, T. Men and Masculinity. Belmont, California: Thomson Wadsworth, 2001.

Collins, R. ed. Historical Problems of Imperial Africa. Princeton: Markus Weiner Publishing, 1970.

Coppa, F., ed. The Encyclopedia of Modern Dictators. New York: Peter Lang, 2006.

Coppa, F., ed. The Encyclopedia of Modern Monarchs. New York: Peter Lang, 2007.

Cope, C. The Lost Kingdom of Burgundy. New York: Dodd, Mead and Company, 1987.

Cork, W. "The Cannon Reconquest of Nasrid Spain and the End of the Reconquista." Journal of Military History. (57(1): January 1993): 43–70.

Cornford, F. trans. The Republic of Plato. New York: Oxford University Press, 1975.

Costain, T. The Last Plantagenets. New York: Popular Library, 1962.

Cowan, T. Fire in the Head. San Francisco: Harper, 1993.

Coyne, J. Why Evolution is True? New York: Penguin Books, 2009.

Creasy, E. Fifteen Decisive Battles of the World. New York: Military Heritage Press, 1987.

Crosby, A. Jr. The Columbian Exchange. Westport, Connecticut: Greenwood Press, 1973.

Crow, J. The Epic of Latin America. Berkeley: University of California Press, 1992.

Cunliffe, B. The Celtic World. New York: St. Martin's Press, 1996.

Curtius, E. European Literature in the Latin Middle Ages. New Jersey: Princeton University Press, 1990.

Davidson, B. The African Slave Trade. Boston: Little, Brown and Company, 1961.

Davies, J. A Discovery of the True Causes Why Ireland Was Never Entirely Subdued. Washington D. C.: Catholic University Of America Press, 1988.

Davies, R. Domination and Conquest. Cambridge: Cambridge University Press, 1990.

Dawson, D. The Origins of Western Warfare. Boulder, Colorado: Westview Press, 1996.

Deacon, R. John Dee. London: Frederick Muller, Ltd., 1968.

Dehouve, D. Historia de las Pueblas Indigenas de Mexico. Tlalpan, Mexico: Centro de Investigaciones y Estudios Superiores en Antropologia Social, 1994.

Dobin, H. Merlin's Disciples. Stanford: Stanford University Press, 1990.

Donogan, B. "Halcyon Days and the Literature of War: England's Military Education Before 1642." Past and Present. (147: May 1995): 65–100.

Duby, G. France in the Middle Ages: 987–1460. Malden, Massachusetts: Blackwell Publishers, Ltd., 1993.

Duby, G. The Legends of Bouvines. Berkeley: University of California Press, 1990.

Durant, W. The Age of Faith. New York: Simon and Schuster, 1950.

Durant, W. Caesar and Christ. New York: Simon and Schuster, 1944.

Edinger, E. Ego and Archetype. Boston, Massachusetts: Shambhala Publications, Inc., 1972.

Eisler, R. The Chalice and the Blade. San Francisco: Harper, 1988.

Eliade, M. The Myth of Eternal Return. Princeton, New Jersey: Princeton University Press, 1991.

Eldridge, C. Victorian Imperialism. New Jersey: Atlantic Highlands, 1978.

Ellul, J. The Subversion of Christianity. Grand Raids, Michigan: William B. Eerdmans Publishing Company, 1986.

Elton, Lord. General Gordon. St. James Place, London: Collins, 1954.

Entwistle, W. The Arthurian legend in the Literatures of the Spanish Peninsula. New York: E. P. Dutton and Company, 1925.

Erikson, E. The Life Cycle Completed. New York: W. W. Norton and Company, 1998.

Esper, T. "The Replacement of the Longbow by Firearms in the English Army." Technology and Culture. (6: 1965): 382–93.

Falls, C. Elizabeth's Irish Wars. London: Methuen and Company, Ltd., 1950.

Farwell, B. Mr. Kipling's Army. New York: W. W. Norton and Company, 1981.

Farwell, B. Queen Victoria's Little Wars. New York: W. W. Norton and Company, 1972.

Fernandez-Armesto, F. The Spanish Armada. New York: Oxford University Press, 1989.

Ferraro, G. and S. Andreatta. Cultural Anthropology. Belmont, California: Wadsworth, 2010.

Fiske, J. The Discovery of America, v. II. Boston: Houghton, Mifflin and Company, 1901.

Fletcher, R. The Barbarian Conversion. New York: Henry Holt and Company, Inc., 1998.

Fletcher, R. Moorish Spain. Berkeley: University of California Press, 1992.

Foley, J. Immanent Art. Bloomington: Indiana University Press, 1991.

Fraser, A. Cromwell. New York: Dell Publishing Company, Inc., 1975.

Frazer, J. The Golden Bough. New York: Avenel Books, 1981.

Friedman, R. Who Wrote the Bible? New York: Harper and Row Publishers, 1987.

Fuente, J., et al. How Culture Shapes Spatial Conceptions of Time. Psychological Science Online First (July 22, 2014.)

Fuller, J. A Military History of the Western World, v. I–II. New York: Da Capo Press, 1954.

Gantz, J. Early Irish Myths and Sagas. New York: Penguin Books, 1981.

Gantz, J. The Mabinogion. New York: Dorset Press, 1985.

Gardner, J. Masculinity Studies and Feminist Theories. New York, Colombia University Press, 2002.

Geertz, C. The Interpretations of Cultures. New York: Basic Books Inc. 1973.

Geoffrey of Monmouth. The History of the Kings of Britain. New York: Penguin Books, 1966.

Giddens, A. The Consequences of Modernity. Stanford, California: Stanford University Press, 1990.

Gimbutas, M. The Civilization of the Goddess. San Francisco: Harper, 1991.

Girouard, M. The Return to Camelot. New Haven: Yale University Press, 1981.

Goldberg, S. Why Men Rule. Chicago: Open Court Publishing Company, 1993.

Grant, M. Myths of the Greeks and Romans. New York: New American Library, 1962.

Graves, A. The Book of Irish Poetry. Dublin: The Talbot Press.

Gross, F. Rhodes of Africa. London: Cassell and Company, Ltd., 1956.

Haas, J. ed. The Anthropology of War. New York: Cambridge University Press, 1990.

Hacker, B. "Military Institutions and World History." Historian, (54: Spring 1992): 425–50.

Hackett, F. Henry the Eighth. New York: Bantam Books, 1956.

Hallpike, C. "Functionalist Interpretations of Primitive Warfare." Man, (8: 1973): 451–70.

Harrison, J. The Second Coming. New Brunswick, New Jersey: Rutgers University Press, 1979.

Hart, D. and R. Sussman. Man the Hunted. New York: Basic Books, 2005.

Hassig, R. Aztec Warfare. Norman: University of Oklahoma Press, 1995.

Hausman, G. Turtle Island Alphabet. New York: St. Martin's Press, 1992.

Hayes-McCoy, G. <u>Irish Battles</u>. Belfast: Appletree Press, 1990.

Heaney, S., tr. Beowulf. New York: Norton, 2000.

Hesse, E. and Williams, H. eds. <u>La Vida de Lazarillo de Tormes</u>. Madison: The University of Wisconsin Press, 1976.

Hicks, D. and Gwynne, M. <u>Cultural Anthropology</u>. New York: Harper Collins College Publishers, 1994.

Hill, C. <u>Antichrist in Seventeenth Century England</u>. New York: Verso, 1990.

Hill, C. <u>God's Englishman</u>. London: Weidenfeld and Nicolson, 1970.

Hill, C. <u>Puritanism and Revolution</u>. London: Secker and Warburg, 1965.

Hill J. <u>Celtic Warfare: 1595-1763</u>. Edinburgh: John Donald Publishers, Ltd., 1986.

Hillman, J. <u>A Terrible Love of War</u>. New York: The Penguin Press, 2004.

Hobsbawm, E. and Ranger, T. <u>The Invention of Tradition</u>. Cambridge: Cambridge University Press, 1983.

Hogue, J., <u>Messiahs</u>. Boston, Massachusetts: Element, 1999.

Holmes, G. <u>The Late Middle Ages</u>. New York: W. W. Norton and Company, Inc., 1962.

Hooks, B. <u>Teaching to Transgress</u>. New York: Routledge, 1994.

Huizinga, J. <u>The Waning of the Middle Ages</u>. Garden City, New York: Doubleday Anchor Books, 1954.

Hunt, L. ed. <u>The New Cultural History</u>. Berkeley: University of California Press, 1989.

Innis, R. <u>Consciousness and the Play of Signs</u>. Bloomington: Indiana University Press, 1994.

Jones, T. <u>The Elder Within: The Source of Mature Masculinity</u>. Wilsonville, Oregon: Book Partners, Inc., 2001.

Jordan, W. <u>White Over Black</u>. New York: W. W. Norton and Company, Inc., 1977.

Jung, C. <u>Man and His Symbols</u>. New York: Dell Publishing, 1964.

Kadir, D. <u>Columbus and the Ends of the Earth</u>. Berkeley: University of California Press, 1992.

Kahn, J. <u>Culture, Multiculture, Postculture</u>. Thousand Oaks, California: Sage Publishers, 1995.

Kauver, G. and Sorenson G. eds. <u>The Victorian Mind</u>. New York: G. P. Putnam's Sons, 1969.

Kay, S. "The Life of the Dead Body: Death and the Saved in the Chansons de Geste." <u>Yale French Studies</u>. (86: 1994): 94–108.

Kearney, H. <u>Science and Change: 1500–1700</u>. New York: McGraw-Hill Book Company, 1971.

Keegan, J. The Face of Battle. London: Penguin Books, 1976.

Keegan, J. A History of Warfare. New York: Knopf, 1993.

Keeley, L. War Before Civilization. New York: Oxford University Press, 1996.

Keen, M. Chivalry. New Haven: Yale University Press, 1984.

Keen, M. The Laws of War in the Late Middle Ages. London: Routledge and Kegan Paul, 1965.

Kennedy, P. The Rise and Fall of the Great Powers. New York: Vintage Books, 1987.

Kerenyi, C. Dionysos. Princeton, New Jersey: Princeton University Press, 1976.

Kinsella, T. The Tain. New York: Oxford University Press, 1969.

Kipling, R. The Collected Works of Rudyard Kipling. New York: Walter J. Black, Inc., 1941.

Knight C. Blood Relations. New Haven: Yale University Press, 1991.

Knight, I. Go to Your God Like a Soldier. London: Greenhill Books, 1996.

Kohl, H. From Archetype to Zeitgeist. Boston: Little, Brown, and Co., 1992.

Kottak, C. Anthropology: The Exploration of Human Diversity, 12th ed. Boston: McGraw Hill, 2008.

Kramer, S. Mythologies of the Ancient World. Garden City, New York: Anchor Books, 1961.

Layard, J. A Celtic Quest. Dallas, Texas: Spring Publications, Inc., 1985.

Lefkowitz, M. and Rogers G., eds. Black Athena Revisited. Chapel Hill: University of North Carolina Press, 1996.

Lefkowitz, M. Not Out of Africa. New York: Basic Books, 1996.

Lerner, G. The Creation of Patriarchy. New York: Oxford University Press, 1986.

Lèvi-Strauss, C. Myth and Meaning. New York: Schocken Books, 1995.

Lèvi-Strauss, C. The Savage Mind. Chicago: University of Chicago Press, 1966.

Lèvi-Strauss, C. Structural Anthropology. New York: Basic Books, Inc., 1963.

Lewis, B. The Muslim Discovery of Europe. New York: W. W. Norton and Company, 1982.

Liddel Hart, B. The British Way of Warfare. New York: MacMillen Company, 1933.

Livy, The Early History of Rome. New York: Penguin Books, 1979.

Lloyd, C. The Structures of History. Oxford, United Kingdom: Blackwell Publishers, 1993.

Lomax, D. The Reconquest of Spain. New York: Longman, 1978.

Luttwak, E. The Grand Strategy of the Roman Empire. Baltimore: Johns Hopkins University Press, 1976.

Lutzker, M. Multiculturalism in the College Curriculum. Westport, Connecticut: Greenwood Press, 1995.

Lynch, J. Multicultural Education. London: Routledge and Kegan Paul, 1986.

Lynn, J. "The Role of the Military Variable in Shaping History." Journal of Military History. (55(1): January 1991): 83–95.

Maalouf, A. The Crusaders Through Arab Eyes. New York: Schocken Books, 1984.

Mack, B. Who Wrote the New Testament? New York: Harper Collins, 1996.

MacLean, P. A Triune Concept of the Brain and Behaviour. Toronto: Toronto University Press, 1973.

Malinowski, B. A Scientific Theory of Culture and Other Essays. Chapel Hill: University of North Carolina Press, 1944.

Malory, T. The Tales of King Arthur. New York: Schocken Books, 1980.

Mallory, J. In Search of the Indo-Europeans. New York: Thames and Hudson, 1989.

Manning, R. Against the Grain: How Agriculture Has Hijacked Civilization. New York: North Star Press, 2004.

Mannix, J. The Celts. Rochester, Vermont: Inner Traditions International, 1993.

Mason, H. Gilgamesh. New York: New American Library, 1972.

Matthews, C. and Matthews, J. The Encyclopedia of Celtic Wisdom. New York: Barnes and Noble Books, 1996.

Mayeski, M. Dhuoda: Ninth Century Mother and Theologian. Scranton: University of Scranton Press, 1995.

MacCana, P. Celtic Mythology. London: Hamlyn Publishing Group, Ltd., 1973.

McCoy, E. Celtic Myth and Magic. St. Paul, Minnesota: Llewellyn Publications, 1997.

McKay, J. et. al. A History of World Societies Since 1500, 4th Edition. Boston: Houghton Mifflin Company, 1996.

MacMullen, R. Christianizing the Roman Empire. New Haven: Yale University Press, 1984.

McNeill, W. Plagues and Peoples. Garden City, New York: Anchor Books, 1976.

McNeill, W. The Pursuit of Power. Chicago: University of Chicago Press, 1982.

Meade, M. Eleanor of Aquitane. New York: Penguin Books, 1991.

Merriam-Webster's Encyclopedia of Literature. Springfield, Massachusetts: Merriam-Webster Inc., Publishers, 1995.

Merriman, R. The Rise of the Spanish Empire in the Old World and in the New, v.I. New York: Cooper Square Publishing, 1962.

Messadie, G. A History of the Devil. New York: Kodansha International, Ltd. 1996.

Meyer, E. Teotihuacan. New York: Newsweek, 1973.

Moncrieff, A. Romance and Legend of Chivalry. London: Bracken Books, 1993.

Moore, R. The Archetype of Initiation. Xlibris Corporation, 2001.

Moore, R. and D. Gillette. King, Warrior, Magician, Lover. San Francisco: Harper, 1990.

Morgan, E. The Puritan Dilemma. Boston: Little, Brown and Company, 1958.

Morris, J. Heaven's Command. New York: Harcourt Brace Janovich Publishers, 1968.

Morris, J. Pax Britannia. New York: Harcourt Brace Janovich Publishers, 1968.

Morris, J. The Welsh Wars of Edward I. New York: Haskell House Publishers, Ltd., 1969.

Mulryne, J. and Shewring M. eds. War, Literature and the Arts in Sixteenth- Century Europe. London: St. Martin's Press, 1989.

Murray, M. et. al., eds. The Making of Strategy. New York: Cambridge University Press, 1994.

Neel, C., tr. Dhouda: Handbook for William. Lincoln and London: University of Nebraska Press, 1991.

Newark, T. Celtic Warriors. Poole, England: Blanford Press, 1986.

Nevins, A. The Gateway to History. Garden City, New York: Anchor Books, 1962.

Nicholls, K. Gaelic and Gaelicized Ireland in the Middle Ages. Dublin: Gil and MacMillan, Ltd.

Nolan, J. "The Militarization of the Elizabethan State." Journal of Military History. (58: July 1994): 391-420.

Oakeshott, M. On History. Totowa, New Jersey: Barnes and Noble Books, 1983.

O'Driscoll, R., ed. The Celtic Consciousness. New York: George Braziller, Inc., 1981.

Offer A. "The British Empire: 1870–1914: A Waste of Money?" Economic History Review. (G.Br.). (46(2): 1993): 215–38.

OhOgain, D. Myth, Legend and Romance. New York: Prentice Hall, 1991.

Oliver, W. Prophets and Millenialists. Auckland, New Zealand: Auckland University Press, 1978.

Oman, C. The Art of War in the Middle Ages, v. I–II. London: Greenhill Books, 1991.

Oman, C. The Art of War in the Sixteenth Century. London: Methuen and Company, Ltd., 1937.

Ong, W. Interfaces of the Word. Ithaca: Cornell University Press, 1977.

Ong, W. Orality and Literacy. New York: Methuen, 1982.

Pacione, M., ed. Historical Geography: Progress and Prospect. London: Croom Helm, 1987.

Pagden, A., ed. Hernan Cortes: Letters from Mexico. New Haven: Yale University Press, 1986.

Panati, C. Extraordinary Origins of Everyday Things. New York: Harper and Row, Publishers, 1987.

Paret, P. Makers of Modern Strategy. Princeton University Press, 1986.

Parker, G. The Army of Flanders and the Spanish Road: 1567–1659. New York: Cambridge University Press, 1975.

Parker, G. Europe in Crisis: 1598-1648. Ithaca: Cornell University Press, 1979.

Patel, K. Multicultural Education in All-White Areas. Brookfield, USA: Avebury, 1994.

Peter, P. Clausewitz and the State. Princeton: Princeton University Press, 1979.

Peters, R. Jihad in Classical and Modern Islam. Princeton: Markus Weiner Publishers, 1996.

Phillips, T., ed. Roots of Strategy. Harrisburg, Pennsylvania: Stackpole Books, 1985.

Pincus, S. Protestantism and Patriotism. New York: Cambridge University Press, 1996.

Pizzillo, J. Intercultural Studies. Dubuque, Iowa: Kendall/Hunt Publishing Company, 1983.

Pomeroy, E. Reading the Portraits of Queen Elizabeth. Hamden, Connecticut: Archon Books, 1989.

Porter, B. War and the Rise of the State. New York: The Free Press, 1994.

Prescott, W. The Art of War in Spain. London: Greenhill Books, 1995.

Prestwich, M. Edward I. New Haven: Yale University Press, 1997.

Purcell, M. The Great Captain. London: Alvin Redman, 1963.

Quatrefois, R. Los Tercios. Madrid: Coleccion, 1985.

Radcliffe-Brown, A. Structure and Function in Primitive Society. New York: The Free Press, 1952.

Rees, D. The Son of Prophecy. Ruthin, Denbighshire: John Jones Publishing, Ltd., 1997.

Reston, J., Jr. The Last Apocalypse. New York: Doubleday, 1998.

Richter, D. The Ordeal of the Longhouse. Chapel Hill: University of North Carolina Press.

Richter, M. Medieval Ireland. New York: St. Martin's Press, 1988.

Ritter, E. Shaka Zulu. New York: Penguin Books, 1978.

Rivers, E. Quixotic Scriptures. Bloomington: Indiana University Press, 1983.

Ross, A. and Robins, D. The Life and Death of a Druid Prince. New York: Simon and Schuster, 1989.

Ross, A. Pagan Celtic Britain. Chicago: Academy Chicago Publishers, 1967.

Ross, J. and McLaughlin, M., eds. The Portable Medieval Reader. New York: Penguin Books, 1977.

Rossi, I., ed. People in Culture. New York: Praeger, 1980.

Saunders, N. The Jaguars of Culture: Symbolizing Humanity in Pre-Columbian and Amerindian Societies. University of Southampton: U.K., Ph.D., 1991.

Sagan, C. The Dragons of Eden. New York: Random House, 1986.

Savaria-Shore, M. and Arvizu, S. Cross Cultural Literacy. New York: Garland Publishing, Inc., 1992.

Scherman, K. The Birth of France. New York: Random House, 1987.

Schlesinger, A., Jr. The Disuniting of America. New York: W. W. Norton and Company, 1992.

Schneider, L., ed. The Idea of Culture in the Social Sciences. Cambridge: Cambridge University Press, 1973.

Seaman, L. Victorian England. London: Methuen and Company, Ltd., 1973.

Scupin, R. and C. DeCourse, New York: Pearson, 2012.

Sherman, W. "John Dee's Brytannicae Republicae Synopsis." Journal of Medieval and Renaissance Studies. (20(1990) 2): 293–315.

Schlain, L. The Alphabet Versus the Goddess. New York: Viking, 1998.

Simpson, L. The Encomienda in New Spain. Berkeley: University of California Press, 1982.

Sitchin, Z. The Twelfth Planet. Sante Fe, New Mexico: Bear and Company Publishing. 1976.

Sleeter, E., ed. Empowerment through Multicultural Education. Albany: State University of New York Press, 1991.

Sleeter, E. Multicultural Education as Social Activism. Albany: State University of New York Press, 1996.

Smith, R. Warfare and Diplomacy in Pre-Colonial West Africa, Second Edition. Madison: University of Wisconsin Press, 1989.

Sommers, C. Who Stole Feminism? New York: Simon and Schuster, 1994.

Spence, L. Spain. London: Bracken Books, 1993.

Spenser, E. A View of the Present State of Ireland. Oxford: Clarendon Press, 1970.

Spielvogel, J. Western Civilization, Second Edition. New York: West Publishing Company, 1994.

Spindler, G. and Spindler L., eds. Pathways to Cultural Awareness. Thousand Oaks, California: Corwin Press, Inc., 1994.

Stevens, P. Patterns in Nature. Boston: Atlantic Monthly, 1974.

Stoianovich, T. French Historical Method. Ithaca: Cornell University Press, 1979.

Talbot, M. The Holographic Universe. New York: Harper Perennial, 1992.

Tarnas, R. The Passion of the Western Mind. New York: Ballantine Books, 1993.

Temple, R. The Sirius Mystery. Rochester, Vermont: Destiny Books, 1987.

Thucydides. The Peloponnesian War. New York, New York: Penguin Books, 1978.

Thomas, H. Conquest. New York: Touchstone Books, 1993.

Tillyard, E. The Elizabethan World Picture. New York: Vintage Books.

Toynbee, A. A Study of History, v. I. New York: Oxford University Press, 1953.

Trattner, W. "God and Expansion in Elizabethan England: John Dee, 1527–1583." Journal of the History of Ideas. (25: 1964): 17–34.

Turney-High, H. The Military. West Hanover, Massachusetts: The Christopher Publishing House, 1981.

Turney-High, H. Primitive War. Columbia: University of South Carolina Press, 1991.

Vance, N. The Victorians and Ancient Rome. Cambridge, Massachusetts: Blackwell Publishers, 1997.

Van Laue, T. The World Revolution of Westernization. New York: Oxford University Press, 1987.

Vansina, J. Oral Tradition as History. Madison: University of Wisconsin Press, 1985.

Vilar, P. "The Age of Don Quixote." Europe. (34: 1956): 3–16.

Vitek, W. and W. Jackson. Rooted in the Land: Essays on Community and Place. New Haven, Connecticut: Yale University Press, 1996.

Warwick, D. and Osherson S. Comparative Research Methods. Englewood Cliffs, New Jersey: Prentice Hall, 1973.

Webb, C. and Wright J. A Zulu King Speaks. Pietermaritzburg, South Africa: University of Natal Press, 1987.

Webb, H. Elizabethan Military Science. Madison: University of Wisconsin Press, 1965.

Weber, M. The Protestant Ethic and the Spirit of Capitalism. New York: Charles Scribner's Sons, 1958.

Weigley, R. The Age of Battles. Bloomington: Indiana University Press, 1991.

Wheeler, E. "Methodological Limits and the Mirage of Roman Strategy." Journal of Military History. (57: 1993): 7–41, 215–40.

Wurzel, J. Toward Multiculturalism. Yarmouth, Maine: Intercultural Press, Inc., 1988.

Yewbrey, G. "A Redated Manuscript of John Dee." Bulletin of the Institute of Historical Research (G.Br.). (50 (1997) 127): 249–53.

"The X-Gene." Discover. 18 (January 1998).

Young, D. Origins of the Sacred. New York: St. Martin's Press, 1991.

Lightning Source UK Ltd.
Milton Keynes UK
UKHW050930010922
408144UK00003B/85